Nomadic
Identities

PUBLIC WORLDS

Series Editors Dilip Gaonkar and Benjamin Lee

MAY JOSEPH

Nomadic

Identities

The Performance

of Citizenship

PUBLIC WORLDS, VOLUME 5
UNIVERSITY OF MINNESOTA PRESS
MINNEAPOLIS   LONDON

Chapter 3 appeared as "Soul, Transnationalism, and Imaginings of Revolution: Tanzanian Ujamaa and the Politics of Enjoyment," in *Soul*, edited by Monique Guillory and Richard Green (New York: New York University Press, 1997), 126–38; reprinted by permission.

Chapter 4 appeared as "Kung Fu Cinema, Frugality, and Tanzanian Asian Youth Culture: *Ujamaa* and Tanzanian Youth in the Seventies," in *SportCult*, edited by Randy Martin and Toby Miller (Minneapolis: University of Minnesota Press, 1999); reprinted by permission.

Chapter 7 appeared as "Bodies outside the State: Black British Women and the Limits of Citizenship," in *The Ends of Performance*, edited by Peggy Phelan and Jill Lane (New York: New York University Press, 1998), 197–213; reprinted by permission.

Poetry by M. Nourbese Philip, from "she tries her tongue, her silence softly breaks," and by Edward Kamau Brathwaite, from *Barabajan Poems*, is reprinted here by permission of the poets.

Published by the University of Minnesota Press
111 Third Avenue South, Suite 290
Minneapolis, MN 55401-2520
http://www.upress.umn.edu

Printed in the United States of America on acid-free paper

Library of Congress Cataloging-in-Publication Data
Joseph, May.
    Nomadic identities : the performance of citizenship / May Joseph.
       p.   cm. — (Public worlds ; v. 5)
    ISBN 0-8166-2636-7 (hc). — ISBN 0-8166-2637-5 (pb)
    Includes bibliographical references and index.
    1. Immigrants—Political activity. 2. Ethnic groups—Political activity.
    3. Minorities—Political activity. 4. Political participation. 5. Citizenship. I. Title.
    II. Series.
    JV6255.J67   1999
    323.6'09'04—dc21   98-43818

The University of Minnesota is an equal-opportunity educator and employer.

11 10 09 08 07 06 05 04 03 02 01 00 99   10 9 8 7 6 5 4 3 2 1

Contents

Acknowledgments

This book would not have been possible without the generosity and support of friends, colleagues, and well-wishers through the years. To P. Rajani, G. K. Mathews, Bert States, Manthia Diawara, Robert Egan, Simon Williams, Gerald Horne, Elliott Butler Evans, Abdul Jan Mohammed, Clarence Walker, Michael Sprinker, Norma Alarcón, Lawrence Grossberg, James Clifford, Michael Taussig, Ngugi wa Thiong'o, Toby Miller, Allen Weiss, Peggy Phelan, Randy Martin, Sandra Richards, Kathy Perkins, Elizabeth Weed, Shirley Lim, Jack Tchen, Margo Machida, Rachel Moore, Barbara Kirschenblatt-Gimblett, José Muñoz, Barbara Browning, Diana Taylor, Richard Schechner, David Van Leer, Micah Kleit, Faye Ginsburg, Barbara Abrash, Una Chayduri, Andrew Ross, and Angela Davis I am most indebted. Their support and encouragement were invaluable. Lawrence Grossberg, Kobena Mercer, Randy Martin, Toby Miller, Dilip Gaonkar, Manthia Diawara, Ngugi wa Thiong'o, Ben Lee, and Philomena Mariani read drafts of this manuscript. Their incisive suggestions were critical in making this a better book. I am especially indebted to Ben Lee and Dilip Gaonkar's enthusiasm for and support of this project. Their commitment was crucial to its realization. I want to thank Carrie Mullen, Jennifer Moore, Laura Westlund, Louisa Castner, and Micah Kleit of the University of Minnesota Press who made the publication of this manuscript a pleasant experience.

A University of California, Santa Barbara Social Science Research Grant in 1989 made possible initial fieldwork on the film/video and theater collectives as well as British Asians from East Africa now living in London.

The generosity of Retake, Sankofa, Black Audio, and Ceddo collectives regarding their archives will never be forgotten. Derek Walcott, Mustapha Matura, Jatinder Varma, Alaknanda Samarth, Rita Wolf, Reece Auguiste, Isaac Julien, Menelik Shabazz, Allan deSouza, Marlene Nourbese Philip, Shani Mootoo, and Ahmed Jamal shared invaluable time and thoughts about the theater, media, and cultural practices. Many thanks also to the Fellows of the Humanities Research Institute at University of California, Irvine, during 1991–92, which provided a challenging environment in which to write. Postdoctoral fellowships at the University of Illinois Unit for Criticism and Critical Theory, Brown University's Pembroke Center, and the Rockefeller Postdoctoral Fellowship at the Asian/American Center at Queens provided a rich network of contexts in which to expand my work. Special thanks also to the inspiring community of international legal scholars for welcoming my interests and sharing their work with me. Stella Rozanski, James Gathii, Celestine Nyamu, Tayyab Mahmud, Vasuki Nesiah, Nathaniel Berman, Anthony Anghie, Karen Engle, Ibrahim Gassama, Neil Gotanda, David Kennedy, and Keith Aoki in particular offered an invaluable community for which I am very grateful. Various sections of this manuscript have benefited from the responses I received from these generous communities. My thanks also to New York University's Tisch School of the Arts and the Paulette Goddard Foundation, which allowed me leave time to finish this manuscript. The gritty environment of New York City and my remarkable colleagues at the Department of Performance Studies, Tisch School of the Arts, New York University, provided a compelling forum for my work.

I want to thank Cedric Robinson, Victor Leo Walker, Leonard Harris, Robert Potter, Tadashi Uchino, Teshome Gabriel, Rosalind Bell, Claude Purdy, Paul Carter Harrison, Mark Rose, Lisa Lowe, and Fred Moten for their support. Smitty and Joan at Revolution Bookstore in New York City were extraordinary resources. For their interest and generosity I will always be grateful. Shishir Kurup, Roger Guenvere Smith, Bina Sharif, and Dan Kwong reminded me why citizenship matters. Allen Weiss and Meena Alexander convinced me that writing could be pleasurable. I am especially grateful to my many terrific students at Performance Studies for sharing their work with me and from whom I have learned much. Their enthusiasm, critical engagement, and support have been a source of inspiration through the years. I particularly want to thank those whose work fueled my own: Sikivu Hutchinson, Anita Cherian, Gitanjali Maharaj, Richard Green, Abdul Karim Mustapha, John McGrath, Fernando Passos, Andre Lepecki, Sansan Kwan, Bertha Palenzuela, Lara Nielsen, Gilad Melzer, Jill

Lane, Jennifer Fink, Rosamond King, Branislav Jakovljevic, Ben Stewart, Jason King, David Kim, Sara Bailes, Yasmeen Feinstein, and Noel Cassiano. June Reich, Richard Green, and Jason King provided much appreciated research assistance. The friendship and humor of Page Leong, Tayyab Mahmud, Ella Shohat, Patricia Hoffbauer, Meena Alexander, Jayati Lal, Joe Simmons, Bob Stam, Meenakshi Ponnuswami, Michael Laessig, Jutka Devenyi, Svathi Lelyveld, Karen Cope, Lisa Bloom, V. Geetha, Supriya, Smrithi Srinivas, Rosemary Coombes, Eugene Nesmith, George Sanchez, and Radz Subramaniam were immeasurably important through these years. Biz, Ted, Joseph, Celine, Alice, Allan, Jaya, and Car provided uncondi- tional love and respite. Finally, to Geoffrey Rogers goes my inexpressible gratitude for having been so untrammeled and entertaining through all this.

1

The Performance of Citizenship

It is a dark rainy night in 1972. A car inches its way through a policed bar-
ricade, interrupted by the surveillance of flashlights. Crowds of Asians are
saying hurried good-byes to Uganda, their homeland until Idi Amin or-
dered their eviction. Melodramatic scenes of terror and fear of the present and future. Sorrowful partings, reluctant leavings. The mise-en-scène
segues into a cartographic map of a journey from Kampala to Greenwood,
Mississippi, from 1972 to 1990. This map cognitively traces a specific archetypal site of inauthentic citizenship for East African Asians: Kampala—
London—Mississippi. In 1991, I sat in a packed downtown Los Angeles
movie house watching Mira Nair's *Mississippi Masala*, with a feeling of déjà
vu sparked by the film's cartographic sequence, startled into remembrance
of things past that, I thought, had been successfully erased. The first few
minutes of the film—scenes of Asians leaving Uganda—awakened long-
buried fears of anti-Asian sentiment in Tanzania, which had tormented my
family on many nights from 1972 to 1975, exacerbated by anonymous
death threats aimed at my father. The persistent anxiety resulted in our
unceremonial departure from Tanzania under less fearful though no less
traumatic conditions than the exile of Ugandan Asians.

The sequence from *Mississippi Masala* unleashed a flood of questions
about this unspeakable past, East Africa of the 1970s. Many Tanzanian

Asians of my generation found themselves adrift in new countries of domicile, with no explanations for the hasty farewells and abrupt departures, no narrative of return to make the leaving more bearable, faced instead with a recalcitrant silence. The visual shock induced by Nair's film reopened questions of immigration and authenticity that had reshaped notions of citizenship in a prior moment of nation formation—the early years of independence, when delineations of authenticity had profound effects on the kinds of citizenship available to non-Africans in former homelands like the East African states of Kenya, Uganda, and Tanzania.

I recall my own efforts at expressively staging citizenship in those early years of independence, my enthusiastic attempts to demonstrate that I was, indeed, a good Tanzanian socialist: marching along with my peers, emulating the best *ngoma* dancers by shaking my hips just so, beefing up my Swahili so that I would be among the handful of Asians accepted into the local Swahili medium secondary schools, singing Swahili songs with the right accent (Asians were constantly mocked for their poor pronunciation of Swahili), trading my skill in drawing frogs and butterflies for help from green-thumbed comrades with my *shamba*, or vegetable garden, so that I would not fail the year. Despite the anti-Asian graffiti present in the streets on the route home, I was determined to prove that I had assimilated. But being defined inauthentic proved a more potent force than my expressive stances. Clearly, more was needed than speaking perfect Swahili—most important, a sense of historicity in relation to this transitioning place of Tanzanian socialist citizenship.

Thus, the question of how citizenship is expressed became crucial in my research into the disaffected space of inauthentic citizenship posed by the large and dispersed communities of East African Asians in India, the Gulf states, Britain, Canada, and the United States. I crossed paths with these enclaves of displaced East African Asians through the years, in Bangalore, Trivandrum, Doha, London, New York, Los Angeles. Many of these people spent years rebuilding their lives; some of them (primarily men) retreated permanently into bitterness. Gradually, there unfolded a peculiar condition for which theories of citizenship do not adequately account: that of nomadic, conditional citizenship related to histories of migrancy and the tenuous status of immigrants. This notion of citizenship extends beyond the coherence of national boundaries and is transnationally linked to informal networks of kinship, migrancy, and displacement, opening up circuits of dependency between communities in Canada, Britain, or the United States and communities in East Africa.

But this later history of renegotiation and rebuilding was haunted by the trauma of dispossession and displacement. Most never spoke of the conditions under which they were compelled to leave. Regardless of regional differences, whether they were from Tanzania, Kenya, or Uganda, their experiences revealed similar concerns about the kinds of citizenship in which they participated, or did not. Their stories posed difficult problems about their relationship to race, class, and nationality. Their children, the generation that came of age in East Africa, raised pointed questions about their compulsory exile but encountered an uneasy, pained silence.

This book is a response to that silence. It investigates the sphere of metaphoric, literal, and performed possibilities available in different arenas of the everyday through which communities and individuals access (successfully or not) the experience called citizenship. It emphasizes the quotidian aspects of performed citizenship through which a nomadic experience of participation is inhabited by those who are marked out as inauthentic citizens. Three questions guided my research: How is citizenship performed under conditions of migrancy? How does the experience of multiple national contexts complicate the enactment of citizenship in the public cultures of nations such as Tanzania, Britain, and the United States? And finally, can specific formations of legal and cultural citizenship be mapped in such an amorphous history of multiple migration? By privileging the period from 1967 to the mid-1970s, when Tanzanian Asians were explicitly accused of inadequately expressing their commitment to socialism, I make connections to other nodes of performed citizenship for those who left East Africa. In effect, these essays trace a journey made by modern nomadic identities and offer a historically contingent approach to narrativizing this period as a series of dramatically transforming moments, locally and transnationally linked. The transnational maps drawn here link socialist and democratic states, Tanzania to Uganda and Kenya, and Tanzania to Britain and the United States as an extended imaginative geography.

A central premise of this book is that citizenship is not organic but must be acquired through public and psychic participation. Citizenship is an ambiguous process vulnerable to changes in government and policy. The citizen and its vehicle, citizenship, are unstable sites that mutually interact to forge local, often changing (even transitory) notions of who the citizen is, and the kinds of citizenship possible at a given historical-political moment. As historians of citizenship such as Thurgood Marshall, George Armstrong Kelly, Will Kymlicka, and Toby Miller suggest, the categories through which we understand and experience full and satisfying citizenship today are profoundly twentieth-century conceptions. They are mutually determined categories, often initiated by the state's need to invent and contain its subjects. Notions of the legal, cultural, and national consequently inflect ideas of who the citizen is and what citizenship entails. Crucial to this understanding are notions of the individual's relationship to the public realm, which transform the possibilities of citizenship in historically particular ways. Such socially determined conceptions of citizenship have emerged in the twentieth century with the increased democratization and liberalization of the state in relation to its subjects.[1] But while there is no simple definition of what citizenship is, or who can be a citizen, we are constantly impinged on as citizen-subjects, operating between the legal, the cultural, and the political, often in tandem, in our everyday gestures.

The essays that follow examine the citizen as a performed site of personhood that instantiates particular notions of participatory politics. More specifically, they probe avenues of cultural and representational practice through which legal and cultural citizenship is accomplished within urban, nomadic communities. The focus here is on the expressive domains inhabited by citizens reinventing themselves according to prevalent notions of authentic citizenship, either popularly or officially defined, whether in the way one holds one's body, the music one consumes, or the kind of theater one produces. Consequently, the expressive enactments of citizenship explored here reiterate the notion that the lifeworld of citizenship entails a network of performed affiliations—private and public, formal and informal—through which the neurons of the state are activated with ideas of a polity.

In the literature on citizenship, there is no easy consensus about what citizenship means, how it is imbibed, and what it entails. Yet the notion of citizenship connotes a sense of engagement with the public realm, generally speaking. Ideas of legal and cultural citizenship that emerge in the following chapters have evolved out of the sites on which I chose to elaborate. The chapters on Tanzania address notions of national and inauthentic citizenship and consequently prioritize the legal dimensions through which ideas of citizenship were inculcated and consolidated. Since the moment I focus on is the first decade and a half of decolonization, the preeminence of the legal in the formation of subjecthood is heightened. The sections on Britain and the United States pay more attention to the cultural aspects of citizenship. This shift is not accidental. The transition foregrounds the difficulties of statehood by juxtaposing the postcolonial African state against an entrenched British state, where the impact of race and immigration in the 1970s brings to a head a cumulative interrelated history of colonial disavowal and postcolonial erasure. The tension within the book, staged as a geographical tension between legal citizenship in a Second World context and cultural citizenship in a First World context, between a socialist state and a welfare state, is a contingent structuring divide. It is relational in that it informs both the Tanzanian and the British sections of the book, while offering a comparative and interconnected approach to reading history across national contexts. The distinction between the legal and the cultural is a slippery one. It is a structural means of locating specific currents, influences, and laws that affect people in distinct ways as migrant subjects. In practice, these are not discrete categories but amorphous spheres of everyday actions. In urban life, the cultural is always contingent on the legal in crucial ways, and, conversely, the legal aspects of Black citizenship profoundly shape the expressive stances of Black cultural producers in Britain, whether through performance, media, or visual art.

Locating enactments of citizenship across national contexts, these cultural readings—of political icons, public policies, presidential speeches, kung fu films, physical education, soul music, revolutionary ideologies, theatrical innovations—reveal the invisible economies that inform popular assumptions about cultural citizenship. Notions of citizenship are infused with public images, official definitions, informal customary practice, nostalgic longings, accrued historical memory and material culture, comforting mythologies of reinvention, and lessons learned from past rejections. Close scrutiny of the ways in which citizenship is actually embodied by the state discloses a scenario filled with the anxious enactments of citizens as actors. The stock characters include authentic citizens; inauthentic minorities; noncitizens with ambivalent political allegiances such as migrant workers, immigrant aspirants, expatriates, and international travelers; emergent political subjects such as youth, women, and the poor. These essays delve into this sphere of nervous enactment to find a transnationally inflected arena of public participation, an imaginative geography of performed sites through which notions of the citizen as a "legal" and "cultural" subject emerge in tandem with the invention of statehood in newly independent nations like Tanzania and simultaneously redefine British and U.S. concepts of citizenship in relation to emigrating communities.

Although cultural displacement and economic displacement are hardly new phenomena, recent historical events have combined to produce dilemmas unique to our time. In the aftermath of anticolonial liberation movements and decolonization, peoples have been uprooted many times over in a single lifetime. One question central to this book is the distinction between legal and cultural citizenship and the intertwined ways in which they are performed under such conditions of migrancy. By emphasizing three specific locales—Dar es Salaam, London, and Los Angeles—as part of an imaginative geography, these essays link East Indians and their nomadic migrations through Africa, Britain, Canada, the United States, and South Asia to widely divergent national constructions of citizenship. These fractured migrant histories of arrival, dispersal, and renegotiation of local and international citizenship exemplify the inchoate conditions in which new ways of thinking about participation in local communities and the national polity develop. Within these nomadic experiences can be traced an imaginative history of the expressive stances linking diasporic subjectivity to legal citizenship, as well as to global concerns about modern citizenship. Through an interrogation of the invisible economies behind minoritarian politics, immigrant struggles for legitimacy, and new political identities within a global public polity, these essays offer a holographic impression of the performance of citizenship in transnationally linked urban contexts and postmodern conditions of statelessness in the late twentieth century.

During the early 1970s, the bourgeois nationalisms that fueled optimistic economic policies in many postcolonial states also provoked intense debates on the meaning of citizenship. Nationalist aspirations forged new notions of a public collective, in the process marking out new categories of noncitizen and stranger within the state. A series of coerced mass migrations resulted: Togolese, Dahomeyans, and Nigerians from the Ivory Coast, Nigerians from Ghana, and Asians from East Africa. These expulsions, literally enforced overnight, were grounded in the crisis of nation-state formation. As the following chapters suggest, for many citizens in these postcolonial states, mobility became a key to psychic survival in a volatile and rapidly changing world.

Theorization about citizenship in African states during the 1960s and '70s foregrounded Western conceptions of the state as a static entity, minimizing its transnational connections even as newly independent nations were delimited by relationships of dependency. This notion of the static state contrasted dramatically with the physical movement of peoples, objects, and mediatized technologies, all of which accelerated disruptive conflict within the national. These translocal and regional disruptions highlighted a neglected arena of social movement theory: the impure space of the early nation-state and its importance as a link between colonial, imperial, and contemporary transnational processes. In contradistinction to the projection of postcolonial states as gripped by underdevelopment, common in generalized observations about Third World nations, the expressions of belonging articulated from the ground up in states like Tanzania, Ghana, and Egypt suggest a more muscular, mobile, and imaginative sphere of Second World citizenship formation that fueled African and Arab socialism as much as it did New Left social movements in Britain and the United States.

By foregrounding this liminal movement in the invention of local and national identities, these chapters emphasize both the performative mobility of the postcolonial state in its hasty embrace of modernity and its dramatic impact on translocal conceptions of citizenship as the very parameters of citizenship shift and consolidate overnight. In these pages, people do not move physically with the rapidity extolled in more current speculations on global modernity. Taking a plane is an event. Traveling to formerly segregated parts of Dar es Salaam is an adventure in spatial dislocation. Being integrated as Asians into local Tanzanian culture is a new sensation, both exhilarating and anxiety producing. Economic frugality under state socialism creates new relationships of time-space compression. The physicality of presence is fetishized: crowds and public displays of national affirmation are more familiar avenues of entertainment than the privatized and voyeuristic pleasures of mediatized spectacles. Authority is locatable in the police, the party, and the political public. The circulation of capital is less fluid than theory would allow, with the recalling of the 100 shilling note and residual feudal systems of accumulation such as the hoarding of gold in the interests of mobility.

This is Tanzania in the 1960s and '70s. Television has not yet arrived, but conceptions of fluid identities, rootedness and dispersal, frugality and accumulation, are being lived at a popular level through urban social practices. Emergent ideas of citizenship in performance are staged against an inchoate sense of personhood in transformation. Mobility and stasis are experienced simultaneously, as institutions, laws, even street names change rapidly, creating a feeling of disjuncture without ever having left the transforming state. It is the era of development theory and structural adjustment, soon to be submerged under the globalizing processes of the new world order.

Movement, Arjun Appadurai suggests, is a social, economic, and imagined condition. The acceleration of temporal and spatial dislocations in the deterritorializing global economy has led to increasingly mobile modes of expressive citizenship. Mass migrations of peoples in conjunction with objects, commodities, and capital flow in different relations of ease generating new disjunctures among states, labor, political ideologies, and citizens.

The resulting tensions of such volatile collisions have given rise to an ambivalent cosmopolitanism in an increasingly democratizing sphere of global citizenship. This new cosmopolitanism simultaneously privileges consumers as the new global citizens while also generating historically new fissures of discord within nationally produced notions of citizenship as a social practice.[2] Appadurai's critical analysis of movement in the production of social biographies offers a means of reading the stagings of embodied citizenship wherein such inventive cosmopolitanism is often negotiated. Movement dislodges the entrenched categories of nation and state by introducing the workings of capital to the production of cosmopolitan as well as local citizenship. It foregrounds the contradictory tensions of consumption through which citizenship is displayed. Movement as a conceptual tool resists easy notions of community or nation.

In the following chapters, I extend Appadurai's conceptual framework of movement and mobility toward specific sites of this new cosmopolitanism that are often neither stable, easily penetrated, legal, nor necessarily progressive in their internationalizing imperatives. On the contrary, the enticing logic of consumption as the great leveler of nations, national identities, and competing modes of citizenship conceals the exclusionary and nondemocratic tendencies embedded in this logic that contradict the hard-fought battles for alternative venues of public citizenship waged by various political identities. Within globalizing discourses of transnational exchange, the seductive metaphors of heightened mobility, advanced at the expense of the political, generate anxiety around the local. At the center of these anxieties is the live body and its unmediated struggle to achieve democratic participation in the city. In tension with the rapid circulation of goods and peoples is the obliquely transforming sphere of performed citizenship foregrounded by live bodies in a globalizing but increasingly locally determined culture within the urban. Where goods, fashions, cuisine, films, cultural artifacts, and kitsch flow with intensified speed, bodies flow in less efficient ways. People in states of dispersal, whether voluntary or coerced, become redundant commodities, and elite businessmen become the implied actors in the mise-en-scène of slowly democratizing spheres of transnational economies.

The new cosmopolitanism is, in fact, neither unequivocally rapid in its circuits of exchange nor politically unfettered by apprehensions over manipulative, efficacious, or progressive public spheres. Instead, as this book suggests, the new cosmopolitanism fractures the idea of easy movements of commodities, consumers, and corporations across regional and national divides by identifying local circuits of exchange within specific urban contexts. It explores the uneasy and politically fraught spaces between migrant bodies in movement across national borders and immigrant bodies in tension with local conceptions of the national and the international within cities. By privileging the performed stagings of citizenship within the urban, it probes the interstices between cultural and legal citizenship, while considering the engines of economic citizenship that drive the need to migrate, relocate, ground oneself in a community, and forge urban public identities.

Notions of citizenship as a performed arena of local public culture highlight the forms of legal self-invention that temper this idea of rapidly circulating commodities, consumers, and corporations across national boundaries. Beginning with early solidarity movements such as Pan-Africanism, Pan-Arabism, suffrage, and anticolonial independence struggles—dramatically coalesced in Bandung and the nonaligned movement of the 1950s—the idea of a global public that could be harnessed in the interests of rights and representation slowly gained visibility as a new arena for staging international citizenship. Twentieth-century pan–identity movements like international socialism and nonalignment had articulated an arena of shared struggle around economic citizenship that created international consciousness about rights in relation to economic participation at local and global levels. This invention of sovereign pan-national identity in opposition to Western-determined conceptions of state and citizenship provided a transnational framework for emerging local social movements in conjunction with international currents of change. Feminisms, Black nationalisms, labor movements, regional and subregional formations staged their own distinctive social identities in relation to existing orthodoxies and entrenched imperial ideologies. Consequently, this idea of staging citizenship, whether in local, national, or international arenas, shaped a transnational conception of performed citizenship. For many minoritarian or antinational social identities, the postnational was a more viable framework than the existing structures of statehood. Alliances among women, workers, young children, Muslims, and socialists were often organized at international or transregional levels, through which these constituencies could gain a hearing not otherwise available at the national level. The identity East African Asian, for instance, emerged under the onslaught of anti-Asian sentiment produced at national levels across East Africa in the 1970s, creating a structure of feeling that was specifically regional in its commitments, longings, and sense of alienation.

Conceptions of citizenship for those struggling against the imperial yoke transformed rapidly from the late 1940s onward, with notions of cultural legitimacy during the decolonizing '60s tied to specific expressions of participatory politics. The self-conscious dramatizations of national visibility politics—such as the feminist and civil rights movements, particularly the Black Panther Party in the United States, as well as the climate in Paris in May 1968—offered new conceptions of participatory citizenship, both invented and nascent, within specific political cultures. These enactments gained popular currency in violently forged nations as they drew on the disparate energies and resources of students, workers, women, trade unionists, intellectuals, and, more troubling, fascist and authoritarian elements, which mobilized populist nationalisms in the interests of the state.

The power of visibility as an embodied act that successfully conceals the ambivalence behind such dramatizations of legitimacy was most effectively staged in these early expressions of performed citizenship. For subjects in transit from one newly invented state to another during the 1970s, the stagings of strategic visibility politics in one state often obscured the experiences of failed community in another national context, for example, in the case of East African Asians who forged new sojourner relationships with India and the Gulf states. Doubt and ambiguity about community or group identities were suppressed in the interest of positivist models of identity. The site of ambivalent political allegiances through which such cultural citizens emerged, anxious and uncertain about their place in the world, remained an unarticulated and repressed sphere of the international conditions of nomadic experience. Falling outside the purview of the national, and appearing in the imaginary of the international as dispersed economic migrants, political refugees, transnational nomads, the relationships moving toward citizenship embedded in these migrant subjectivities have yet to be accounted for as they migrated from one host state to another. For many nomadic communities in the twentieth century, these spheres of belonging have often been contingent rather than homogeneously constituted.

The global displacement of East African Asians is one such symptomatic site of citizenship in dispersal during this internationally volatile period of fervent nationalisms and Cold War realignment. As this community found itself in hastened states of nomadic disruption, contributing to a more widespread pattern of petit bourgeois migrancy, it raised new questions around the kinds of citizenship available, accessible, and performed in conditions of communal and territorial dissolution. This minor history of East African–Asian migration forces open the discursive dilemma of connecting the neglected history of Asians in Africa to that of metropolitan sites in the North such as Britain, Canada, and the United States, and urban locations like London, New York, Los Angeles, and Toronto. Such discontinuous trajectories produce new tensions within discourses of minority citizenship in an international framework, as they rub against established national minority politics and immigration naturalization policies. Such communities have forced the question of nomadic citizenship in a global market as they create fresh sources of tension between former homelands and new countries of domicile.

Culturally, these tensions are staged on a local level. For instance, the presence of East African Asians in the United States forges new historical connections to Africa between African Americans and Asian Americans. Their presence also accentuates the strategic essentialisms and hybrid pluralities of U.S. identity politics versus the messier realms of cultural citizenship in the Second and Third Worlds. This presence brings into tension the discourses of migration, immigration, and cultural citizenship through which nomadic subjects have to carve out a credible political and legal space, often within the crevices of legitimate minoritarian identities. By juxtaposing African socialism, Tanzanian Asian, Black British, and Asian American expressions of citizenship, the following essays lay out an alternative discourse of citizenship in formation, highlighting the competing citizenscapes that shape the political imaginary of urban nomads.

In the United States, the expressive stagings of citizenship in the culture of new immigrants enact the need to reinvent community in the interstices of political visibility. Often such stagings coalesce around former histories, current allegiances, and future possibilities, accentuating the arenas of ambiguity that are more successfully bound in the public expressions of national minorities. What gets elided in these utopian stagings of imagined community are the struggles to link former political histories with what Lauren Berlant describes as the practice of private citizenship in the United States. "The practices of citizenship," Berlant argues, "involve both public-sphere narratives and concrete experiences of quotidian life that do not cohere or harmonize. Yet the rhetoric of citizenship does provide important definitional frames for the ways people see themselves as public, when they do."[3] However, such a pedagogical project of transforming people into "private citizens," though immensely appealing to the often conservative and mercantile emigrating communities, poses several obstacles for immigrants in transitional frames of reference.

Publicly proclaiming one's identity, a distinctly U.S. expression of democratic political performance, is a sphere of experience that must be acquired. As an avenue of political embodiment, it is neither obvious nor easily emulated. For new immigrants, the spheres of performed visibility in the United States accentuate the conflicts between political cultures. For many immigrants, staging political identities in former states such as East Germany, Czechoslovakia, and Tanzania was viewed with suspicion. As Michael Ignatieff points out, in much of the world people are not free to pick or choose their relations to the political. In the 1970s, Argentina abolished citizenship entirely, while citizenship in Mao's China was available only at the expense of all private rights, and citizenship in Julius Nyerere's socialist Tanzania discouraged identitarian politics and individualism in the interests of the larger public good.[4] Under such conditions, the public performance of identity often involved broader political concerns grounded in social unrest rather than individual desire. For immigrants from authoritarian states, being discreet or traveling incognito was a safer strategy. Most important, the relationship between state, individual, and public arenas of performed identity in such states was more tightly regulated, subordinating the private to the public through systems of bureaucracy and surveillance. Consequently, gestures toward particularisms were likely to provoke unpleasant sanctions.

Acquiring cultural citizenship in the United States, then, involves a complex coming to terms with former political histories, as new immigrants find themselves at the juncture of African American and Asian American cultural histories. East African Asians forge links with Asian American and African American political and social formations and at the same time attempt to articulate a tangential former history of Asian struggles for African citizenship and the resulting travails of nomadic belonging. The unresolved political issues that such a project raises concern the possible links and crossovers that connect former histories of citizenship with current struggles for domicile in the newly adopted home of the United States. How do immigrants, migrants, and nomads imagine, perform, and invent themselves anew or insert themselves into the unfamiliar politics of place and arrival?

New York City offers a visceral grounding for such a scenario of multiply layered migrations. The dense concentration of diasporic South Asians from Latin America, the Caribbean, Africa, Britain, and the Subcontinent complicates any simple notion of Pakistani, Indian, and Bangladeshi citizenship. Former struggles of diasporic South Asians for cultural legitimacy in British Guiana, East Africa, the Caribbean, and Britain are repressed in the new struggles for a piece of the American pie. On the other hand, racial antagonisms in former states, where Asians are often categorized as Black, are relegated to the past as the new configuration "Asian American" supersedes Black to produce new alliances of a different historic strain.[5] For the dispersed, rapidly changing, and divided South Asian communities in the United States, expressions of cultural legitimacy are simultaneously isolated nationalistic gestures of solidarity with former homelands like Pakistan and India, and disconnected from their shared histories of migration and nomadism over the past two hundred years. Disparate strains of disaffiliation and nationalism are publicly displayed across the generational divide. This narrative continues to focus on the physical movement from nation A to nation B as the site of radical disjuncture, rather than the invisible economies of disruption, migration, and nomadism that have linked these diverse transnational communities in more meaningful ways to other diasporic migrants.

Citizenscapes in Performance

An implicit premise of the ensuing chapters is that commonsensical ideas about participatory democracy inform the underlying logic of performance, understood here as both a conceptual tool and a social practice. As a genre and mode of discourse, however, the phenomenology of performance has rarely made explicit connections between epistemological/political meanings of citizenship and its own logic as a social practice. Historically, the ontology of performance has assumed a shared political framework because of its implied national coherence. Consequently, the question of citizenship never arose as a primary agent in the manufacture of culture and taste. But increased democratization of the public sphere has dispelled the myth of seamlessness within which social life, political identities, and lived practice are presumed to smoothly coalesce. In its wake, a contestatory public sphere has generated inquiries into the kinds of citizenship these sites enable.

The neologism *citizenscape* provides a framework for exploring these multiple avenues of citizenship. In tandem with Appadurai's taxonomy of scapes, the following chapters offer a series of citizenscapes, vignettes of nomadic citizenship in ambivalent relations to official and available discourses about private and public citizenship. Socially and politically produced conceptions of participatory democracy inform the phenomenological experience of performance as they conjoin with available and imagined vehicles for constructing contemporary citizenships. The multiply structured and structuring arena of performance as a lived and invented practice of social relations involves a self-conscious realization of citizen as subject. It heightens and, more often, naturalizes ideas of participatory citizenship as part of a broader culture of democratic rights, often obscuring real tensions and limits existing within contemporary democracies, whether socialist or welfare states. By foregrounding the ambivalent and performative sites of participatory citizenship, these readings of citizenscapes unravel the dissonances inherent within shifting notions of citizenship as lived experience, in the process giving substance and context to the seemingly amorphous experience of nomadism. Only by taking into account overlapping narratives of various citizenscapes can a holographic conception of modern citizenship emerge.

Twentieth-century conceptions of participatory democracy have been nuanced by communist, socialist, postcolonial, and totalitarian cultures of citizenship, producing slippages and hybrid genres within specific political cultures such as socialist Tanzania or the British welfare state. These contaminations of ideological absolutes rupture the pristine conceptions of how citizens are produced, and how public life makes available a variety of possibilities within and outside official discourses of citizenship. These citizenscapes reiterate the idea that democratic participation is neither a homogeneously constituted experience nor a utopian place of free and unfettered production of rights.

From Jean-Jacques Rousseau, John Stuart Mill, Joseph Schumpeter, and Julius Nyerere to Carole Pateman, Toby Miller, Seyla Benhabib, Lisa Lowe, Lauren Berlant, Issa Shiuji, Yoweri Museveni, and Mahmood Mamdani, debates over the limits and possibilities of the citizen as participating agent suggest a more complex relationship between the rhetorical and conceptual realms of democratic ideals, and the performed spheres of their enactments. As many theorists of participatory democracy suggest, there have always been radical disjunctures of varying proportions among the myth of participatory democracy, everyday practices available to different constituencies within the polity, institutions of governance, and the potentially democratic masses. Such disjunctures have produced national and context-specific interpretations and expressions of rights and representation. These context-specific articulations often reveal contradictory ideas of public citizenship. Hence, the phenomenological experience of citizenship as an embodied condition becomes a locus for exploring these competing desires, conflicts, and potentialities.

While theorists of participatory democracy may quibble about the degree of participation available or its progressive possibilities, none disagrees that the inherently performative nature of citizenship is simultaneously learned, cultivated, and improvised as a total work of citizenship in formation. Performance emerges as an implied sphere rather than an actually located process. It is the self-conscious enactment of the legal, cultural, and social structuring logics in postindustrial citizenry. In democratic theory, arguments about the role of participatory politics and the extent to which democratization of the polity can remedy the elitism inherent in specific notions of democratic participation distinctly incorporate notions of performance without inquiring into the possibility of such a category within strategies of citizenship. The idea of citizenship as a performing sphere that transforms the abstraction "the people" into individuated political subjects and participating citizens lurks within both classical and contemporary perceptions of citizenship. But many theorists, while incorporating notions of performed citizenship, fail to translate the spheres of enactment through which a participatory polity can be realized.

Within performance theory, on the other hand, the preoccupation with citizenship and the polis—from Aristotle, Shakespeare, Machiavelli, Corneille, Racine, Diderot, down to twentieth-century theatrical innovators—opens up a pantheon of citizenscapes staged between master and slave, foreigner and citizen, city dweller and peasant, citizen and noncitizen. In the work of Corneille, Racine, and Diderot, debates hinged on French manners and decorum through which permissible notions of Frenchness could be projected in the larger interests of cultivating ideas of French public culture. In twentieth-century nationalisms, the intersecting histories of national theaters and democratizing publics foregrounded theatrical activity within the state as a laboratory for experiments in public cultural citizenship.

In the work of early movement theorists Émile Jacques Dalcroze, Rudolf von Laban, and Mary Wigman, a fascination with staging large groups of youth in gestures of mass consent offered a display of public citizenship in performance. These early spectacles created a visual language for the staging of citizenship through public participation and highlighted the individual choreographer's autonomy and authority in relation to groups of performers. In Soviet theater of the 1930s, Vladimir Mayakovsky and Vsevold Meyerhold struggled to find a balance between private subjectivity and the pressure to create images of communist citizenship. Both rejected the erasure of private citizenship and the need to manufacture public citizenship through ideological submission to socialist-realist aesthetic values. Resisting these prescriptive imperatives, issued by Anatoly Lunacharsky on behalf of the Soviet state as the main components of legitimate cultural work, both innovators found themselves written out of cultural citizenship with tragic consequences. Finally, during the 1970s, Paolo Freire in Brazil, Augusto Boal in Peru and Brazil, Ngugi wa Thiong'o in Kenya, and Safdar Hashmi in India experimented with ideas of participatory politics as a pedagogical approach to staging democracy through grass-roots movements. Boal, Freire, and Thiong'o evocatively explored the possibilities between a democratizing public sphere and the politicization of the masses as citizen-subjects.

The work of all these practitioners was fueled by the tensions between self-conscious stagings of public citizenship through particular enactments of the national, and private iterations of local allegiances through specific local discussions about participatory citizenship (or the lack thereof). For all these practitioners, the theater was a highly visible arm of the state, through which notions of public taste, public citizenship, and private access to new identities could be visited in covert and tangential ways. The citizenscapes emerging out of these closely monitored stagings of participatory politics, often under authoritarian regimes, implicitly staged the tensions between public and private citizenship. In almost every case mentioned, the director-choreographer's success depended on conforming to, or at least negotiating, the party line. For some, the venue's elasticity allowed them to circumvent traditional or imposed ideologies of personhood, whether revolutionary, authoritarian, or democratic. But for others, failure to adapt led to loss of theater and later execution (Meyerhold), suicide (Mayakovsky), exile (Thiong'o, Boal, Freire), murder (Hashmi), and a more fractured dissemination of these experiments as manifestos of democratic performance pedagogy.

Nomadic Citizenship

To reiterate, the story of citizenship for those born in this century has often consisted of the forced and voluntary migration across states. With the proliferation of nations in the twentieth century, the relationship between legal and cultural citizenship for urban nomads has foregrounded the complex spheres of everyday life through which citizenship is enacted. How citizenship is accomplished has acquired central importance as borders are reconfigured and new regional or economic identities redefine older ones. As these newer economic, corporate, and regional identities emerge, they do so in tandem with the layered histories that have influenced contemporary notions of peripheral, alien, or minority citizenship.

One such sphere of minority experience is that of nomadic citizenship. The accelerated pace of modern migration has generated more exceptions to national identities than the formulations of nationalisms reveal. For many peoples during the second half of this century, migrating many times over—as immigrants, refugees, economic migrants—has become a common experience. Individuals or even entire communities have found themselves in transit for years, moving from one temporary residence to another, frequently within the state (as in communist and socialist relocations of people, and postcolonial urban migrations), often under conditions of legal uncertainty. As a persistent, transnational condition, this tenuous existence sunders the relationship between passport and citizen and challenges any tidy division between citizen and noncitizen. The political, legal, economic, and cultural nomad has been forced to perform citizenship across as well as *within* national boundaries, a practice referred to here as nomadic citizenship.

As both an imposed condition and process of negotiation, nomadic citizenship suggests the ambivalent, lucrative, unconscious, and itinerant ways in which migrant subjects live in relation to the state. Nomadic citizenship delegitimates the state as arbiter of identity and citizenship. For communities dismissed as economic migrants—Mexicans in Los Angeles, Asians in Uganda, the Lebanese in West Africa—nomadic citizenship enables the articulation of psychic and social boundaries of legitimation through which they exist as cultural citizens within the state that disavows them in subtle and overt ways. Nomadic citizenship fractures coherent categories of belonging, offering instead the incomplete, ambivalent, and uneasy spaces of everyday life through which migrant communities must forge affiliations with majority constituencies. Nomadic citizenship comprises a series of unstable relations through which ideas of citizenship, nationality, and sovereignty are invented along the road to statehood, even as the importance of the state recedes and transnational corporations tighten their hold on the social and imaginative biographies of citizens as consumers. Nomadic citizenship maps the transversal, nonlinear arenas of postnational identification.

The performance of citizenship became prominent in decolonizing societies over the past half-century as sovereignty struggles raised difficult questions about the relationship between nationality and state formation. Simultaneously contesting the validity of the Western nation-state while constructing national identities for themselves, postcolonial states embodied both the precariousness and promise of citizenship. From the 1940s to the '70s, many states established between the two World Wars consolidated notions of the national while reiterating conceptions of postcolonial conglomeration. For example, Indonesia, Egypt, Kenya, and India aligned themselves along broader pan-identities in an effort to navigate increasingly bipolar globalizing influences. In solidarity movements such as the nonaligned movement of the 1950s, Afro-Asian liberation movements, and the revolutionary nationalisms of Second and Third World states, the staging of postcolonial state formation always extended beyond the national. It was postnational in that it was already bound by the transnational discourses of colonial territories, regional identities, precolonial cartographic mythologies, and Cold War and postcolonial sovereignty struggles. The performance of modern citizenship in many Third World countries increasingly inclined toward the pan-national in its regional identifications and geopolitical specificity. Such theatrical stagings of statehood were expressed in the emergence of independent India and Pakistan in 1947, and Tanganyika (now Tanzania) in conjunction with its neighboring countries, Kenya and Uganda, during the 1960s.

Some of the most dramatic enactments of modern citizenship have occurred between these amorphous boundaries of the national and the postnational. During the early years of decolonization, numerous African states were racked by serious crises precipitated by attempts to relate citizens to noncitizens, host countries to migrant communities, authentic nationals to hybrid nationals produced as inauthentic. Popularly remembered through the forced repatriations of Arab Swahilis from Zanzibar; Dahomeyans, Togolese, and Nigerians from the Ivory Coast; Tutsis from Rwanda; Kenyan Luo and Asians from Uganda; and Yoruba and other Nigerians from Ghana, these crises demonstrated that the condition of nomadic citizenship was more systemic than exceptional and exposed the conflicting legacies of colonial policy and the rule of newly self-governing states. In retrospect, the compulsory repatriations of specific communities to former homelands might be described as dramatic stagings of the new nation-state's sovereignty. They performed both the promise and limits of citizenship that shaped national identities in the postcolonial era.[6]

During the 1970s, Tanzanian Asians found themselves deeply embroiled in a struggle for cultural citizenship, both in Tanzania and newly adopted homelands. A crucial question plagued their search for legitimacy in Tanzania: were non-Africans capable of politically progressive ways of being within the socialist African state? Further, was citizenship some mysterious biologically determined right, or a place of self-invention and the sociopolitical production of rights? Moreover, as this community, along with Kenyan and Ugandan Asians, struggled in new countries of domicile, the specter of former lives as political subjects with fraught relationships to the process of citizenship haunted their imaginings of political desire. For many East African Asians, the trauma of failed citizenship enacted through coerced departures raised troubling questions about strategies of performing citizenship. Ghost narratives around failed citizenship combined with a new history of migration to countries with a pronounced culture of participatory democracy. Most important, the baggage of non-identitarian, though particularistic, public identities demanded by Tanzanian socialist citizenship conflicted in crucial ways with the more privatized political identities featuring an older history of staging dissent and producing consent, such as that of British working-class culture.

Economic migrancy shaped the reinvention of East African–Asian citizens as British, Canadian, U.S., and Indian subjects. Their anxieties as legal and cultural citizens combined with postmodern conditions of migrancy. In the United States, many East African Asians, particularly the Gujurathi Patel communities, bought motels at transient points along freeways, in small towns, at crucial junctions along the U.S. grid of cities, establishing a new economy of nomadic citizenship. In Britain, Ugandan and Kenyan Asians reestablished themselves with differing degrees of success. Small duka traders at corner shops in London related tales of middle-class life in Uganda and the violent trauma of hasty departures without a penny to their name. Many found the uncertainties of life in Britain intolerable and expressed a desire to return to Uganda. Their desire has now been realized on the twenty-fifth anniversary of the Asian expulsion. Uganda's president, Yoweri Museveni, has galvanized a return of Ugandan Asians to their former homeland. One wonders what new strategies of affiliation this younger generation of Asians raised in Britain, Canada, and the United States will bring to Uganda.[7]

What unfolds in this unstable site of voluntary nomadism is a conflicted history of transnational longing, simultaneously invoking lost homelands like Uganda, originary moorings like India, new countries of domicile like Dubai, the United Arab Emirates, and Qatar, and future places of self-invention within a rapidly narrowing geopolitical terrain. In this panorama of differing political cultures that impinge on the formation of diasporic subjectivity is the tenuous place called citizenship, a chasm to be filled with incomplete desires of community and allegiances. This ephemeral place of imagined and available rights is a performed as well as rhetorically produced avenue of personhood, whereby peoples invent themselves in relation to, and in tension with, existing constructs of participatory politics. Clearly, the kinds of imaginings invoked in socialist Tanzania during the 1970s were quite different from those offered to displaced Tanzanian Asian immigrants by a transitional socialist government in India during the height of Indira Gandhi's Emergency of 1977, and certainly different from the authoritarian regimes of Gulf states such as the United Arab Emirates and Qatar. Nomadism generates a physical delinking of citizenship from national longing, of political desire from community strategies. It is within this postmodern condition, following the hopeful postindependence struggles for emancipatory forms of citizenship, that nomadic subjectivities must locate a place from which to articulate ideas of political belonging.

The recent history of East African cultural politics include a tangent—the dispersals of various minorities—linking the region to other geographic and political contexts. Therefore, to lend a national coherence to a profoundly transnational history, regionally as well as internationally, would be to elide an important (though minor) dimension of this contemporary history. Moreover, within East African states a tension existed between the narrative of place deployed by the state and the intricate microeconomies that shape life as a citizen within a specific city such as Dar es Salaam. As opposed to the structural theories that made the economies of African states transparent as statistics, the citizenscapes of everyday life demystified the notion of a homogeneous socialist state, a notion advanced even as the state dealt with an urban crisis characterized by tremendous mobility across socioeconomic and geographic boundaries. While the early postcolonial socialist state focused on the agrarian, the emphasis in the neglected cities was on achieving the good life as much as empowerment. These citizenscapes reveal the fact that socialist transformation in Second World states like Tanzania was not only about survival but about allowing for the psychic biographies of migrants to inflect the new social mapping.

2

Citizen Nyerere

Charisma and Postcolonial Authority

The early years of postcolonial statehood brought with them an anxiety over authority fueled by the long period of anticolonial struggle. In various African and Asian nations, this anxiety often congealed around evocative nationalist leaders linked to liberation struggles, later reconfigured as heads of secular, independent states. The biographies of Mahatma Gandhi in India, Sékou Touré in Guinea, Gamal Abdel Nasser in Egypt, and Julius Nyerere in Tanzania dramatize the transformation of fragile, even reticent figures into charismatic, rhetorically powerful, publicly efficacious leaders of the new nation-states.

In his typology of legitimate authority, Max Weber proposes three ideal types: traditional, legal-rational, and charismatic. Because the idea of traditional authority, in which power is produced through customary practices, has been dismissed as obsolete by many Weberians, and charismatic authority is considered authoritarian and therefore dangerous, legal-rational authority has been recognized as the only viable type for the modern state. In opposition to legal-rational authority, Weber ascribes charismatic authority to patriarchal power rooted in the economic needs of everyday life, endowing the holder with specific gifts of the body and spirit believed to be supernatural and available to a select few.[1] The

Weberian charismatic individual is motivated by a divine mission and is therefore set apart from other mortals, treated with devotion by virtue of the magical, heroic, and shamanistic qualities he is thought to embody. It is immaterial whether the charismatic individual actually possesses any of these qualities, since he is perceived as an extraordinary being charged with a messianic task.

Weber locates the rise of the charismatic leader in periods of political, religious, physical, psychic, and economic disruption. The charismatic leader is bred in dysfunctional social conditions. He does not depend on traditional bureaucratic or political structures. Since his authority is ordained from supernatural realms, the charismatic individual draws on and manipulates the psychic domain of mass adulation. His power lies in his ability to coerce absolute subservience by persuading followers of his right to lead and their obligation to serve. In the economy of charisma, money means little, mercantilism even less. Rather, the charismatic leader mobilizes obedience by rejecting rational action and harnessing the ecstatic and the devotional. Not surprisingly, the unquestioning adulation that the charismatic leader demands and receives is conducive to tyrannical megalomania.[2]

If economic alienation, religious crisis, and social dislocation pave the way for the rise of charismatic leaders, their success depends on ameliorating the hopelessness and frustration that allow charisma to emerge in the first place. Though located outside bureaucratic structures, charisma catalyzes a sense of purpose within the larger social construct. Thus, the charismatic leader fills a void in the national or local imaginary by infusing it with a semblance of political agency.

The development of a postcolonial leadership cadre reflects a breakdown or blurring of Weber's self-contained ideal types. The struggle for sovereignty in postcolonial states demanded complex representational strategies, often drawing on the devotional, customary, and rational simultaneously. The figure of Gandhi is a case in point, where ideas of the saint, lawyer, and Hindu nationalist syncretized to form a radically modern revolutionary subject. Gandhi's political evolution dispels the assumption that prescriptive forms of authority are necessarily detrimental to the interests of the citizenry. On the contrary, it demonstrates that the history of colonialism compelled a rethinking of universalist categories of knowledge in local and context-specific terms. Colonial subjugation structurally demanded a charismatic figure who could mobilize abject peoples toward the visionary ideal of freedom. Within the context of militarized colonial power, charismatic authority had to be invented by activists, intellectuals, and revolutionaries through informal means, such as Gandhi's famed Dandhi (Salt) March and other strategic displays of resistance, in order to accrue charisma on the scale necessary to achieve decolonization.

The enactment of postcolonial authority through Julius Nyerere's performance as charismatic leader reveals the invisible mechanisms through which that authority is constituted. While inventing notions of a historically new modern subjectivity—that of the postcolonial citizen—Nyerere's enactment of charismatic authority goes beyond a simple reading of effective or ineffectual head of state. The charisma of Nyerere draws attention to a phenomenon that resounded in many nascent postcolonial states, that of agrarian-based political cultures imbued with the cult of personality.

The link between charismatic power and the postcolonial agrarian state has historic roots. The genealogies of twentieth-century serfdoms suggest that emergent nationalisms were often mobilized through revolutionary incitements of peasant abjectness.[3] The mythologies of nation formation often developed around individuals, as demonstrated by the legendary figures of Mahatma Gandhi, Toussaint-Louverture, and Vladimir Lenin.

This accrual of charisma around the revolutionary-turned-nationalist uplifter of the rural masses was a crucial and evocative arena of public performance in the postcolonial state. It forged notions of both local emancipatory strategies and broader international solidarities through contradictory stagings of progressive socialist leadership, with varying degrees of coerciveness. What is important to distinguish here is the self-conscious and performative agency through which postcolonial charismatic authority is enacted as opposed to the transparent and discrete ideal types in Weber's grid. Performative ideologues—including, among others, Jomo Kenyatta of Kenya, Kwame Nkrumah of Ghana, Sukarno of Indonesia, Fidel Castro of Cuba, Sékou Touré of Guinea, Jawaharlal Nehru of India, Tito of Yugoslavia, and Nyerere—occupied this ambivalent terrain between ideology and the embodiment of ideology with an unambiguous commitment to inventing the postcolonial nationalist state. Kenyatta drew as much from notions of traditional authority in Gikuyu culture as he did from his history as a freedom fighter in the Mau Mau struggles. Similarly, other charismatic Third World leaders, from Indira Gandhi and Aung Sung Syu Kyi to the Ayatollah Khomeini and Nelson Mandela, have also mobilized the rational, spiritual, and customary to legitimize their bid for power.

In the twentieth-century histories of socialism, the charisma of socialist pedagogues has been as much a part of their strategies as their rhetorics. It is this alchemy of power combined with the secular manifestation of ideology that eludes available critiques of the kinds of political cultures that emerged during the 1960s and '70s. This power looms large behind the question, how could one person wield so much authority, accrue so much legitimacy in the name of the state? And what was specific about the political cultures of the 1960s and '70s across the Second and Third Worlds that narrativized particular states around the charismatic individualism of their figureheads, often deemed "fathers of the nation"?

Secular Identities, Public Personhood

Tanzanian socialism during the 1960s and '70s was a unique mix of utopian possibility, traumatic change, extravagant state ideology, and radical social transformation charismatically articulated through the figurehead of Julius Nyerere. His role as president of Tanzania from 1962 to 1985 brought into play the power of charisma, the theater of the state, and the production of modern socialist Tanzanian personhood in a public way.

The publicness of Nyerere's persona was a historically new kind of subjectivity—secular, socialist, and mediatized. His public performances as head of state made available a lexicon of public personhood that, prior to independence, had been inaccessible to Tanzanians. The notions of public personhood invented by Nyerere, and his development of charismatic authority, gradually engendered a public sphere of participatory politics. Its historic particularity as a turning point in the development of modern postcolonial subjectivity is interesting because it is located at the threshold of new kinds of embodiment.

Nyerere's charismatic public demeanor interwove a socialist pedagogy for the rural and urban proletariat by exercising an instructive and educative mode of political address. African socialism as envisioned by Nyerere in the early 1960s was a personal project in decolonization as much as it was an experiment in decolonizing the state. Rather than create a veneer of participatory democracy, Nyerere tested the ideas of a charismatic socialist pedagogy. Implicit in such a pedagogy were conceptions of authority that drew on interaction with and commitment to students and rural peasantry, while simultaneously rejecting attempts at hagiography. The state and head of state often blurred, as the conditions of decolonization were read as a personalized transformation of Nyerere's vision, a directorial debut in the invention of a fledgling state.

This convergence of state formation and charismatic authority encapsulates the way in which the narrativization of the state is reduced from an experiment of terrifying historic proportions to a manageable process. How better to contain the immense sense of possibility generated by independence than to localize its enormity around a personality that gives material shape to the amorphous thing called "the state"? What more effective vehicle for inventing the state than public pedagogy, becoming teacher—or *mwalimu*—to all citizens, as socialist practitioners like Chairman Mao, Zhou Enlai, and Lenin had before? Ho Chi Minh, Castro, Nkrumah, and Léopold Sédar Senghor were others in a long line of charismatic visionaries that formed the backdrop to Nyerere's invention of a public persona: that of the socialist intellectual head of state, the political philosopher as grassroots activist, the *mwalimu* of a radical African socialism in strategic opposition to global capitalist logic.

As pedagogue and actor of insurgent statehood, Nyerere trod the volatile terrain of Cold War tensions, nonaligned nation solidarities, pan-African struggles for sovereignty, and continuing resistance to the powerful dependence economies of neoimperial organizations and multinational corporations. His articulation of postcolonial socialist citizenship clashed with the vast psychic economies through which notions of nationness and statehood are mobilized against international pressures to conform with superpower ideology. For Nyerere, the daunting task of proving the viability of nonaligned socialism against the odds of Cold War economics demanded a fully vigilant and *frugal* performance of socialist citizenship. Always conscious of the performative realm necessary for progressive state socialism, Nyerere proposed a notion of frugality that is both contemporary in its lived reality and reflexive in its political commitment. Socialist modernity offered a way out of the grip of dependency for nonalignment adherents such as Nyerere.[4]

Tanzanian socialism demonstrates the informal connections between the charismatic leader and the creation and containment of a socialist public sphere. Often responding more to the promise of an idea than its materialization as an economically viable reality, the public enthusiastically endorsed Nyerere's vision of socialist citizenship. Its efficacious sense of a public socialist culture produced a belief in a socialist possibility, despite socialism's international framing as a failed experiment. This sense of a public socialist commitment depended on the charismatic authority conferred on the state as well as on its anthropomorphized symbol, the body of Nyerere.

Baba Wa Taifa / Founding Father

The iconic and performative power of Nyerere, in his collarless, khaki "Tanzanian suits," is emblematic of the visual and psychic affect embodied by a particular generation of revolutionaries. The intellectual freedom-fighter-turned-nationalist leader framed as the founding father (*baba wa taifa*) of the nation-state accrues charisma around the body of Nyerere. However, what distinguishes the iconic power of Nyerere from other leaders of his generation are the subtle politics of the autonomous self that emerges through a revolutionary-style nationalism.

The charismatic authority that imbued the presence of Nyerere allowed a public and modern conception of political autonomy to emerge. Such public visual and aural representations of political autonomy stand in tension with colonial repressions of native representations in the struggle for modern subjectivity. For the fledgling African state, the struggle for independence was also a struggle for representation against the ethnographic narratives that limited the colonized's access to sovereignty and autonomy.[5] Enlightenment ideas of development and progress infantilized natives and legitimized colonialism as a civilizing and Christianizing mission. Natives were never granted personhood. On the contrary, as Siba Grovogui points out, Africans were expected to surrender to the colonial power their right to sovereignty and related privileges. As disavowed subjects—people without personhood under colonial law—the idea of autonomy was even less possible in the eyes of the colonial. Consequently, the emergence of the postcolonial state as a modern idea ensconced in tradition had to be contended with at a visual and performative level. The postcolonial state not only had to be invented from nonexistent or depleted material resources but would have to provide contemporary mythologies, emblems, and iconic representations of modern citizenship through which postcolonial subjectivity could be enacted, overnight.[6]

By foregrounding the charismatic individual and the autonomous self as the markers of the postcolonial state, the image of Nyerere as powerful orator emphasizes presence as a function of postcolonial subjectivity. Nyerere's production of presence becomes a historically new visual representation. It moves the narrative framing of the modern African state away from its colonial representations of tribal and customary practices to its secular and transnational links as an East African postcolonial formation. His evocative style of politics functions as the disclaimer of modernity that the colonized must be civilized. Rather, it presents a critique of the ethnographic eye of the West, by emphasizing a historically dispossessed modern subjectivity—that of the postcolonial revolutionary intellectual.

The image of Nyerere in conversation with farmers, workers, and students made possible during the 1960s ideas about modern African subjectivity that colonialism had repressed and contained. It raised the historical pertinence of a particular modern subjectivity—erudite, radical, politically astute, rhetorically powerful, a product of the colonial encounter that reconfigures the relation of colonized and colonizer in new terms. For Nyerere, postcolonial subjectivity involves not just exchange between the elites and comprador class of the Third and First Worlds but, rather, a radical destabilization of race, caste, and class through the implementation of socialist Africanization. Nyerere bears the burden of history as a transitional figure because of what he could mobilize by embodying a stylish frugality. His performance of charismatic authority raises questions about the reasons for its success as a strategy during the early years of decolonization in many Third World states.

Most important, Nyerere's iconic power reinforced a belief in the idea of the state and its possibilities during the 1960s and '70s. His presence as a popular demagogue far outdistanced his role as emblem of the state to provide a new idea of the socially conscious, publicly involved, and politically committed citizen of the socialist state. It provided a new vision of the autonomous but collectively involved self, deeply concerned with the project of decolonizing the economy and forging a new idea of national identity that would be a modern socialist one. Nyerere consciously moved away from the ethnographic narrative that reduced African subjectivity to its diverse kinship and belief systems without accounting for its contemporaneous shifts under colonial rule. He represented a prescriptive way out of Tanzania's ethnographic dilemma toward a socialist modernity adapted for local needs.

The power enveloped by Nyerere's presence during the first decades of independence is historically significant because of the particular location in which the first generation of postcolonial intelligentsia found themselves. Having struggled against imperial occupation to achieve sovereignty and democracy, they were then faced with new internal pressures and the expectations of the ruling elite. As a historically new juncture, the public persona of Nyerere struggled with the contradictions between the monopolistic power of a one-party system and the idealistic image of a participatory polity, where the people's voice matters. It mediated between the promise of democracy and the anxieties of anti-imperial economic policies. Through a publicized performance of frugality and spartan living in the interests of a larger social good, Nyerere merged policies of self-reliance with a personal politics of minimal needs to offer a lived example of participatory socialist citizenship.

Nyerere's brand of individual autonomy emphasized the importance of the individual within the community through the invisible economies of charisma. It bridged international socialist pedagogy and local concerns through the lens of anticolonial struggle, incorporating the aura of revolutionary freedom-fighter-turned-nationalist leader. Nyerere self-consciously imbibed charisma, that invisible domain of power that mobilized masses in the invention or revolutionary transformation of territorial sovereignty and endowed the initiate with the mythology of the founding father.

Always gendered masculine in popular discourse, charisma for the revolutionary-radical-turned-head of state is a place of becoming—around its performative efficaciousness lies the aura of authority. With Nyerere, this careful performance of authority was remarkable in its rhetorical and argumentative open-endedness, privileging a pedagogic interactiveness over a proscenium declamation. Rejecting the ostentatious pomp and forbidding distance typically indulged in by founding fathers and heads of state, Nyerere embraced a self-effacing involvement with the people. He despised entourages. He often traveled discreetly in his presidential sedan with only one other car for security, unlike Jomo Kenyatta, who in his heyday created a spectacle with his motorcade of fifteen red Mercedes.

Power for Nyerere lay in conspicuous discretion about the personal and public engagement with students, peasants, and urban proletariat. Scenes of his digging a trench for water pipes with members of the National Service, visiting a class in Ruvu, assisting the relocation of people to *Ujamaa* villages in the Dodoma district by mixing mud for making bricks emphasized his investment in rural development during the early '70s as a sign of socialist citizenship. Nyerere's 134-mile walk to Mwanza for the Tanganyika African National Union (TANU) conference of October 1967 with rural women, old people, and youths who had marched long distances in support of the Arusha Declaration staged the idea of socialist citizenship in terms of physical commitment to public displays of solidarity.

The Mwanza trek is memorable for its staging of change on a human scale. Echoes of Gandhi's Salt March reverberating in the background, Nyerere's gesture of walking—the most common form of transport in rural areas—announced a new era of people-centered change, to be accomplished from the bottom up. Nyerere's organic approach to policy making—going directly to the people to find out their needs, debating the viability of various programs with farmers and other villagers, while personally demonstrating how to implement government policies of self-reliance—activated rural areas as privileged locales for change. In the process, his policies inadvertently polarized the urban and rural, human-scale development and industrial/technologized economies of scale, disregarding the importance of the urban in the revitalization of rural development. This dichotomy captures the contradictions in Nyerere's charismatic authority as an intellectual-policy-maker-turned-postcolonial-leader.[7]

Emergent Publicness as Visual Modernity

The rise of Nyerere as a charismatic presence must be viewed against notions of publicness prevalent at the time. Colonial administrative policies had produced two types of modern subjectivity, broadly conceived as modern and tribal. The first was the arena of life that came under the jurisdiction of colonial law, and the second that which came under the purview of customary law and native authority.[8] Colonial subjects were interpellated through these two legal systems, producing changing notions of modern subjectivity while simultaneously relegating Africans to the faceless identity of native.

Within this double realm of competing epistemologies, one colonial, the other native modernity, notions of community rights and individual rights emerged around the concept of proprietary ownership of land. Early modern colonial ideas of the individual therefore developed in relation to community, corporate, and individual rights, often in conjunction with each other.[9] Conceptions of public individualism took shape in the shift from the absence of private property in precolonial Africa to contemporary forms of property ownership through the development of landlordism and peasantry.

However, until the surreptitious manifestations of anticolonial resistance through the popularization of struggles for self-governance, the modernity of native subjectivity never gained public visibility. On the contrary, as the testimony of Joseph Kimalando, one of TANU's founders, suggests, colonial authority depended on maintaining the nebulous status of African civil servants during the late 1920s. Kimalando, a law clerk, states that as the nascent African Association formed with political advice from an Indian lawyer, the alliance generated anxiety in and was denounced by the colonial press.[10] The association with Indians was condemned by the British because they feared that the anticolonial struggle in India would be transported to Dar es Salaam, a breeding ground for political activism in the 1930s. What was then amorphous local discontent against discriminatory racial policies might assume coherent form through contact with Indian and Arab nationalist strategies of public resistance to colonial authority.[11]

Kimalando's observation is crucial to understanding the emergence of a postcolonial conception of publicness. As he argues, colonial authorities were both ruthless and anxious about the systematic displacement of local power through the importation of cheap Indian labor. This transaction served a dual purpose: it kept the local populations unskilled and at levels of invisibility that would prevent any threat to the colonizers, and it introduced a buffer class between white power and Black labor. However, this happy arrangement was tainted by the knowledge that with the import of semiskilled and technically proficient labor came the possible exchange of ideas about insurrection and resistance. The inciteful potential of the idea of publicness embedded in such notions would have hastened the idea of a free, modern African subject.

Kimalando's rise to political consciousness during the late 1920s and his political visibility by 1946 through the African Association, of which Julius Nyerere was a member, suggest that a sense of the need to conceptualize publicness was already nascent among African civil servants at the time. Growing awareness of other anticolonial struggles (such as the Mau Mau during the 1940s), poor working conditions, salary inequities, and racial discrimination catalyzed the formation of the Tanganyika African National Union (TANU) on 7 July 1954. The founding of TANU can be viewed as an epistemological break within the history of social movements in Tanganyika. It marked the shift from the colonial identity of Africans as civil servants to that of an emergent anticolonial subjectivity, the nationalists. As a modern Tanganyikan organization, TANU encapsulated the rights of indigenous citizens without a state, deprived of power to self-governance within their own territory. TANU marked the advent of public political representation through the galvanizing of a nascent, organized, local counterpublic. Both Kimalando and the Nkrumah-inspired Mwalimu Nyerere rose to public prominence as TANU's first representatives. Nyerere was elected as TANU's first president that day, initiating the move to create a public through political participation.[12]

Hence, the emergence of the public individual as a secular entity entitled to a spectrum of rights and aspirations symbolized a new kind of modern personhood—the decolonized African subject. Julius Nyerere's projection of public individualism set in motion a language of visual modernity, making available decolonized conceptions of African subjectivity. It was a sense of personhood dramatically different from the tribal and nativist articulations nurtured and kept alive through the policies of indirect rule. Indirect rule was a system of institutional segregation devised by the British in their colonies. It perpetuated and maintained the regime of differentiation that was exercised in colonial Africa and that subsequently was reformed and redefined after independence.[13]

The visual modernity embodied by Nyerere operated at a number of different levels. At the level of the individual, it created the space of an emergent postindependence subjectivity that was sovereign, contemporary, and secular. Most important, it consolidated the idea of the public personality in relation to the modern Tanzanian subject. Nyerere symbolized the tensions between prior histories of subjection and contemporary expressions of sovereignty, the complex junctures of neocolonial influence activated by the reconfiguration of Soviet, Chinese, and Western interests in Tanganyika. Through newspaper articles, radio speeches, public appearances, and photographic reproductions, his presence created the context for enunciating a public that had never before been possible.

The period of postcolonial reconstruction demanded that Nyerere perform various ideological and national interests in his public demeanor and speeches. Initiating a new kind of historical process visually, the public individualism enacted by Nyerere offered the idea of a local public personality for the first time. This new articulation of authority further dismantled dichotomous assumptions about dominating and subordinating subjects of colonialism, by playing out the complex boundaries of postcolonial hegemony. The emerging idea of public individualism marked a condition of becoming, of surviving the past and making sense of the chaotic present, of working toward the future. In this sense, Nyerere's charismatic individualism represents the state of cultural transformation from trauma to recovery. It captures the hope, apprehension, and nationalist sentiment that gripped the postcolonial state at the time.

Born into a minor ethnicity, the Zanaki, in the village of Tabora, Tanganyika, a Christian in a predominantly Muslim country, and trained as a schoolteacher at Makerere University in Kampala, Uganda, Nyerere's own fractured subjectivity unconsciously played out the shifting grids of class, gender, ethnicity, religion, and geographic location through his policies. Through self-reliance, nonracialism, and nationalization—policies key to his socialist program—he strove to reconcile the tensions of location through which subjectivity is constituted. Simultaneously incorporating and negating the complexities of subjectivity in the interests of a larger public good, Nyerere's public individualism dramatically conflicted with his policies of self-effacement and negation of presence. His policies emphasized rural community development at the expense of the urban—which included diverse migrant enclaves—and repressed ethnic tensions under the guise of socialist citizenship, thus restraining the kinds of minoritarian strife that tore apart other emerging states. In opposition to the conflicting interests and identities of divided and discontinuous agents of political change, Nyerere's policies suggest the strategic curtailing of sub-jectivities to create an appearance of a cohesive, monolithic subjecthood.[14]

Nyerere and Crowds

In the interest of developing the appearance of a cohesive and consensu-ally constituted state, Nyerere's political strategies included forging the idea of a tangible public. Central to this conception was the crowd. The crowd in early Tanzanian culture could be seen as a crucial site for galva-nizing and manipulating postcolonial subjectivity. During the early 1970s, crowds represented a critical mass of national subjectivity, bringing to-gether fragmentary identifications in powerful displays of solidarity. The crowd emerges during this period as a new kind of public entity with a new kind of historic possibility. The crowd set in motion conceptions of a public postcolonial subjectivity, activated by local Tanzanians in relation to the head of state. Nyerere and the crowd—in Mnazi Mmoja Park, at the National Stadium, at the Karimjee Hall, in the streets of Dar es Salaam, at the State House grounds—actualized a historically new relationship between the modern individual and the collective.[15]

This new relationship is that of an emergent participatory polity: be-tween charismatic authority and the democratic crowd. While anticolonial resistance had drawn together different ethnicities in the spirit of national fervor, the renegotiation of the populace as a postcolonial polity demanded new approaches to politics. In his speeches from 1952 to 1965, Nyerere carefully and insistently lays out the tools and strategies necessary to ac-tivate such a postcolonial public—discussion, equality, and freedom. For Nyerere, "discussion is one essential factor of any democracy, and the African is expert at it."[16] However, this transition to democracy was a painstakingly orchestrated one that rejected considerations of a two-party system in the interests of national unity and cohesiveness. Class hierarchy was rejected as a foreign import. "Traditionally the African knows no 'class,'" Nyerere argued. "I doubt if there is a word in any African language which is equivalent to 'class' or 'caste.'"[17] By deploying notions of classless-ness derived from African social structures, Nyerere developed a new dis-course of African democracy, one in tension with Western concepts. In his early formulation of democratic participation, found in "The African and Democracy," Nyerere expresses doubts about the suitability of Anglo-Saxon democracy for Africa. He challenges the ideas of government em-bodied in some of the West's most cherished documents by exposing their contradictions:

It was possible for the framers of the Declaration of Independence to talk about "the inalienable rights of Man" although they believed in exceptions; it was possible for Abraham Lincoln to bequeath to us a perfect definition of democracy although he spoke in a slave-owning society; it was possible for my friends the British to brag about "democracy" and still build a great Empire for the glory of the Britons.

These people were not hypocrites. They believed in democracy . . . but they lived in a world which excluded masses of human beings from its idea of "equality" and felt few scruples doing so. Today, in the twentieth century, this is impossible. Today, the Hungarys, the Little Rocks, the Tibets, the Nyasalands, and the Bantustans must be explained away somehow. They are embarrassing in this century of the Universal Declaration of Human Rights.[18]

Nyerere's approach to democratic participation drew more from what he called tribal socialism. It shaped the foundation and objective of his policies for African socialism, *ujamaa*, or familyhood:

We, in Africa, have no more need of being "converted" to socialism than we have of being "taught" democracy. Both are rooted in our past—in the traditional society which produced us. Modern African socialism can draw from its traditional heritage the recognition of "society" as an extension of the basic family unit. But it can no longer confine the idea of the social family within the limits of the tribe, nor, indeed, of the nation. . . . Our recognition of the family to which we all belong must be extended yet further— beyond the tribe, the community, the nation, or even the continent—to embrace the whole society of mankind. This is the only logical conclusion for true socialism.[19]

In this early blueprint for African socialism, Nyerere inscribes notions of authority, participation, and pedagogy by drawing on existing cultural practices of discussion and consent. His public performance as teacher of the nation reinforced what he outlined in his conceptions of *ujamaa* as familyhood, setting up a powerfully evocative and direct relationship between head of state and political subjects. This relationship predetermined the head of state as *mwalimu* (teacher) to the crowd of citizens, as Nyerere employed discussion and encouraged public participation in the creation of a political public. This political public was a univocal, consensual public, a one-party democracy self-consciously formulated in opposition to the multiparty democracies of Western nations. Consequently, the political public was only one emergent site of publicness, the one consolidated through the performance of crowds—crowds of farmers, students, workers. The crowd in the early postcolonial state, strengthened by its visual and heterogeneous anticipation of national affirmation, demarcated the dramatic change from the silenced voices under colonial bureaucracy to the visceral depth of a people in consent. What is important about the crowd in early Tanzanian political culture is its formulation as a democratic socialist crowd: it was the extension of the idea of a socialist state.[20]

The crowd consolidated Nyerere's conception of a one-party nation in spatial terms. Most important, this crowd occupied the spaces of Dar es Salaam en masse, in ways that were not possible under colonial segregationist policies. European and Asian spaces were reclaimed as Tanzanians migrated across the invisible markers of colonial segregation, undoing the racist logic that formerly shaped the city. Schools, shops, hotels, streets, houses, gardens, and beaches acquired a "local" look under the Africanizing and nationalizing measures adopted by TANU. Students streaming through the Asian section of Upanga, workers leaving the docks and railways heading across the visible class lines of housing toward the workers' estate areas of Temeke and Chang'ombe, domestic workers and laborers walking the long distances across the class and race lines of unaffordable accommodations toward Kariakoo, Illala, and Magomeni—all marked the slowly reconfiguring tensions of class and ethnicity operating in the city.[21]

Conceptions of a public sphere in a desegregating city most evocatively take hold in the national imagination through crowds in performance. With the heady accumulation of dramatic political events, a sense of history-in-the-making energized the crowds, strengthening the spatial realization of the city as an emblem of the nation. Independence, the creation of the Republic, the army mutiny, the establishment of the Organization of African Unity Liberation Headquarters, and visits by various heads of state exposed the Dar es Salaam citizenry to an idea of politics that was popular as well as tangible.[22]

Crowds in Mnazi Mmoja Park listened to the first speeches of the Arusha Declaration with nationalist pride. Crowds along Lumumba Street heard of the new Africanizing measures. Crowds gathered along Sokoine Drive and Kivukoni Front to welcome visiting dignitaries. Student crowds performed socialist group exercises with sticks and clubs for state holidays. Dance troupes performed *ngomas* (folk dances) on the streets during national holidays and Saba Saba. These were some of the avenues through which a dynamic conception of a national public began to emerge in the spaces of the postcolonial city of the 1960s and early '70s.[23]

While these sites consolidated a popular sense of an emerging national public within the city, other avenues of publicness were constituted under interests widely divergent from that of the national culture. Alternative publics continued to coexist in tense relationship with state attempts to create a proletarian public sphere closely regulated by socialist policy. Many of these often dispersed publics had a long and sometimes informal tradition of affiliation and social expression under British colonial rule. They had frequently been subjected to oppressive laws restricting public displays of group solidarity and had been crucial in fomenting the seeds of counterauthoritarian sentiment. The African Association, the diverse East African Islamic literary communities that during the 1930s nurtured early discussions of Swahili nationalism, and the different branches of the East African Indian Association were all avenues of intellectual exchange, political organizing, and social gathering that had either officially or surreptitiously existed under British rule and would lead new lives under state socialism.

During the early years of decolonization, these diverse religious and social groupings originating in Tanzania's different ethnic communities were permitted to maintain their sectarian cultural practices while also participating in the larger, secular socialist sphere of political life as citizens. This relative freedom of expression generated a wide array of local publics within Tanzanian Asian communities as well as in the broader culture, giving rise to an eclectic network of work associations, clubs (jazz, football, radio, street-corner), and entertainment groups, communicating through the exchange of local news.[24]

In contrast to the dominant public image of Asians as traders or businessmen, the elaborate social institutions of Asian cultural life demonstrated complex fissures across caste, class, language, immigrant histories, and professional occupations. As opposed to the monolithic construct of the mercenary middlemen of Tanzanian society, the various avenues of civil society created by Asians expressed a heterogeneous and nationally divergent community of people. Bohoras, Gujerathis, Ithnasheris, Muslims, Hindus, Punjabis, Goans, and Parsees belonged to private social networks, which often subsidized private schools and social institutions such as the Khalsa Club, the Kerala Kala Mandalam, the Goan Institute, and the Patel Brotherhood, to name a few, until the nationalization policies following the *ujamaa* declaration of 1967 put an end to such multiple allegiances.

At the time of Tanganyikan independence, Asians owned considerable amounts of land around Bagamoyo, Tanga, Kilwa, and other towns, holding a monopoly on buildings and commercial enterprises. They also occupied substantial portions of land around the edges of Dar es Salaam, since this area had been part of the Asian sector under colonial rule.[25] With such a powerfully entrenched business community whose history of assimilation, integration, and collaboration with local Tanganyikans was as tenuous and ambivalent as it was with Indians outside their own narrow communities, the possibility of incorporating new modes of citizenship seemed precarious and uncertain.

Faced with the daunting task of introducing democratic citizenship in the context of glaring economic and infrastructural inequities, Nyerere's rhetoric of nonracialism was an attempt to soften the transition from European and Asian minority hegemony to the hard-won sovereignty of African majority. His policies of nationalization and Africanization are crucial in the history of East African–Asian identity formation for their particular efforts to avoid race conflicts while forging ahead with the business of nation building. Nyerere's philosophically compelling arguments against race tensions—what he called "nonracialism" in the interest of the African majority—came up against entrenched and volatile arguments for more overtly anti-Asian legislation from nationalist sections of the party. In the climate of economic nationalism that fueled anti-Asian sentiment in Milton Obote's and later Idi Amin's Uganda and Jomo Kenyatta's Kenya, Nyerere's policies seemed fair, even reasonable, ironically providing a respite for Asians fleeing Uganda and Kenya. While on the one hand the nationalizing measures in Tanzania dramatically affected most Asian involvements in East Africa, Nyerere's charisma provided a gloss of equanimity to what seemed at the time catastrophic measures for minority non-African entrepreneurship in East Africa. The trauma of financial loss did not prevent Asians from hanging black-and-white photographs of Nyerere in their living rooms, a tribute to his charismatic impact as leader of the nation.

3

Ujamaa and Soul

Transnational Desires for Soul

In November 1969, Julius K. Nyerere, president of Tanzania, outlawed "soul music." The ban was accompanied by warnings that the state would take action against soul nightclubs that ignored state policy.[1] A popular explanation for the ban was the need to curb the perceived Americanizing influences locally embodied by the thriving soul clubs, and nationally to insist on less conspicuous consumption. The excessive display of pleasure and leisure epitomized by local bars and discos jarred the official policy of *ujamaa*, or frugality as a way of life. The ban on soul clubs was explicitly articulated in transnational terms. It was a conscious effort to promote local as well as national expressive forms while controlling the kinds of non-Tanzanian influences that introduced forms of consumption in opposition to the state ideology of economic and socialist restraint. The ban generated distinctions between the city and the country, between "American" influences in urban popular culture—whether through clubs, musical genres like funk and soul, or lifestyle—and expressive, urban forms grounded in local cultural practices. The ban against soul clubs marked the city of Dar es Salaam as a transnationally mediated locale, whose urbanity contained ideologically contradictory expressive forms that went against the philosophy of *ujamaa*.

The ban was eventually lifted. But at the time, the move to censor soul clubs and the popular culture of migrant, cosmopolitan Dar es Salaam coincided with an expansion of investment in rural development. Performances of *ujamaa* policies permeated daily life in myriad ways through the economic and public displays of frugality. Ideas of individual freedom considerably narrowed the interests of the public good. Intrusion of the state into both public culture and avenues of the private generated discreet modes of enjoyment, with new meanings and commodities accruing around the notions of soul culture after 1969. Where previously soul culture and African socialism had forged a symbiotic expressivity in the public spaces of the city—clubs, discos, radio programs, posters, street culture, high school—the new official anxiety around the meanings and appropriations of soul created popular dissent and surreptitious circulations of soul consumption.

Revisiting 1970s socialism and soul culture from the vantage point of the United States in the '90s raises important questions about the structures of enjoyment embedded in the anticapitalist stance of many emergent socialist states such as Tanzania during the early years of decolonization. Most critiques of '70s socialist cultures readily dismiss socialism as having no soul, the inherent assumption being that only capitalism can provide leisure enjoyment through the free and ideologically uncontaminated flow of consumption. Such binary critiques oversimplify the relationship of citizens as consumers to state formations. These critiques further elide the intricate and subtle strategies with which state ideologies such as capitalism and socialism, and cultural commodities such as soul culture, mediate and blur the boundaries of political rhetorics through transnational economies of consumption.

The disparate diasporic sites of soul culture allow for a more nuanced reading of the connections and slippages between citizenship, transnational political ideologies, and cultural commodities. During the 1970s, conflicting ideologies, international capital, transnational affiliations within Cold War politics, and the expansion of a Pan-African popular culture all converge in soul culture. Its international dissemination raises the question of how cultural commodities from the United States were deployed as state propaganda to counter the rising fear of socialism within and beyond the United States.

The export of U.S. entertainment industries through the State Department as part of its international foreign policy during the Cold War masked the ideological boundaries of consumption.[2] In the antisocialist propaganda launched during the Cold War, socialism is marked out as a deracinating, de-eroticizing politics of scarcity. Socialism becomes an undifferentiated blank space with a functionalist understanding of need. What is erased in this reductivist definition is the spectrum of cultural forms generated through ideologically contradictory strategies of production and reception. This circulation of cultural commodities by way of official and informal spheres of consumption opens out the subtler areas of enjoyment through which an indigenous socialist youth culture emerges. Such circuits of exchange demand a more inflected reading of enjoyment under international socialism.

This chapter traces some of the sites of enjoyment produced within Tanzanian notions of *ujamaa*, or self-reliance. Afro-American soul culture of the 1970s opened up sites of socialist longing through its informal dispersal into underground urban Tanzanian life. Operating ambivalently within the seductive and exploitive boundaries of U.S. imperialism—consumerism being the new face of imperial expansion—soul prompted an international as well as local resurgence of Pan-African desire in Tanzanian popular culture. The circulation of Afro-American popular culture through dramatically different ideological and geographical terrain beyond its national context foregrounds the complexities of transnationalism. It accentuates the implications of transnationalism for contingent and specific nationalisms both within the United States, such as Black nationalism, and in other nations such as Tanzania. It reveals the inherent paradoxes of a Pan-African aesthetic of political and rhetorical possibility under socialism. Its mobile cultural capital and global repercussions during this period suggest a complex array of issues that disappear when Afro-American culture is viewed only within the U.S. context. The mobility of Black culture as a transforming commodity adds yet another dimension to the critiques made by Gladstone Yearwood, Ed Guerrero, Manthia Diawara, Jacquie Jones, Michele Wallace, and Mark Reid: of the misogyny, the criminalizing of Black communities as an underworld of hustlers, the pathologizing of Black masculinity, and the one-dimensional plots and characters found in many Afro-American pop-cult texts.[3]

Soul culture was caught in the transnational economy of traveling commodities, serving during this time as an ambassador of official U.S. culture abroad. Sports through the performance of the Harlem Globetrotters and Muhammad Ali, Black music, Blaxploitation cinema, and the struggle for visibility in Afro-American popular culture are read and translated differently outside the domain of their national context. The impact of Afro-American culture during the 1970s far exceeds the boundaries of the United States, as the work of Paul Gilroy, Ngugi wa Thiong'o, and

Manthia Diawara, among others, demonstrates.[4] Soul's transnational circulations connect with Tanzanian socialist possibilities for enjoyment in subtle and provocative ways.

Ujamaa *as Soul*

Tanzanian socialism was predicated on a conscious anticolonialist move to delink from the West's imperial obsessions. Beginning with independence in 1961, the rhetoric of postindependent Tanzania (whose name was itself forged out of the violent struggle for independence, joining Tanganyika and Zanzibar to form Tanzania) was the optimistic and self-conscious attempt at a socialism that would create its own autonomy as a nation-state. Education and the social imaginary would be decolonized through the new ideology of *ujamaa.*

This radical move to invent an African socialism of self-reliance was contingent on collaborative negotiations with Tanzania's neighbors, Uganda and Kenya. *Ujamaa* offered the possibility of a self-contained state whose citizens would devote their services to the sovereign nation, with the greater good of the Federation of East Africa in mind. *Ujamaa*'s logic of sacrificing individual desire on the altar of public good was intended to achieve a radical delinking in the present while laying the foundation for a more egalitarian and self-reliant society in the future. The concept of self-reliance implicitly assumed that radical conservatism in the short term would allow for a form of liberal socialism in the long run.[5]

The rhetoric of the unified state produced by Tanzanian socialism generated many regulative logics in the interest of an egalitarian and educated civil society. One such logic was the production of citizens as agents. The Arusha Declaration of 1967 was a self-conscious move to animate citizenship as a pedagogical exercise in the nation's performance as a newly independent state. The declaration's philosophy of governance and economics of self-reliance would redefine the participation of indigenous peoples as actors within their own state. The Arusha Declaration produced a system of state control whose rhetoric announced a radical realignment of private interests as state interests, through policies that articulated the redistribution of wealth, land, and international dependency relationships. The declaration was an elaborate philosophical argument to disengage from the systems of capital that would create neocolonial economies subordinate to and dependent on former imperial powers. Consequently, by the late 1960s the nationalization of land, buildings, private property, businesses, and education had created a monolithic state-regulated economy through which cultural work could emerge, but on radically nationalist and social-ist terms.[6]

Tanzanian socialism struggled to define a progressive possibility while setting up state apparatuses for the social regulation of desire. In other words, most forms of consumption were legitimated, funded, and con-trolled by the state. Cultural production and distribution were an exten-sion of state ideology, without the extreme forms of policing that such regulative logics took in China or the Soviet Union, for instance. Under Tanzanian socialism, self-reliance allowed plenty of leeway within schools, entertainment, leisure, and political associations to create an elaborate and multilayered society yet to be articulated as civil society. The negotiation of cultural citizenship in such a newly independent state would have to play out in the interstices of formal and informal popular culture, such as Tanzanian soul culture.[7]

Pan-African Longing and Soul

Tanzania's sympathies with Leninist and Maoist ideologies existed in tense relation to the ideological agenda of the United States. Blaxploitation film and Afro-American cultural production circulated in such a transnational economy as socialist commodities embodying capitalism's mobility. The particular significance of the transnational circulation of commodities from the United States during this period lay in its embodiment of Cold War political tensions. Afro-American cultural production circulated inde-pendently of mainstream U.S. ideology; its "internationalism" tapped into local Pan-African sensibilities.

The visuality and aurality of Afro-American commodities influenced local Tanzanian subcultural practices of youth culture and style. It gener-ated an internationalist patina of modernity experienced by local Tanza-nian youth as a transnational desire for Pan-African belonging. This Pan-African youth style activated resistance to forms of state authoritarianism and opened up contingent modernities that exploded West/non-West narratives of both the Cold War and state socialism. Pirated, legitimate, and bootlegged Afro-American culture permeated Tanzanian youth self-invention, circumventing the social regulation of political desire through the contradictory identification of "Americanness" as Blackness.[8]

The transnational commodification of soul raises difficult questions about consumption as it travels, translates, and is reinvented through local-ized receptions and circulations of meaning. The material effects of these formal and informal circulations of soul in the West, as well as in what were referred to as developing nations and newly emergent African states such as Tanzania, were a complex and rich conglomeration of imagined readings. The co-optations, evocative linkages, and rhetorical connections generated in Tanzanian popular culture through these commodities elaborated on the tensions, promises, and betrayals of modernity. They invoked the Black feminist radicalism of June Jordan, Maya Angelou, and Angela Davis; the struggle for rights of *Cleopatra Jones;* the urban decay and class politics in James Brown's 1974 albums *Hell, Payback,* and *Reality;* the anticolonial strategies of *Superfly TNT;* the cosmopolitan extravagance of Grace Jones; and the Pan-African longings of Aretha Franklin, Muhammad Ali, and Miriam Makeba.

This sphere of ideological contestations, where Blackness signifying Americanness blurs the boundaries between state regulation of desire and spectatorial seduction by capitalist consumption, demonstrates the antagonistic sites of enjoyment as agency. Enjoyment becomes crucial to expressing forms of cultural citizenship. As consumers of commodities, citizens negotiate contradictory identifications as free agents within authoritarian states. In this site of pleasurable social antagonism, Ron O'Neal, Tamara Dobson, James Brown, Angela Davis, and Muhammad Ali represent struggles against state exploitation, whether capitalist or socialist. They embody the appeal of capitalist self-fashioning signified by their lifestyle and the intoxicating promise of a fully democratic, capitalist state. They realize a transnational sense of Black radicalism through their free and open performance of dissent and insurgency within the international imaginary, as Black feminists, Black communists, Black guerrillas, Black Muslims, or international Black pop icons. They perform a modernity that disrupts the economic rhetorics of scarcity and dependency by proposing transnational links of solidarity and struggle.

The question of cultural capital is another route along which the international repercussions of soul travel. In Tanzania, the cultural capital embedded in these commodities needs to be read in conjunction with the anti-imperial, anticapitalist sentiment of *ujamaa,* the philosophy of self-reliance expounded by Julius Nyerere. Nyerere's experiments in African socialism were a radically utopian struggle to escape the West's economic grip. Tanzanian socialism combined an eclectic and nonpartisan attitude of cultural open-mindedness toward both the East and the West, while limiting avenues of consumption in the interest of the nation's greater good. The closing of imports and exports, and the blocking of private enterprises and public opportunities for international trade, homogenized the avenues of consumption in unprecedented ways. Chinese stationery,

Chinese shoes, Chinese books, and Soviet-sponsored machines, railway technology, teachers, and books became the visible representations of this homogenization. So, while at any given time commodities such as sugar, milk, or luxury items of any kind except locally produced fabrics and other goods might be unavailable, one could always buy rubber-soled Bata shoes with plastic uppers, or yellow HB pencils, or notebooks with Marxist slogans stamped "Made in China" marking their ideological legitimation.

In this narrowly construed international public sphere, the possible imagined spaces more immediately invoked Castro's Cuba, Tito's Yugoslavia, Mao's socialism, or Brezhnev's Soviet solidarity. Alternative modernities were imagined primarily through music, of which Afro-American music and the new glut of Hollywood films geared for Third World countries—such as Blaxploitation films and Westerns—comprised a considerable portion. The kung fu movies of Bruce Lee, Jim Kelly, Richard Roundtree, and Ron O'Neal competed for attention in a market flooded by spaghetti westerns, Russian, Hong Kong, and Chinese kung fu movies, Hindi melodramas, John Wayne, and Clint Eastwood. Films like *Shaft in Africa*, *Cleopatra Jones*, *Superfly TNT*, and *Sheba Baby* created an eclectic and nuanced kung fu–loving, Hindi "flim"–acquainted, Western genre–immersed Tanzanian audience whose Pan-African imaginings resonated most immediately with the gun-toting, Afro-haired heroine of the platform shoes, taller than any white man around, and perhaps a bit too tough, though always cool in her ultraBlackness. (This was the early '70s: killing Native Americans was not cool, but it was less cool to kill Blacks on screen.) Here was an imagining of the democratic possibility that appealed to Tanzanian socialist youth dreaming about a more seductive kind of social transformation than *ujamaa* promised, a transformation that would incorporate red, wet-look jackets, fabulous bell-bottomed trousers, bad Lamborghinis, and soulful revolutionaries like Superfly driving down the disappearing highways of economic modernity. (I would have swapped my kangas and kitengas for your crimplene, or terrylene, or blue jeans—if only you had crossed my path.) A seven-shilling fantasy, a complete contradiction of one's socialist sympathies and convictions, but benign because one has the Pan-African thread to legitimate it.

About Sex Machines, Black Moses, and Soulful States

The early 1970s drew on a broad range of Pan-African styles to fabricate a local and specifically Tanzanian cool, and the Godfather of Soul, Mr. James Brown, was very much part of this screeching, screaming, and evocative culture of emergent nationalisms and their dissonant resistances. Caught between the powerful rhetoric of the coherent, homogeneous African state and its populace of diverse ethnicities, religions, and languages, the subtext of *ujamaa* was the nagging and volatile question of Tanzania's heterogeneous citizenry of Arab, Chinese, Indian, Persian, and African extraction who practice Muslim, Christian, Sikh, Ismaili, Hindu, and indigenous religions. The rise of economic nationalism in Uganda, which resulted in the expulsion of its Asian citizens in 1972 by Field Marshall Al Hadj Dr. Idi Amin Dada, further exacerbated a climate of fear and anxiety within East Africa's Asian communities of second- and third-generation citizens. Like a *bui-bui* in the afternoon light just before the four o'clock rains, one question hung loosely around the politics of Tanzanian belonging during the 1970s: could Tanzanian Asians have soul?

The answer to this question was crucial because like soul music soul-style politics were tied to a distinct yet inexpressible soulness of contemporary Tanzanian modernity. Beginning with Julius Nyerere's own production of a certain cosmopolitan and urban-style politics—the collarless safari suits and *kitenge* shirts, the organic intellectual as self-styled pedagogue or Mwalimu of the newly independent state—soul style permeated national fashion. Following a longer international tradition of Black radical intellectuals as self-styled revolutionaries/leaders such as Malcolm X, C. L. R. James, Martin Luther King Jr., Kwame Nkrumah, Léopold Sédar Senghor, Jomo Kenyatta, and W. E. B. Du Bois, Nyerere practiced a soulful socialism, emancipatory in its vision. Socialist-style politics for Nyerere were first and foremost internationalist in the organizing metaphors of revolution, proletarian radicalism, New Left complexity, Black and Third World solidarity, while materially located firmly in myths of soil and roots, and national as well as Pan-African philosophies of belonging.

For a generation of Tanzanian Asians growing up under *ujamaa*, caught between Nyerere's vision and the parochialism of ethnic particularities such as being Muslim, Ismaili, Christian, Sikh, or Hindu, self-fashioning an aesthetic of cool became crucial. As new subjects of the socialist experiment, their struggle for cultural citizenship and belonging was linked to a Pan-African utopia and the fabrication of an East African–Asian brand of cool. Tanzanian Asian youth of the late '60s and '70s were self-conscious about assimilation, integration, and acquiring soul in the eyes of the nation. But could Asian teens do the boogie or the bump? And if they did, why only within their segregated ghettos and enclaves of their petit bourgeois fiefdom? If only they could, they would have donned Afros, shades, platform shoes à la Shaft, Angela Davis, Miriam Makeba, Fred Williamson,

James Brown, and Diana Ross. But the creation of Asian cool was to be negotiated on ethnically specific terms, mediated by the Hindi films and Muslim cultural practices of popular everyday life.

If East Africa were to come to terms with its Asians—the Pakistani, Indian, and Chinese communities whose migrations to the East African coast were as old as the slave trade—Asian youth might function as the bridge. Youth and their education provided the testing ground for the new nation's invention as a confident and self-reliant state. The streets, parks, roads, and parade grounds became the public spaces of youth education, within which Asians had to negotiate Tanzanian soul. At a time of large-scale youth mobilization through sports, drills, *ngomas* (folk dances), marches, public addresses by Mwalimu Nyerere and other Tanganyika African National Union (TANU) apparatchiks, the formal and informal circulations of soul carried no small weight. For Asian youth, this was a time to recover a certain kind of soul for themselves as citizens. Asians had participated in the articulation of Black consciousness. They had struggled alongside other Tanzanians against imperialism. But this isolated history of a tenuous minority had been submerged by a resurgent nationalism, and Tanzanian Asians were precariously perched as undesirables. Though ambivalently situated, Hindu, Muslim, Sikh, Ismaili, Confucian, Buddhist, Jain, Zoroastrian, and Christian, largely Goan, populations of Asian Tanzanians were simultaneously transformed by soulful socialism.

Many of these communities already bore complex histories of migration, coming from South Asia, Mauritius, other African countries like Uganda and South Africa, with powerful experiences of persecution, poverty, and antiminority sentiment. In this context, funky self-invention was a site of great social antagonism for Tanzanian Asian youth. Urban Asian youth subculture, located primarily in Dar es Salaam, drew on James Brown, Angela Davis, the Black Panthers, the music of soul, and the masculinist discourse of Black American radicalism, which traveled and translated into locally specific terms. "Soul" was scrawled in public places; James Brown's "sex machine" was scribbled on high school walls, motor bikes, and necklaces; the gold chain and shades of Isaac Hayes (better known as Black Moses) had their very local Hindi movie versions; phrases like "dig," "soul sister," and "soul brother" slowly shaped a nascent discourse of Asian cool in its interpretive reinventions of Black cool, mingling with Tanzanian socialism's mandatory *ndugu*, or comrade.

For Tanzanian Asian teen culture of the '70s, soul offered the possibility of cultural citizenship, of "integrating" through an international Black cool. When Asians were expelled from East Africa in the early 1970s, their ambivalent relationship to the production of East African soul became imbricated with questions of authenticity. Did Asians not have enough soul to pass? Always sojourners vis-à-vis their political stakes in East Africa, Asians both constructed themselves and were read as being ambivalent about East African citizenship during the early '70s. Soul embodied a certain Tanzanian essentialism that would continuously produce its minority citizens as not having enough soul for Tanzanian socialism. For East Africans during the '70s, Asians would never have soul enough for the new nation-state.

Traveling Internationalists and People Who Never Move

For Tanzanians nurtured within a socialist internationalism articulated through the state's founding rhetoric of freedom and unity, *uhuru na umoja*, travel was crucial to a Pan-African imagining. The mystique of mobility was linked to an aesthetic of Pan-Africanism. The African National Congress used Dar es Salaam as its headquarters throughout its turbulent years; exiled South African nationalists, writers, and intellectuals continuously traveled to and from Tanzania, using it as a mediating place for future revolutions. Nyerere's support of Frelimo and liberation struggles in Angola, Namibia, Mozambique, and South Africa situated Tanzania in complex ways to other African states, and in turn, the idea of a certain Black internationalism shaped the ideology of the Tanzanian state.

Miriam Makeba, the soul of South African music at the time, had a Tanzanian passport, and her marriage to Stokely Carmichael linked East Africa indirectly to the Black Power movement in the United States.[9] The continuous front-page coverage of Angela Davis, George Jackson, the Black Panthers, and the emergence of a style politics simulating Afro-American hairstyle and fashion blurred the boundaries between the harsh reality of U.S. racism and the broader rhetorics of empowerment and revolution that Black American visuality and music made possible. Here was a Black modernity that imagined and fashioned new agents of history both cinematically and aurally for postcolonial Tanzania. The encounter with ideologies at the level of the visual, aural, and phantasmic escaped the rigid boundaries of state control, where the rhetoric of class and labor precluded the articulation of gender, transnational desire, and consumption as forms of cultural citizenship, and Blackness as a traveling aesthetic.

Colonialism and its economic aftermath, postindependence scarcity, established travel as a class-determined space. Unless you were an expatriate making the mandatory trip back to a place that had already forgotten you, only the privileged could afford to travel. In other words, in the national imaginary the proletariat did not move, but in fact, migrancy into cities rose exponentially. Postindependence economic strategies and agrarian restructuring prompted a massive movement of peoples between Dar es Salaam and the rest of the country. On the one hand was a strong invocation of land and agriculture that gave a renewed sense of rootedness and on the other were the dramatic changes wrought by industrialization and expansion necessary to sustain the modernity of self-reliance, locked between utopian visions of economic delinking and large-scale assistance from transnational companies from China and the Eastern bloc countries. In such a space of conflicting codes, a cosmopolitan character like Ron O'Neal's Priest in *Superfly TNT* has more in common with Tanzanian popular imagination than the rhetoric of state socialism, while both coexist in their contradictory pleasurability. As Priest, O'Neal is a nomad in Europe. He drives coupes in Rome, speaks Italian, travels to Senegal, has lived in France, England, and Norway, is chased by paparazzi, helps a West African Francophone revolutionary (played by Roscoe Lee Browne) overthrow colonialism in a West African nation called Umbia, befriends a fellow African American expatriate (Robert Guillaume) living in exile in Rome who sings in Italian—all to a script by Alex Haley, directed by Ron O'Neal, with music by Osibisa.

While negative critiques of *Superfly* (directed by Gordon Parks Jr., with a soundtrack by Curtis Mayfield) and its sequel *Superfly TNT* are numerous and valid, I want to point out the contradictory spectatorial pleasures for an urban Tanzanian audience embedded in Priest's evolution from a dolce vita–style nihilist to active historical agent. *Superfly TNT* provides the imaginative terrain of agency for a kind of popular hero who is allowed a political and visual modernity not otherwise available to the average Tanzanian citizen. The translation of Priest as a traveling hero is linked to his African American ethnicity. Priest's cultural and economic capital is translatable in specific ways for a local Tanzanian as a mobile and seductively insurgent agency, simultaneously Western and anti-imperial. In *Superfly TNT*, there is style, radicalism, a critique of capital, and real dollar value attached to the historic visibility of Afro-American visual modernity in '70s Tanzanian popular imagination.

Tanzanian soul culture shaped the structural feel of urban youth socialism and its Pan-African imaginings of revolution. Along with film, radio was the primary vehicle for disseminating international culture, as there was no television and scant visual representation of pop icons. All official forms of entertainment were mediated by the state and hence bore the signs of its legitimacy. As the most popular and versatile site of mass consumption, the radio generated disparate and heterogeneous audiences. Seventies Tanzanian nationalism deployed the popular appeal of soul music among other forms of popular music, to fill the material vacuum in times of economic hardship. As records were largely unavailable and certainly unaffordable, funk operated as an inventive terrain in a context of scarcity (where very little goes a long way), oddly congruent with policies of self-reliance. The visuality of Aretha Franklin's numerous hairstyles and fashions, Isaac Hayes's style politics, James Brown's closing gestures with the mike, the Jackson Five's spectacles, all would be encounters to be had as a traveler or in exile, new but familiar resonances experienced as a dislocation from the specificity of the United States. Invoking a specific time (the 1970s), place (Dar es Salaam), context (radical socialism), and technology (the radio and spool tape), these would be texts to be revisited on new terms, on different terrain in diaspora.

4

Kung Fu Cinema and Frugality

Ujamaa and Tanzanian Youth in the 1970s

In the opening scene of his performance piece "In Between Space," Shishir Kurup, a Los Angeles–based Asian American performance artist, narrates growing up in Mombasa, Kenya, in the 1970s:

> We live over here in Pandya House, a tenement building with shops and of-
> fices below. Over here is the Regal Cinema which exclusively plays American
> shoot-'em-ups, Italian spaghetti shoot-'em-ups, and Chinese Kung-Fu-'em-
> ups. Sam Peckinpah, Sergio Leone, Run-Run Shaw, Raymond Chow. Tickets
> are two shillings and forty cents for rows A–J (which work out at about a quar-
> ter in American cash), 3/6 for rows K–Z, and 4/8 for the balcony. In this thea-
> ter Eastwood is badass, McQueen is cool, Bronson is tough, and Bruce Lee
> can kick all their asses. Shane and Shaft and Superfly and Cleopatra Jones. We
> hear names like Thalmas Rasulala and Lee Van Cleef. Eli Wallach is the Ugly,
> Yul Brynner the King, and I the kid with the open mouth stuffing popcorn
> down my throat. In the Indian film houses, Rajesh Khanna, "Shotgun" Sinha,
> Dharmendra, reign supreme. Amitabh Bhachan isn't quite the god he is soon
> to become and Zeenat Aman is the babe of all our nocturnal emissions.[1]

What Kurup invokes for Mombasa could be found elsewhere in East Africa at this time. Seventies cinema had a transnational impact that intertwines broader ideological, nationalist, Pan-Africanist, and anticolonialist sentiments in the local cultural politics of production and consumption. In the midst of Cold War tensions, nationalist fervor, state sovereignty, and a visible Pan-African solidarity, East African popular culture is a crucible in the competing international ideologies of socialism, communism, and capitalism across and within national borders. The simultaneous transnational figuration of these ideologies had an impact on local cultural politics within Third World socialisms.[2]

In Tanzania, for example, experiments in socialist democracy foregrounded education and cultural nationalism as primary tools for solidifying the fledgling state. Tanzanian youth were mobilized toward the broader goal of promoting a socialist youth culture. The harnessing of youth in the interest of national culture influenced possible subjectivities, pleasures, and forms of spectatorship. This in turn affected the styles and self-fashioning consumed and publicly exhibited by youth.

In this chapter I investigate some of the connections among diasporic South Asian youth culture, state socialism, and transnationalism by considering the immense appeal and wide circulation of Bruce Lee and kung fu cinema during the 1970s in Tanzania. I examine the early years of nation building through the mobilization of youth from the subjective standpoint of my experiences as a Tanzanian Asian youth under the Africanization and nationalization measures enacted in Dar es Salaam during the 1960s and 1970s.

The popular practices of *ujamaa*, Julius Nyerere's implementation of Tanzanian socialism, coalesce in provocative ways with the phenomenology of kung fu spectatorship. Juxtaposed, they generate a montage of urban Tanzanian youth culture around the "performance of frugality." By suggesting here that ideologies are enacted, I dislodge the structural/functionalist approach to socialism and instead probe the phenomenological avenues of self-invention for youth within the discourses of the state. In this chapter I unpack the realms of imaginative self-fashioning that shape Tanzanian Asian youth culture under African socialist modernity.[3]

From 1962 to 1985, Tanzania developed a uniquely pedagogical approach to state formation that was known as *ujamaa*. In his controversial policy paper, "*Ujamaa*: The Basis of African Socialism," Nyerere distinguishes Tanzania's experiment in nation building, grounded in village communalism, from other strategies:

> *Ujamaa*, then, or "familyhood," describes our socialism. It is opposed to capitalism, which seeks to build a happy society on the basis of exploitation of

man by man; and it is equally opposed to doctrinaire socialism which seeks to build its happy society on a philosophy of inevitable conflict between man and man. We in Africa have no more need of being "converted" to socialism than we have of being "taught" democracy. Both are rooted in our past—in the traditional society that produced us. Modern African socialism can draw from its traditional heritage the recognition of "society" as an extension of the basic family unit.[4]

Ujamaa implemented "villagization," a system of rural development based on communal self-reliance.[5] This policy move asserted a number of ideological strategies aimed at decolonizing the state. Nyerere countered Western notions of the nuclear family by offering an African-derived conception of communalism stemming from indigenous kinship networks that are extended. He proposed *ujamaa* as a community-based system of development that shares available wealth rather than accumulates it in the interests of the individual. *Ujamaa* was obviously a radical departure from capitalist forms of development, but also represented a shift in emphasis from Soviet and European socialism toward indigenous customs that shaped local practices of governance. *Ujamaa* villages would not be created through the violent collectivism of Soviet communism. Rather, local transformation would be accomplished through a paradigm of familyhood.[6]

The philosophical underpinnings of *Ujamaa,* or self-reliance, were grounded in a destabilization of Western theories of modernization. For Nyerere, the dilemmas afflicting recently decolonized and exploited African states demanded specific local strategies of development. Consequently, Western periodization narratives, with their focus on urbanization imposed on newly independent states such as Tanzania, demanded critical reconsideration. The conscious effort to critique Western notions of modernity, combined with a policy of nonalignment articulated by the Bandung conference and Afro-Asian nations, generated alternative approaches to African modernity. *Ujamaa* was one such approach. As a radical measure to escape the dependency relationships of Western aid sources, this policy privileged the rural over the urban and attempted to redress class inequities by emphasizing the majority constituencies of peasants and workers over the minority urban bourgeoisie.[7]

As a theoretical argument, *ujamaa* functioned as a critique of modernity on several levels. It consciously attempted to create a nonaligned African socialist theory of economic development that was organic and people centered. It operated as an ideological vehicle for Africanization, by drawing on indigenous as well as international philosophies of social change in a uniquely Tanzanian model that privileged the agricultural majority. And it drew on tradition as a contingent, shifting, and inseparable part of the modernization process, as a corrective to the simple dichotomy of tradition versus modernity prevalent in modernization theories, where tradition implies backwardness.

Internal criticisms of the Tanzanian experiment dispelled utopian hopes of finding ways to resist Western forms of accumulation through the government creation of *ujamaa* villages. Instead, this vision of a pastoral communalism, democratic in spirit and free from the ills of landlordism, gave way to a complex hierarchy of centralized power. Women, children, and the urban and rural poor were marginalized in these socialist initiatives.[8] But during those electrifying early years, as policies were still unfolding, the air was thick with the promise of change.

Frugality and Tanzanian Asian Youth

Urban youth emerged ambivalently under the sign of *ujamaa*, with its emphasis on rural development and the engagement of youth in economic self-reliance activities. On the one hand was a palpable feeling of social change: literacy programs, racial integration of the school system, Africanization of education through the introduction of Swahili as the medium of instruction, modernization of the curriculum with the introduction of new science, modern mathematics, and civics, which resulted in students trying to talk and behave like socialists. On the other hand was a distinct antiurban logic fueled by *ujamaa*'s principles. Teachers and pupils of primary and secondary schools in Dar es Salaam were obliged to practice socialist tenets through agricultural projects, the goal of which was to inculcate a sense of responsibility toward the larger community, presumed to be agrarian. The resulting tensions created new sites of antagonism and invention for urban youth.[9]

The performance of frugality was one such avenue of self-invention that emerged in the tension between urban youth and antiurban policies. Frugality in *ujamaa* was a structure of feeling between the logic of consumption and the practice of anticonsumption under policies of economic self-reliance. As theorized by Nyerere, frugality was a strategy for culturally delinking the youthful state.[10] It offered opportunities for personhood, drawing on indigenous African socialism through the inculcation of a national consciousness of self-reliance. Sports, dance (*ngoma*), marching, farming, and national service were all aspects of this performance of frugality. These spheres of physical embodiment were practiced as state-implemented technologies of care for youth.

Rising anti-Asian and antiurban sentiment under intensive Africanizing measures connected the frugality of Tanzanian Asian youth culture to *ujamaa*. One site of this connection was the popularity of kung fu cinema during this time. The reception and translations of kung fu instantiate the struggles of frugality that shaped a non-African Tanzanian youth constituency under socialist modernity.

The early 1970s saw an influx of Hong Kong, Chinese, and American kung fu cinema into urban Tanzanian popular culture. As part of a larger international film market of Hindi films, Italian spaghetti Westerns, Soviet exports, American Westerns, and the very popular Blaxploitation films, Bruce Lee's *Enter the Dragon* (1973) generated a passion for kung fu among urban South Asian–Tanzanian youth. Popular song lyrics like "Everybody was kung fu fighting," posters of Bruce Lee on the streets of Dar es Salaam, the fetish for the nunchaku and black-cloth Maoist shoes, the speedy martial movements of beachside wrestling matches, side kicks, and one-finger push-ups—all were extravagantly popular. The Mao suits worn by groups of railway technicians from China and North Korea brought to Tanzania during the '70s—and worn by Lee as well—carried a certain chic for local Asian youth. Images of Jim Kelly, Fred Williamson, Tamara Dobson, Pam Grier, Grace Jones, and Richard Roundtree also circulated as representations of "America" or the "West."[11]

The heterogeneity of '70s Tanzanian youth culture was inflected by an inherited colonialist logic of residential segregation. The popular youth cultures of minorities such as Asians were visible in Asian parts of the city, such as Mosque Street and Upanga. Bollywood (Hindi) cinema played at downtown movie houses like the New Chox, Avalon, and the Odeon, as well as the popular drive-in theater. Amitabh Bhachan, Rajesh Khanna, and Zeenat Aman embodied a hip Indian diasporic popular sensibility, but the rise of Bruce Lee as a charismatic and diabolical Asian superhero operating between communist and capitalist economies ruptured the boundaries of an otherwise segregated urban Asian Tanzanian youth culture.

The popularity of Hong Kong and Chinese kung fu cinema, epitomized by Bruce Lee films, created a multiethnic spectatorship within the implicitly segregated city of Dar es Salaam. As an ambivalent sign of Maoist socialist and American self-invention, Lee's films opened up desire and pleasure within contradictory sites of citizenship such as the movie houses, the rapidly integrating movie audiences, and American popular culture itself. Lee and the cinema he popularized shifted the binaries of the Black/white axis of race discourse in the reception of popular cinema by presenting a predominantly Asian visual field for a heterogeneous Tanzanian audience. In the process, Tanzanian spectatorship drew on new definitions of pleasure, social space, and emancipatory possibilities within an African-style socialism, forging a realm of visual modernity through the rhetoric of frugality and a radically new technology of the self. The economy of kung fu movement echoed a local aesthetics of the frugal, unadorned, but active socialist body, capable of serving the state. This empathy, combined with Maoist-inflected rhetoric and narratives of capitalist versus revolutionary, youth versus feudal lord, and decadence versus scarcity, resonated with the structure of Tanzanian socialist pedagogy.

Kung fu foregrounds an abhorrence of any technology other than the self as a means of juridical and revolutionary intervention, highlighting the importance of frugality as an everyday strategy. It does this through the striking absence of guns or bombs, a genre formula that is theatrically fastidious in its austere focus on the frugal body. By inscribing capitalism and decadence onto the body, socialist notions of self and spatiality emerge in Lee's films *Enter the Dragon, Fists of Fury* (or *The Big Boss*), *The Chinese Connection* (or *Fist of Fury*), and *The Return of the Dragon*. In contrast to the deindividualized rhetoric of Tanzanian socialism, however, Lee valorizes the disenfranchised masses on whose behalf he fights but foregrounds the individualistic self as problem solver.

The question of what kind of pleasure this contradiction produces for socialist youth links kung fu cinema to Tanzanian socialist technologies of self. Kung fu spectatorship brings together the disjunctures among the material frugality of the socialist state, the aesthetic frugality of unadorned martial bodies combating capitalist evil (such as landlords), and the excess of the spectator consuming Hong Kong and American cinema in a culture of anticonsumption. Watching kung fu cinema stages the tensions generated by a desire for transnational circulation of commodities under conditions of scarcity. It performs the ambivalence of frugality as it invites spectators to consume globalizing commodities such as Hong Kong cinema, structuring a transnationally linked sphere of enjoyment.

Struggling between the seductive machines of First World technologies of the body and everyday life under conditions of frugality within African socialism, youth consumed kung fu, with its contradictory play on gender, sexuality, and masculinity. These dimensions were otherwise silenced under the centralized one-party state of the Tanzanian African National Union (later the Chama Cha Mapinduzi), whose privileged forms of cultural citizenship were inflected by its proletarian and agrarian-based policies of socialist belonging.

Decolonization, Governmentality, and the Invention of Youth

The circulation of kung fu cinema in '70s Tanzania reveals the particular methodological, ideological, and aesthetic dilemmas embedded in the category "youth" during the first decades of decolonization in an African socialist state. The problem of theorizing "youth" outside a European/U.S. framework lies in the epistemological assumptions of Anglo-American youth subcultural theory, predicated on the established sovereignty of the state within which forms of late-capitalist culture produce notions of self, education, leisure, location, community, hegemony, and rebelliousness. Consequently, much theorizing in youth studies of the 1970s and '80s assumes certain institutional orthodoxies regarding the forms of state legitimation of cultural and legal citizenships, through which notions of youth culture as pathology and moral panic have emerged in Britain and the United States.[12]

The work of scholars of the Birmingham school of cultural studies, addressing representations of white and Black working-class youth in Britain, has been crucial to such an analysis.[13] Although the theories of the Birmingham school offer approaches to reading "youth," the particular contexts of socialist states such as Tanzania caution against drawing easy parallels between youth formations across national and political cultures. The heterogeneity of Tanzania's 120 ethnicities, for instance, complicates concepts of difference advanced by Anglo-American youth discourse. A dialogue of homogeneity and hybridity, of authenticity and inauthenticity, molded the discourse on race as these heterogeneous communities emerged as a socialist majority wary of its commercially successful non-African communities, such as Asians.

As opposed to the longer history of nation formation out of which Anglo-American subcultural theory emerges, the recentness of postcolonial sovereignty creates the epistemological and historical bind of theorizing youth within a contingent modernity-in-formation. The early writings of Nyerere are insightful here, providing ongoing political analysis of the institutional, cultural, and representational practices of colonial bureaucracies, that articulated "young people" in discrete and obvious ways in the interests of the mother country.[14] To counter the debilitating neglect of youth in the colonial era, Nyerere proposed a radical approach to educating young people, initiating policies to update and Africanize the curriculum, introducing African history and Swahili as the language of instruction. He critiqued the anthropological model of Christian missionaries civilizing indigenous populations, through which the colonial bureaucracy sought to perpetuate itself. Instead, he proposed postcolonial pedagogical strategies of Africanization for decolonizing youth culture. Such a syncretic modern approach to cultural delinking was intended to reverse colonial penetration rather than presume monocultural isolation.

For Nyerere, education was crucial for decolonizing the state and consolidating the socialist nation. With the implementation of Swahili, a visibly socialist Swahili youth culture was forged as national culture. Schools were nationalized and generated a secular, nationalist, anticolonial youth culture. Under the secularity of nationalization, ethnically diverse schools coexisted, shaping varied conceptions of youth in relation to the state, to religions such as Islam, and to the intraethnic cultures within which youth existed in Dar es Salaam. Former colonial institutions such as the Boy Scouts and Girl Guides; technical institutes teaching needlework, cooking, and carpentry; the sports clubs; and Christian groups like the YWCA and YMCA articulated Tanzanians as "youth." Thus youth emerged as a diverse, polylingual, multidenominational constituency.

For Tanzanians in the 1960s, a hegemonic "national" culture was still struggling to be articulated through delinking, nationalization, indigenization, vernacularization, and self-reliance.[15] "Youth" was a founding category for the radically socialist state, and state policy demanded that the socialist commitments of youth be affirmed through physical expressions of solidarity. These performances of socialist commitment, consolidated around projects of self-reliance, were mainly agricultural, where young socialists trained in notions of communal responsibility. Like Lenin and Mao, Nyerere prioritized youth in his experiments with African socialism—signaled by the Africanization of education—and while this focus situated youth in a powerful relation to the emergent state, expressive youth cultures had to negotiate multiple forms of co-optation or containment. The struggle to create a cohesive national youth culture in opposition to the colonial legacy of "Englishness" fabricated by the machinery of schooling, church, jurisprudence, administration, and bureaucracy became a new orthodoxy against which subcultural forms emerged.[16]

The theory of youth conceived by Nyerere was informed by the antiimperial strategies of many African intellectuals and revolutionaries, including Patrice Lumumba, Kwame Nkrumah, C. L. R. James, Walter Rodney, Frantz Fanon, Léopold Senghor, Samora Michel, Tom Mboya, and Ngugi wa Thiong'o. For Nyerere, youth was a pedagogy of nation formation. This contrasted with the colonial neglect of youth during the 1940s and '50s. Under such contending ideological and cultural terrains of antagonism and desire, youth emerged as a new orthodoxy, a rhetoric of statehood both conformist and radical in its larger political aim.[17]

Nyerere's self-conscious theorization and implementation of youth culture in Tanzanian public life was dialogically linked to the international public sphere. His pedagogy of youth—the mobilization of youth in the interests of the state—should be viewed in the context of the instrumental role played by the internationalist youth movements of communist states in the Soviet sphere, China, and other Third World nations. His long-range goal was to forge alliances across African states to overcome the pressures of dependency economies, that surfaced as the new face of imperialism. Striving for a Pan-African post-nation-state federation, he deployed the language of radical social democracy on historically new terms—socialist, nationalist, and Pan-African. The resulting solidarities and contradictions of these three contending ideologies produced a locally vibrant African socialist youth modernity.[18]

Lenin-Mao-Nyerere: The Performance of Statehood

Ujamaa emerged as a new anti-imperial and egalitarian logic of self-help. Its central figure was the nation's youth, on whose shoulders rested the future of nation building. *Ujamaa* sought a self-reliant state that had decolonized ideologically, phantasmatically, and territorially. It was symbolized by school youth working in public spaces. Among other activities, such work involved tending the *shambas* (state-owned vegetable gardens), marching, planting trees along city roads, clearing public spaces, and maintaining school compounds.[19]

In *The Tasks of the Youth League*, Lenin locates youth as the fundamental base of the production of statehood and lays out a pedagogy for youth citizenship, arguing that "we must deal in detail with the question of what we should teach the youth and how the youth should learn if it really wants to justify the name of communist youth, and how it should be trained so as to be able to complete and consummate what we have started."[20] Nyerere's treatise on nation building closely follows Lenin's prescription for modern education, formulating a specifically Tanzanian-based model for African socialism. Elaborating on what "proletarian" culture might signify for Tanzania, Nyerere's foremost project was the modernization of education through the mobilization of youth. Interpreting Lenin's formula for educating the youth leagues by "learning, organizing, uniting and fighting," Nyerere introduced an array of activities to generate what Lenin calls the "shock group" of youth who can help "in every job . . . displaying initiative and enterprise."[21]

Suburban vegetable gardens were central to this project. Lenin elaborates on the vegetable garden as a means of abolishing disparities between classes, particularly the intelligentsia, by dissolving the division between the theory and practice of communism. "The members of the League should use every spare hour to improve the vegetable gardens, or to organize the education of young people in some mill or factory," Lenin writes, in order that they may view labor differently from the way they did in the past.[22] This idea became central to the category of youth in Tanzanian socialism, as the policies of *ujamaa* approached the schooling of youth through the implementation of physical activities such as gardening in the name of nation building. Young socialists had to participate in grassroots economic self-reliance activities, of which agricultural projects that involved tilling the land were an integral part.[23]

Youth emerged as a decolonizing postcolonial public sphere through which the newly independent nation-state became manifest. Parades, marches, and *ngomas* (folk dances); children waving flags by roadsides as Nyerere and other state functionaries drove by; compulsory large-scale youth drills with clubs, hand gestures, sticks, and guns; and mandatory summer camps linked the schooling of youth to the creation of good citizens. Learning how to wield a *jembe* (hoe) and maintain a *shamba*, growing one's own vegetables, was a crucial component of the curriculum in many high schools. The use of the word *ndugu* (comrade) for both genders and the radical move to make Kiswahili the primary means of instruction at school and university were important corollaries. The compulsory marching every day before and after school and the regime of sweeping and dusting one's own school compounds followed Lenin's advocacy of youth organizing the cleaning of city blocks or villages. Hence one could observe the primary students of Dar es Salaam walking to school with brooms and school boxes. This was an elaborate and persuasive instrumentalization of the category youth within the national culture, and the shape of modernization under African socialism.[24]

Nyerere's visit to China in 1965, the publication of the Arusha Declaration in 1967, and the nationalization of banks and industries in the public and private sectors earlier that year consolidated his Leninist/Maoist notions for a new African democracy forged and sustained by youth. The establishment of organizations such as the Tanzanian National Service and policies such as "Education for Self-Reliance" cohere with Maoist principles of producing the state through the training of young people as citizen-workers. Along with this ideological hybridization came an influx of cultural commodities in the guise of North Korean table tennis coaches; Chinese books, stationery, and shoes; Soviet mathematicians and physics teachers; Chinese engineers for the Tanzanian/Zambian railway project; Soviet export cinema; and kung fu cinema à la Raymond Chow, Lo Wei, Run-Run Shaw, and Warner Bros.[25]

Technologies of Frugality: Kung Fu and the Ambivalence of Enjoyment

"Hong Kong invaded the U.S. film biz this weekend as 'Rumble in the Bronx,' starring Jackie Chan, and 'Broken Arrow' directed by John Woo, scored a one-two punch at the box office," wrote Andrew Hindes for *Variety* in February 1996.[26] *Rumble in the Bronx* soared to the top of the box-office hits with an estimated gross of $10 million, followed closely by the John Travolta vehicle *Broken Arrow* at $8.3 million. Retrostyle '70s are back, complete with bell-bottoms and flared synthetics. Kung fu is making a '90s return in New York, with tae kwon do, hapkido, kick boxing, karate, aero-boxing, Thai boxing, and Brazilian capoeira providing a range of martial art–inflected styles of choreography. Christian Slater quotes Bruce Lee in the opening sequence of *Broken Arrow*, and Jackie Chan comes into his own in the United States with *Rumble in the Bronx*, no longer a shadow of Lee, though citationally invoking him. Observing this, I am reminded of another time of plastic clothes, bell-bottoms, platform shoes, Afros, and Bruce Lee.

Lee's first film was *Fists of Fury* (originally titled *The Big Boss*; 1972), directed by Lo Wei and produced by Raymond Chow. This anticapitalist/antifeudal propagandist film is closely linked to populist socialist rhetoric that privileges the laborer or peasant, embodied most dramatically by Lee himself in his Chinese worker suits. Like the rest of his films, *The Big Boss* presents a field of contested class and race relations to a public of peasants and workers. Social space in Lee's films demarcates narratives of good versus evil, urban versus rural. There is the corrupt foreman of the ice factory in *The Big Boss*, the drug lord/capitalist entrepreneur Mr. Han in *Enter the Dragon*, and Rome-based American mafiosi in *Return of the Dragon*.

The Big Boss did not attain great popularity in Tanzania until the success of Lee's Warner Bros. venture *Enter the Dragon* (1973), directed by Robert Clouse, produced by Weintraub and Heller in conjunction with Raymond Chow, and scored by Lalo Schifrin. This phenomenally successful film broke the predominantly Black/white cinematic field of race constructed by the deluge of classical Hollywood narratives in Dar es Salaam. The hegemony of Hollywood was interrupted only by a modest glut of Hindi films frequented by a largely Asian Tanzanian audience. Lee's international stardom problematized the narrow spectrum through which race was constituted in Tanzanian popular cinema. As both Mahmood Mamdani and Isaac Shivji note, this was a time of simmering anti-Asian sentiment, exacerbated by legislative moves to nationalize Asian businesses. These developments had far-reaching repercussions for a cultural politics of race in Tanzania.[27]

Enter the Dragon was spectacularly successful, playing to packed houses in Dar es Salaam throughout the early '70s. Its seductively racist narrative provides an exciting sense of internationalism that in retrospect is merely a Hollywood rendition of the starving exotic Oriental enclave much fetishized by the British and Americans: Hong Kong as a colonial metropole. The aura of kung fu's internationalism in Enter the Dragon is a trans-Pacific fantasy, both Orientalist and pro-American, with chop-socking Asians, Shaolin temples, and chop-socking Westerners. The opening sequences locate Hong Kong as a cosmopolitan fetish of the Pacific—for capitalists, secret agents, martial artists from both the East and West, and drug lords. John Saxon, Bob Wall, and Jim Kelly provide the spectrum of Westernness through which Lee's own transnational identity is realized, both Asian American and Hong Kong Chinese. In the film, Lee is an agent of the British government working against Chinese criminals. The Asian American Lee is joined by the Anglo-American John Saxon and the African American Jim Kelly, setting up an imperialistic relationship between travelers and natives, juxtaposing Vietnam refugees in Hong Kong Harbor with evil Chinese landlords, and martially trained youth against the cosmopolitan sportsmen/travelers from the West.

Enter the Dragon raises interesting questions about the visual and narrative ambiguity of spectatorial pleasure in a postcolonial context. The colonialist ideology of British and American hegemony in Hong Kong is barely concealed in the good Americans/bad Asians plot: the American trio's exploits in Hong Kong frame them as heroes liberating the people from exploitive landlords. For audiences in a nonaligned, anti-imperialist state such as Tanzania, this idea of "the good" was discrepant enough, but the contradictions were heightened by local Tanzanian politics regarding landlordism and Africanizing measures. The issue of local landlordism was a crucial rallying point of economic nationalism. Hence the visual pleasure of restoring Western hegemony through the overthrow of local landlordism conflicted in diametrically opposing ways with issues of African sovereignty.

Another axis of spectatorial ambiguity is that posed by Jim Kelly, whose popularity as an African American actor provided a visual hook for Tanzanian spectatorship in more ways than one. Kelly flees police brutality and white supremacy in Los Angeles and belongs to a Black Power enclave in the form of a Black karate school. He exemplifies a notion of American cool that resonates with Tanzanian notions of Pan-African cool, as he wears red bell-bottoms and an Afro and embodies a style of politics in sync with Black nationalist sentiments in Dar es Salaam during the '70s. Kelly complicates the politics of white and Asian American masculinities pitted against generic Oriental masculinity by introducing the violent race politics of Los Angeles. He marks the Pan-African connections to Asia through ideological solidarities with Third World struggles, the martial arts, Asian religions, and the transnational exchange of socialist kitsch. But, as Kelly's death in the film reduces the complexity of his narrative presence to a prior, stereotyped racist representation, it produces a resistant reading that inflects the closure of the film. In a sequence reminiscent of a lynching, Kelly's body is impaled on a hook with chains and lowered into a vat of acid. The stereotypical racist solution of the death scene negates the potentially imperialist fantasy tale of Westerners cleansing the world of evil. Instead, the haunting specter of racism in the imperial home fractures the colonialist self-righteousness behind "Americans" rescuing the "Orient."

The film's gender politics are equally complex. Whereas at first it replicates the misogynist and sexist logic of early mainstream kung fu cinema through the production of women's bodies as objects of pleasure, the figure of Angela Mao, a hapkido black belt, as Bruce Lee's sister, Su Li, offers a new kind of representation. Mao kung fus her way through a battalion of Han's men, preferring suicide with a piece of glass to the horror of rape at the hands of the malevolent American, played by Bob Wall. Angela Mao embodies a new kind of socialism—an agent against patriarchy and traditional notions of femininity who dismantles the coordinates of gender role–playing as she opens up other ways of socializing women's bodies. Mao creates a transgendered space outside familiar representational forms, performing the martial-socialist body of the comrade. Discarding gender binarisms, Mao enacts both the promise of kung fu, as a site of social militancy, and its failure. She enacts its promise by demonstrating that she can fight better than most men, with an indestructible sense of self. Her socialist body echoes closely with the popular transgendered practice of calling all persons—irrespective of gender—comrade or *ndugu*. Her death, however, performs its failure by reiterating the reductive ways that gender and sexuality work to subject women's and other minority bodies to violence.

The tensions of race, gender, ethnicity, and masculinity raised in *Enter the Dragon* foreground the transcultural misreadings through which Bruce Lee gained international popularity. The film highlights the complex ways in which Lee himself is situated as a hybrid Asian American, binationally affiliated, working in Hong Kong and California. Lee was an American citizen and had opened schools of jeet kune do in Seattle and Oakland. His multicultural clientele included such African Americans as karate champion Jim "Kung Fu" Kelly, Lew Alcindor (who later took the name of Kareem Abdul-Jabbar), and the judoist Jesse Glover; Anglo-Americans such as Steve McQueen, James Coburn, and Stirling Silliphant; Asian Americans such as Japanese American judoist Taky Kimura and Filipino American escrimaist Dan Inosanto; and others, such as Roman Polanski.[28]

Tanzanian cultural politics of the early '70s are also tied to the rabidly nationalist anti-immigrant sentiment expressed in Lee's films. He is pro–Chinese peasant, anti-Japanese, anti-Soviet, and anti-Western in *The Chinese Connection* (1972), directed by Lo Wei—a xenophobia expressed in the beatings of a Japanese Bushido boxer and a former Soviet champion boxer. Combined with the film's attempted critique of 1930s colonial Shanghai, this produces a confusing mélange of condemnation and racist stereotyping. The Japanese occupation of Shanghai and the northern provinces as depicted in *The Chinese Connection* resonates with the strong anti-Asian sentiment perpetuated at the time in Tanzania, situating the immigrant petit bourgeois entrepreneur in antagonistic relation to the interests of the nationalist masses.

In *Return of the Dragon* (1973), Lee plays a country bumpkin from Hong Kong who avenges the harassment meted out to his restaurateur relatives by an underworld ring of immigrants from the United States and other countries. Typical of most of his films, the climax is structured around a choreographed fight sequence, in this case his encounter with the American Chuck Norris in the Roman Coliseum. Lee asserts his anti-Western perspective by destroying all threats to his relatives' future in Rome, epitomized by Norris, only to discover that there is no place outside capital itself when he learns that his uncle is in league with the criminals.

Lee died before completing *The Game of Death* (1974), set in Bangkok, but its structuring ethnocentrism is nationalist in contradictory ways. Lee demonstrates the superiority of Chinese kung fu over other forms by decimating a Korean hapkido specialist, an escrima stylist, a Japanese samurai, and a Black boxer played by Kareem Abdul-Jabbar.[29] Jingoistic ideological content, bare-bones dialogue, and often atrocious production qualities—none of these detracts from Lee's kung fu performance. His choreography creates contradictory spaces for the participation of heterogeneous subjectivities that constitute the audience under the faceless charisma of statehood itself. The power of his films lies in his cultish persona and brilliance of movement, but the popularity of his films in Tanzania accrued a narrative depth that the plot and diegesis could not.

Lee was clearly the first transnationally situated Asian American actor simultaneously working for very different markets in Hong Kong, Hollywood, and the Third World. His transnational interests created divergent pressures on his status as a megastar across Asia, Africa, and other Third World countries. The international economies of kung fu filmmaking and its distribution also blurred the distinctions among ethnicities and national contexts. For Tanzanian Asian youth, there were few or no distinctions among the films of Hong Kong, mainland China, and Warner Bros. Kung fu cinema was generically read as mainland Chinese or Maoist, and Chinese cinema was reduced to the kung fu genre.

Technologies of the Self: Foucault's Askesis and Nyerere's Frugality

A reading of kung fu enables one to revisit the informal avenues of enjoyment under East African '70s socialism. Bruce Lee's popularity as an *uchina* (Chinese hero) at this particular juncture is interesting for many reasons, one being that he privileges what I would call a technology of frugality, or the body as a weapon of frugality. Lee's technology of frugality was a philosophy of efficient and minimal action, whereby the opponent's weaknesses are utilized to fuel the self's power. For Lee, a little is enough. Frugality became a voluntary technology of plenty, an articulation of agency. Lee's cultivation of an aesthetics of frugality on-screen cohered with Nyerere's theory explained in a 1965 speech to the nation:

> In February I went . . . to China, and there I learned one very important thing . . . they are a frugal people. . . . it would be very foolish of us . . . individually or as a nation, to appear as rich as a country like America. Everyone knows that we are not rich. And the only way to defeat our present poverty is to accept the fact that it exists, to live as poor people, and to spend every cent that we have . . . on the things which will make us . . . more educated in the future.[30]

Such a reading of China seems simplistic and reductive from the vantage point of the 1990s, as contemporary forms of capital and exchange have permeated even the much-desired frugality of that country. Still, such an aesthetics laid out by Nyerere has broad implications for a phenomenology of frugality through which youth forges avenues of enjoyment.

A phenomenology of frugality is structured around imaginative embodiments of little-as-enough, of anticonsumption, of which kung fu partakes. The choreography of kung fu trains the body as a weapon of vigilance. It hinges on a technology of self otherwise relegated to the state through the police, the military, sports, national youth service, and other forms of regulative socialization. Kung fu valorizes an aesthetics of self-governance closely aligned with forms of control that produce and sustain state-saturated societies such as Tanzania.[31] In such societies, the individual, articulated as youth, is produced through various institutional regimes and practices as the vigilant and productive machine of the state. Youth becomes a technobody whose every action and enjoyment should be directed by a pedagogical practice of statehood.

One aspect of such an aesthetics of frugality is the ascetic and athletic care of the self. In his lectures on the technologies of the self, Michel Foucault discusses how the practice of *epimelesthai sautou* ("to take care of oneself," "the concern with the self") was a crucial philosophy in Hellenistic Greek cities.[32] Through a close reading of the Socratic dialogues, Foucault argues that Socrates considers his mission useful for the city, in fact "more useful than the Athenians' military victory in Olympia—because in teaching people to occupy themselves with themselves, he teaches them to occupy themselves with the city."[33] Foucault links the care of oneself and the city to Christian asceticism eight centuries later and its edict to know oneself.[34]

As part of this meditation, Foucault elaborates one of the three Stoic techniques of self, *askesis*, described as a remembering—not a disclosure—of the secret self: "It's the memory of what you've done and what you've had to do."[35] The two poles of this principle are *melete*, or meditation, and *gymnasia*, "to train oneself." As Foucault points out, there is a spectrum of intermediate possibilities as well.[36] Bruce Lee's choreography occupies this intermediary possibility of the care of the self, which by extension becomes a care of the youthful body in the city through a performance of gymnastic frugality, kung fu.

In Bruce Lee's films, the meditative self, physical training, and the juridical process work in mnemonic fashion to restore order to the chaotic youthful city. The striking presence of gangs of young men training in kung fu schools (whether Chinese or Japanese), the comparative absence of women as agents, and the group movement of youth across the city in search of justice link kung fu to notions of male sociality in the modern metropolis. Lee's choreography reads as a performance of informal juridical practices of urban youth. The fight sequences emphasize an urban reclusiveness, enacted in the crowded street, in public spaces like the Coliseum, or in the winding alleys of Macao, restoring order to the chaotic urban landscape. The economic theories of frugality advanced by Nyerere and Foucault's technologies of self merge in Bruce Lee's choreography of the self and the city.

Kung Fu, Radical Historical Subjects, and Feminist Imaginings

In a broader context, kung fu choreography embodies a viable technology of self for people of small frames, implicitly critiquing conventional masculinity. Though Lee's style of kung fu, wing chun fist, is popularly associated with male homosociality, its origins lie in a form developed by Yin Win Chung, a Buddhist nun from mainland China, that she invented as self-defense for females and people with small frames. Hsiung-Ping Chiao suggests that wing chun fist emphasizes speed as opposed to strength and notes that Lee learned it at age thirteen from Yip Man, the sixth-generation master of the wing chun fist school.[37] The privileging of speed over strength is an important factor in understanding the wing chun fist form in terms of a radical historical subject such as the martially trained Buddhist nun in thirteenth-century China who first developed it. This provides an explicit link between feminism and kung fu, which opens arenas for the negotiation of gender through movement and choreography within kung fu history and as a visual representation of women breaking boundaries within public space.

The connections between kung fu and feminist interpretations of martial movements are not evident in the visually gendered identities of early kung fu cinema, much of which preserves the status quo of men as fighters and women as sexual objects. But although '70s kung fu cinema maintains the dichotomy of docile women and warring men, the occasional ruptures are startlingly uncompromising and even empowering. For instance, the emergence of new historic subjects such as Angela Mao ("Lady Kung Fu," discussed above), Black kung fu expert Tamara Dobson, and martial artists such as Chen Hsin, Chen Kuan-Tai, Meng Fei, Wang Tao, and Tanny dismantles orthodox notions of gender, valorizes androgyny, and creates transgendered choreographies, diminishing the conventional framing of male martial bodies.[38] These brief choreographic ruptures challenge stereotypes of women as weak, dependent, or victimlike by showing women decimating dozens of young men through dexterity, intelligence, extra-ordinary skill, and strength. Hollywood's Tamara Dobson, along with Hong Kong cinema's Angela Mao and Tanny, popularized muscular fight-ing bodies, martial movements, lesbian desire, and a campy style of femi-ninity. Before lipstick feminisms came platform feminists, giving patri-archy the karate chops it never expected.

Kung fu–kicking special agent Cleopatra Jones (Tamara Dobson), six feet two inches tall with platform shoes and packing a cosmopolitan cool, demonstrates a connection between feminist critiques and a Black radical-ism that is mobile and internationalist. In *Cleopatra Jones* (1973), the pro-tagonist fights drugs in her own community and still finds time to organize antidrug maneuvers in Turkey. Her worldliness, her articulation of power and gender in visually novel terms, suggests other ways of being Black within capital. In *Cleopatra Jones and the Casino of Gold* (1975), she is part-nered with dart-throwing British superagent Mei Ling Fong (played by Tanny), a historically new on-screen alliance grounded in lesbian desire. Actually, in this film power and desire are constructed along the axis of same-sex identification and antagonism among three women: Shelley Stevens, Dobson, and Tanny. The irreverently antipatriarchal undercurrent in the film's spectatorial field opened up alternative imaginings in '70s youth culture: the martial art for small frames gained currency among teen femi-nists as self-defense and a technology of care *from* men.

Kung Fu and the Emergence of New Historic Subjects

Bruce Lee shattered the hermetic secrecy of kung fu by teaching it to any-one who wanted to learn the form, raising provocative questions about kung fu and race. Lee's master-student relationship with African Americans like Jesse Glover, Kareem Abdul-Jabbar, and Jim Kelly and the estab-lishment of Black martial art schools in Los Angeles and elsewhere in California attest to the form's eclecticism, transnational malleability, and appeal to all frames and cultures. The widespread popularity of kung fu in Blaxploitation films links the martial art to Pan-Africanist and Black na-tionalist embodiments of the care of the self, in which the self becomes a tool of revolution, for fighting drugs, white hegemony, injustice, and the state. The films of actors/sportsmen like Jim Kelly, Tamara Dobson, Pam Grier, Jim Brown, Fred Williamson, Richard Roundtree (*Shaft*, 1972), Ron O'Neal (*Superfly*, 1972), and Kareem Abdul-Jabbar are noteworthy exam-ples. Jim Kelly's *Black Belt Jones* (1972) features a Black karate school with a picture of Bruce Lee hanging, shrinelike, in the background. In *Enter the*

Dragon, Kelly is seen leaving his fellow martial artists at a school in Los Angeles before going to Hong Kong, and the association of martial arts with the training of Black men to survive in a hostile police state is explicit.

The works of Michele Wallace, Gladstone Yearwood, bell hooks, Manthia Diawara, Mark Reid, and Ed Guerrero, among others, address the misogyny, sexism, and stereotyping of African Americans in Blaxploitation cinema of the 1970s, while also marking the possibilities these films held for the development of Black cinema.[39] Building on the analysis of such authors, it becomes possible to read the cultural capital of Blaxploitation cinema as it circulates and translates in ways that exceed its reception in the United States.

Early blaxploitation superheroes made possible a new kind of visual pleasure for Tanzanian Asian youth. The spectrum of martial art styles popularized by Bruce Lee's jeet kune do and other forms of karate and judo incorporated into kung fu by Kelly, Williamson, Brown, Dobson, and Abdul-Jabbar, presented a technology of self that was aesthetically synchronous with the conditions of frugality in Tanzanian popular culture. As a sophisticated choreography for a martially oriented militaristic dance, it suited the local emphasis on discipline and sport. This linking of kung fu to Black struggle in Blaxploitation films rearticulated resistance and revolution across ideological lines, and the Pan-African implications of Black struggle resonated with popular Tanzanian youth sentiments of the time, particularly in its practice of frugality as a style of movement. The body is the only machine of action: there are neither guns nor any other autonomous technologies apart from the self.

Kung fu cinema's connection to a diasporic schlock consciousness in the '70s is complicated by its relations to race, gender, the Cold War, and the more transnational imaginings perpetuated through kung fu kitsch. Lee's films, in particular, are visually disorienting as the eclectic ethnicities of the actors and landscapes blur the distinctions between context and period. The visual field is "Chinese." However, the actors are of Thai, Malay, Japanese, and Chinese ethnicity; the landscapes are those of Hong Kong and Thailand; and the badly dubbed dialogue unwittingly creates a Brechtian alienation effect through its asynchronous sound.

Still, kung fu's connections to Tanzanian socialism, Black nationalisms, Bollywood fight sequences, emergent feminisms, and a diasporic youth consciousness of '70s kitsch have returned today with a '90s twist. Spinoffs from kung fu cinema have been more important than the genre itself, nostalgically evoked in the hyperviolence of contemporary Hollywood films. Its embeddedness in an aesthetics of frugality inadvertently raises the question of how frugality travels across national and political cultures. The globalizing influences of Hong Kong cinema and its particular translations in Tanzanian popular culture as a mediating space between scarcity and excess, between "Asianness" and Tanzanian Asians, and between capitalist kitsch and socialist ideology open up the intricate transnational linkages in the circulation of meaning generated through the consumption of movies.

Tanzanian socialism took youth as central to its project. As A. G. Ishumi and T. L. Maliyamkono state, "This ideological conditioning was carried to its extreme in the teaching of civics, a school subject dubbed Political Education since 1967, which resulted in virtually all pupils trying to talk, act or behave like socialists. This was indeed an ideological success, even though, in retrospect, it may have been more deceptive and pretentious than real."[40] The particular embodiments, translations, and cultural capital of socialism were closely linked to the informal ways in which youth imbibed and made local forms of socialist desire, whether in antagonism or consent.

An important part of the mechanics of state formation was the performance of frugality, the emphasis on communal self-reliance as exemplified in the practice of *ujamaa*. As I have shown, there is a formal parallel between the performance of frugality and the youth culture of '70s Tanzania. The gender ambiguity of win chung fist and the appeal of an explicit "technology of self" to a consciousness of nation building offered a nascent transnational aesthetic of frugality for emerging expressive youth cultures.

With the state appointing itself as the home of youth through the rhetoric of family, and the head of state assuming the role of teacher or father of the nation, the paternalistic formulations of socialist practice became linked to state control. Whereas Nyerere's more stringent critics have dismissed his experiments in socialist pedagogy as authoritarian, I argue here for a more nuanced consideration of a critical and daring experiment in grassroots social transformation as it interfaces with global popular culture. The philosophy of self-reliance articulated in *Ujamaa* was farsighted and utopian, but doomed to be structured as failure by the West. Instead of dismissing forms of postcolonial citizenship in peripheral states as failures, however, we need a more capacious reading of the kinds of desire, longing, and imaginative reinventions that fill up the abstract spaces of state formation.

5

Nomadic Citizenship

Nomadic Identities / Migrant Histories

While creating possibilities for new types of community, many postcolonial states have seen radical disruptions of old ones. In the throes of nationalist struggle, the violent legacy of the colonial encounter transformed local communities into transitory, nomadic, and fraught areas of postcolonial migrancy. Over a single generation, people have lived through cataclysmic dislocations, from the colonial to nationalist then postcolonial state, to transnationally situated communities. For those displaced by these seismic changes, the correlation between national identity and country of citizenship has been shattered irrevocably. Such dramatic reconfigurations of ideas about homeland, nation, and adopted country have created new dilemmas about how communities perform cultural citizenship in conditions of transnational migrancy.

The ragged history of East Indian migration is illustrative. The movement of this dispersed and heterogeneous community—at times coerced, at others self-induced—has been a volatile one, tracing a path from colonial India to East Africa, the Caribbean, Panama, Surinam, and British Guiana in the nineteenth century, and later Britain, Canada, and the United States via itinerant sojourns in the Persian Gulf and Southeast Asia. Often moving three, even four times in the space of a lifetime, East

Indian migrants have incorporated multilayered relations of belonging into their narratives of individuals and communities in transit. In spite of the complexity of this history, however, immigrant Indian struggles for cultural, legal, and economic citizenship have been subsumed by mercantilist accounts of travel and trade.

As a microhistory of both East Indian migration and of nomadic citizenship, the conditions under which many East African Asians came to be defined as undesirable in the 1960s and '70s offers an opportunity to recover this repressed history. Spurred by policies designed to promote economic decolonization that targeted Asians as the enemy, the migration highlighted the tentative relationship between nation and citizen, as neither passport nor birthright proved to be an adequate qualifier of citizenship. The fate of Asian citizens of Kenya, Tanzania, and Uganda presumably interlocked with the interests of sojourner East African Asians, many of whom held British passports. However, for Ugandan Asians, the fragility of this connection became apparent when, in September 1972, those who wished to remain in Uganda watched British Asians scramble for flights out of the country under order from Idi Amin to leave within ninety days.[1] For Kenyan Asians, the disavowal of rights attached to passports had been staged in 1968 with the passage of the Commonwealth Immigrant Act, under which they were refused entry to Britain on racial grounds. For Tanzanian Asians, who had constructed an uneasy identity as socialist citizens, economic nationalism and anti-Asian sentiment forced them to confront their tenuous purchase on modern African identity.[2]

In this climate of insecurity and impending crisis bred by official policy and informal mechanisms of delegitimation, East African Asians began to ask searching questions about the nature of citizenship. Who is a citizen? How can citizenship be enacted? By what criteria is citizenship determined? The early tremors of uncertainty regarding citizenship staged in the exodus of Kenyan Asians under Jomo Kenyatta's orders had sown the seeds of anxiety. This was aggravated by Britain's denial of their rights as British subjects. In Uganda, hostility toward Asians, galvanized by Milton Obote's fiscal strategies and violently concretized by Amin's antisocialist propaganda, demonstrated that legal citizenship offered no guarantee of authenticity within the imaginative borders of economic nationalism. For many East African Asians who left the region in the 1970s, their abrupt emergence as an undesirable minority catalyzed a dramatic and painful rupture with the past.

As a very specific migrant history connecting East Africa to Britain and North America, the trajectory of East African Asians poses certain questions about the staging of political identities. The multiple migrations of this diaspora over the past fifty years highlight the importance of visibility politics in states of nomadic citizenship. This little known history traverses the discourses of race and specific nationalist struggles linking the Black and South Asian diasporas in the twentieth century. In nineteenth-century Fiji, British Guiana, Mauritius, and Trinidad, for instance, the growing presence of peoples of Indian descent by way of a system of indentured labor greatly fractured conceptions of race, nationalism, and class in the colonies. Although often played off against peoples of African descent by colonial administrators, Indians forged new solidarities with Africans that were articulated around issues of labor, rights, and sovereignty. Their intertwined accounts of insurrectionary strategies and local liberation struggles against the colonial yoke suggest the tumultuous landscape within which modern political identities were formed.

While the histories of East African–Asian communities differ in their specificities, they share a common experience of silence about the particularities of this passage. Their troubled but persistent allegiance to nomadic citizenship opens up the spaces between the politics of race and the history of migration.[3] Similarly, the minor history of Tanzanian Asians sheds light on conceptions of nomadic citizenship as a condition of postcolonial subjecthood. Spaces opened up by such multiply migrated communities bring into focus some of the incidental, though no less traumatic, collisions of displaced nationalisms, such as the tenuous identification of East African Asians with nostalgic nationalist sentiments for the Subcontinent and, more locally, the ongoing struggles for national citizenship within Tanzania and across East Africa.

An "East African–Asian" Imaginary

Like many other diasporic communities with nomadic histories, East African Asians created regional cultural moorings with specific local resonances. In Uganda, Kenya, and Tanzania, the presence of Asians generated an informal transnational diasporic link that was simultaneously a locally grounded and dispersed history of belonging. Indo-African contacts in the coastal towns of Bagamoyo, Zanzibar, Dar es Salaam, and Mombasa preceded the Christian era. These older mercantile trans–Indian Ocean connections acquired new meanings under Arab, German, Portuguese, and British occupations in the region, and as the intercontinental exchange in commodities included slaves, colonial labor, and women on both coasts.[4] Resultant migrant and entrenched communities of Asian businesses flourished around the Uganda railway and the trade routes in East Africa as well as the Indian Ocean littoral. Gujarathis, Ismailis, Ithna Asheris, Bohoras, Khojas, Sikhs, Jains, Malayalees, Goans, and Tamils created microcommunities of affiliation across small towns in British and German East Africa. Shaped through circumstances of arrival and dispersal, their diverse relationships to local nationalist politics open up interesting questions about how such communities participated as cultural citizens in the adopted state or as part of a more dispersed, imagined community—under African socialism, for example.[5]

One arena of strategic political importance that dramatized the fissures within modern citizenship concerned the role that East African Asians would take in local politics during the early years of decolonization. In the newly independent Tanzanian state, for example, Asians were firmly committed to local economic policies of Africanization and nationalization. This commitment was constantly tested, however, by the question of how to perform cultural citizenship as Tanzanian Asians without being erased under the new policies of nonracialism, which radically reconfigured inherited colonial structures of race with Africanist and nationalist inflections. These policies implicitly demanded the public display of citizenship while also indicating that commercially prominent non-African communities should restrain themselves as a minority power and take a backseat to the majority political culture of the independent nation.

This postcolonial interface of continental political identities posed fresh questions. What was the relationship of older hybrid East African identities to the newly emerging political identity of the postcolonial state? What was the relationship of Tanzanian Asians to African socialism? To Pan-African politics? To national politics? What discursive influence did these interwoven Afro-Asian communities have on the cultural hybridity of the region? Would these communities forever be consigned to a nomadic existence? Were they expected to accept a sojourner-like status? Or did they have a stake in the nation's fate as great as other Tanzanians? What sort of participatory politics would demonstrate their nationalist commitment and allow them to acquire legitimacy as citizens within the African state? For Tanzanian Asians, the feeling of illegitimacy in their production of cultural citizenship coexisted with a broader structure of feeling distinctly East African, and this contradiction shaped expressions of solidarity and socialist commitment throughout the 1970s.

Such anxieties of legitimation must be viewed in a broader context of older migrations in the Indian Ocean, and the particular economies through which South Asian populations operated under British colonial rule and later under the emergence of new nation-states. Colonial commercial involvements across empires required a steady source of cheap labor to provide an economic buffer between colonizer and indigenous peoples. As a result, Indian indentured labor and colonial African labor were regulated by British colonial policies through different mechanisms of need and security. Within the context of the movement to abolish slavery in the British colonies during the early 1800s, Indians emerged as an abundant source of "voluntary" contract labor, willing to undertake the long trip across the black water, Kala Pani, of the unknown.[6]

Thus, the trade in Indian contract labor accelerated in the mid-1800s, gradually displacing the global trade in Africans that had sustained the emerging world capitalist system before the abolition of slavery. The resulting system of indentured labor from India to the British colonies joined the history of Indian migrations to that of African migrations in both the old and new worlds through colonial laws governing civil, political, as well as land rights of colonized peoples within the Empire. Under the burden of plantation economies, these laws inflected Indians and Africans differently from their earlier pre-British, trans–Indian Ocean links, which were largely mercantile. Articulated as Hindu versus indigenous African, transient labor versus settler/slave, customary practice versus common law, subtle relationships to local legitimacy divided these communities of exploited labor in the interest of colonial hegemony.

The cumulative effects of Arab, Portuguese, Dutch, German, and British expansionist interests in the Indian Ocean subsequently generated new maritime relations of power between India and the Indian Ocean rim region of the East African coast, Mauritius, the Seychelles, Zanzibar, and the Maldives. A new axis of this emerging maritime economy was the trans–Indian Ocean migrant labor, which became a powerful source of divisiveness within East African cultures. As a migration that was deliberately organized to compensate for and supplant local power, Indian labor— in the form of clerks, artisans, teachers, *duka* traders, and supervisors— became an integral component of Britain's system of indirect rule, in both Africa and the Caribbean. In the roles of middlemen, intermediaries, petty shopkeepers, and mercantile businessmen, Indians filled the bulk of the middle stratum opened by the British East African colonial structure, playing ambivalent roles of subjugation and ownership, sustaining both the colonial and insurgent economies through the trade in guns, ammunition, and metal works.[7]

Another arena of emerging transnational maritime exchanges of power were the capitalist economies of empire that generated new relationships of race and labor through intercontinental expansionist interests. For East

African–Asian migrant labor, this exploitive economy was offset by the need to forge new imaginative links among African, Arabian, and Indian land masses of older mercantile trade routes. This mobile transoceanic connection became a crucible of modernity, as it shrank the spaces between former homelands, new places of belonging, and trade ports. An emerging imaginative geography connected the seaports of Dar es Salaam, Zanzibar, Pemba, Mombasa, Muscat, and Aden to the ports of Kutch, Bombay, Goa, Cochin, Madras, and Calcutta, weaving older histories of trade and commerce with the newer history of colonial subjugation. Local traditions around Cochin on the Kerala coast, for instance, underwent cultural transformations while incorporating shifting Arab, Indian, and European mercantile interests in the Indian Ocean trade. With the quickening pace of maritime travel, bodies, communities, ideas, and culture were shed more rapidly at ports of call, in the transient moorings of ships in passage and the harsh encounters of culture shock. Arab, Muslim, Jewish, Chinese, Hindu, and Persian influences in pre-British Indian Ocean culture during colonialism traveled across neighboring island states through *dhow* (Arab sailing boats) traders, generating a local hybridized ecology of Afro-Indo-Arab culture with Anglophone, Lusophone, and Francophone inflexions. *Taarab* music, Swahili Muslim culture, Islamic artisanal details by Indian craftsmen in Zanzibari and Mombasa architecture, and a trade in textiles and spices that predated European colonial penetration offered a complex network of syncretic influences within East African coastal cultures, while Arab, Persian, and East African cultures had an impact on indigenous peoples of coastal villages in India as well.[8]

This seasonal practice of free migrations in old East Africa as well as a thriving maritime economy of trade between Indian Ocean states are irrevocably transformed with the advent of British domination. The introduction of militarized British rule represented a new global hegemony in which all natives were not equal.[9] Colonial policies delineated distinctions in the monetary value of different colonized peoples—African, Asian, and Arab. Under the elaborate colonial logic substantiated by natural law, paleontology, and administrative policy, indigenous peoples bore different cultural capital as embodiments of labor.

Colonial law explicitly articulated Indian indentured labor as itinerant and sojourning through a variety of policies in relation to family emigration, property ownership, representation rights, and an ambiguous subaltern status, with some room for mercantile mobility. Viewed as both a commercial convenience and an economic threat by the British, Asians were dissuaded from establishing permanent roots in Uganda, for instance, and instead were directed toward commercial areas that Europeans were disinclined to exploit and in which Africans were denied entry. Working as middlemen at the interface of colonial subjugation and growing resentment among indigenous peoples, Asians forged a precarious balance between white power and a Black majority. In Uganda, Asians could not obtain freehold land in most areas, nor was there any mechanism for their incorporation into the segregated society of European elites and African subjects. In addition, Asian government clerks and their families were given six months' paid leave home every four years, which encouraged them to maintain affiliations in their native country.[10]

Colonial policies that produced Indian migrant labor as temporary in the African and Caribbean colonies were informed by the crown's awareness of increasing insurgent sentiments fueling anti-British feeling across colonial India. Furthermore, the trans–Indian Ocean migration of laborers, merchants, and *duka*-wallahs who serviced railway sites in East Africa brought with it the ideas of anticolonial and proletarian movements that had stimulated peasant struggles through the nineteenth and early twentieth century in colonial India. Contrary to colonial and postcolonial historical accounts of the region, in which this massive movement across the Indian Ocean is marked by passivity and abject silence, a complicated sphere of political activity developed between Asians and the British, between Asians and Africans, and between East African Asians and Indians on the Subcontinent.

What unfolds in the early twentieth century is a cross-fertilization of ideas about insurgency against the British fomented across race, class, and caste lines in East Africa, and influenced by African (Maji Maji and later Mau Mau), Arab, and Indian nationalist struggles. These ideas in turn taught Indians returning to India from East Africa to view caste, class, and power differently from their compatriots who had never left India. Early twentieth-century nationalisms were more intertwined and transinfluential, inspiring subaltern agency across national boundaries. Arab nationalisms, in particular, strongly influenced African and Indian struggles for sovereignty, while African strategies for achieving self-governance borrowed much from Gandhian and Nehruvian ideas. Kenneth Kaunda found inspiration in Gandhi, while Kwame Nkrumah and Julius Nyerere aligned themselves with Nehru, Tito, Nasser, Castro, Bandaranaike, and Sukarno in a policy of nonalignment that committed them philosophically to strategies of self-reliance, the promotion of peace, and radical redistributions of power and resources in the international economic and social order.[11]

The struggle for liberation and territorial sovereignty along the East

African coast and the Indian Ocean rim states was staged in this crucible of hybridized Afro-Indo-Arab culture, but with European markers carved by the British, Dutch, French, Germans, and Portuguese. Emerging postcolonial states demarcated the histories of former trading port cultures from the struggles for modern citizenship. Older historic links formed through the Indian Ocean trade in goods and spices metamorphosed into the potentially threatening presence of Asians in East Africa. Old migrations and cultural connections assumed new meanings of neocolonial dependency. The peculiar role of the Indian in East Africa gained hypervisibility as the old face of colonial exploitation dramatically changed hands from white power to African sovereignty. Asians quickly emerged as the residual reminders of foreign occupation, regardless of their integrated and interdependent role within local economies. As hybridized Swahili cultures coalesced around Africanizing national identities, Asian communities found themselves situated as outsiders within the nationalist agenda. Once again, in the postcolonial era, they emerged as transient and expendable.

Modern Subjectivities / Emergent Citizenship

In the transition from a colonial periphery to a newly independent nation during the 1960s, Tanganyika (now Tanzania) rapidly created mechanisms for decolonizing the state along with working ideologies of national culture and sovereignty.[12] A fervent nationalism swept the country, producing a rhetorically cohesive and optimistic postcolonial state. In the crevices of the nation's body, its Arab and Asian minorities hastily assessed their pasts and speculated on the uncertainty of their futures.

The tumultuous transformation to postcolonial statehood propelled the need to radically dismantle the colonial myth of an infantilized African culture with no history of its own. Genealogies of Africa as the creation of colonial migrations, further mystified by its wealth of indigenous customs and rituals, created pressure to reconfigure historiography on modern, secular, and national terms. Jean-François Bayart points out that "it is still possible in France to write excellent monographs on African kingdoms which completely ignore the colonial or postcolonial State, to which such kingdoms have belonged for a century." As Bayart emphasizes, studies of contemporary modernity have been unable to integrate Africa's volatile historicity. The categories of thought that shape contemporary political conceptions like democracy, authoritarianism, and totalitarianism have been conceived, debated, and refined on the basis of historical experiences that exclude Africa.[13]

Fully conscious of this political legacy of external periodization, in which African states are considered transitional in the slow path to modernity, Julius Nyerere actively critiqued simple distinctions between traditional African societies and modernizing forces imposed by colonial intrusion. He shaped public awareness of dependency relations through his policies for national integration and launched a program called villagization, or *ujamaa vijijini*, with a concerted attack on modernization theories that privilege urbanization. The concept of *ujamaa* (self-reliance), embedded in everyday life, was central to Nyerere's critical stance. By shifting the focus of policy from the few modernized elite to the rural proletariat, he urged the new historiography in directions that challenged Western notions of modernization. For Nyerere, an African historicity would need to be based in the political and cultural histories of its rural majority. In this new historiography, Tanganyika's 120 "tribes" would be foregrounded, and a rearticulation of the state in terms of its nonsectarian national majority would be implemented with haste to undo a century of exploitation and disempowerment.[14]

This focus on the national and its constituent ethnicities—effected in the interest of creating what Bayart refers to as "historicity"—made Tanganyika's non-African minorities irrelevant other than as cases of exceptionalism. Efforts to redress the systematic negation of local cultures and knowledges under colonial rule directed Tanganyikan political discourse toward the national and the local over the transnational and the migrant. The question of legal, cultural, and economic citizenship emerged as the most evocative and contested site of national affiliation. Policies addressed concerns of national identity, provoking in the process a whole new set of questions regarding modern identities and emergent subjectivities in postcolonial Tanganyika. As symptoms of this volatile and changing terrain of citizenship, East African Asians would emerge as redundant or vulnerable scapegoats.

Nyerere's early speeches (1952–65), published as *Freedom and Unity/ Uhuru na Umoja*, reflect the multiple levels of struggle for national sovereignty, from the galvanizing of African interests under colonial repression to the demarcation of specifically Tanganyikan and, more broadly, East African conceptions of citizenship. Central to Tanganyikan conceptions of citizenship would be the move to delink race from political representation. As Nyerere pointed out in his public addresses from this period, colonial policies had operated under strictly racial lines, with Africans, Indians, and whites designated as separate constituencies. The city of Dar es Salaam was segregated by race. The Legislative Council in 1957 included "ten Africans, ten Europeans and ten Asians"—in other words, the African population, a majority at 98 percent, was allocated ten seats, while the non-African minority received twenty. Indigenous rights to land were ignored, the bulk of which was parceled out to white farmers and Asians along with ninety-nine-year leases. This elaborate construction of colonial space along racial lines demanded radical redress.[15] Nyerere's attempts to forge a sovereign state involved asserting the rights of the African majority and rectifying the inequities of land distribution and access to education. After centuries of exploitation, the attainment of majority rights made the question of minority non-African rights a peripheral and highly contentious forum of concern. The delicate question of national citizenship for non-Africans such as Asians and Europeans, as well as non-African Tanganyikans whose Swahili, Arab, and Indian ancestry challenged any simple notion of national identity, marks Nyerere's early pronouncements on Tanganyikan citizenship.[16]

Public expressions of territorial sovereignty prior to independence demarcated concerns around race and rights in relation to economic action for the sovereign citizen. Nyerere was explicit about the struggles involved in gaining majority rule and African sovereignty. Arguing for racial equality as a central tenet in 1952, he vehemently rejected the colonial system of "equal" political representation in which Europeans, the smallest minority, held as many legislative seats as the majority African constituency and the minority Arab and Asian communities. Instead, on the eve of independence he offered a vision of East African diversity:

> We appeal to all thinking Europeans and Indians to regard themselves as ordinary citizens of Tanganyika; to preach no Divine Right of Europeans, no Divine Right of Indians and no Divine Right of Africans either. We are all Tanganyikans, and we are all East Africans. The race quarrel is a stupid quarrel, it can be a very tragic quarrel. If we all make up our minds to live like "ordinary sort of fellows" . . . we will make East Africa a very happy country for everybody.[17]

This was a premonition of things to come, as the race quarrel very quickly threatened to become a tragic quarrel during the early years of independence. Already in 1959, two years before independence, Nyerere gestured toward the impending collisions between Tanganyikan citizenship and the racialized discourse of colonial inequities:

> At present, the African can see that his quarrel is not with the non-Africans . . . but with the colonial system. . . . He does not . . . degenerate into any sense

of personal grievance against Asians or Europeans. But when Independence comes, we must tackle this economic complication quickly. . . . the economic problem brings us back to the "race" problem.[18]

The determination to hasten majority control over resources during the postcolonial phase of the 1960s resulted in rapid policy changes mobilized around economic nationalism. Reflecting these concerns, Nyerere's public speeches addressed national property, the Africanizing of the state, and the early nationalization measures of 1962 to 1965 with the policy papers on *ujamaa*, citizenship, education, and property ownership.

Under increasing pressure to Africanize and nationalize the state, to create a "local look," the subtle colonial logic that produced Asians as mercantile communities in states of economic migrancy began to unravel. A policy circular on Tanganyikan citizenship released by Nyerere on 7 January 1964 sounded the death knell:

> On 9 December 1961, the vast mass of people of this country became citizens of an independent country; Tanganyika citizenship became a legal fact. There were, however, a few people whose legal right to become citizens of this country meant renouncing citizenship of another nation. These people had two years in which to make their choice. This period of grace has now expired. Since 9 December 1963 we have known exactly who are citizens of this country by right of birth. . . . There is no longer any uncertainty about whether a person is a citizen or not; the period of transition is over.[19]

This policy statement had far-reaching implications. It underscored the tension between former colonial subjects and emerging binational identities such as the minority non-Africans and binational Africans, and between immigrant citizenship and national identities. Embedded in the policy statement are the contradictions between legal citizenship and cultural legitimation. It suggested that authenticity of citizenship coheres with legal citizenship: becoming a Tanganyikan citizen made one an authentic Tanganyikan.

Those denied legal citizenship—as many Asians were under the pretext of lost applications—faced the possibility of being branded inauthentic. The demarcation between legal and cultural citizenship became crucial as it simultaneously assumed a correlation between birthright citizens and legal citizens, and disavowed non-African birthright access to legal citizenship. Further, as the impending crisis of Zanzibar in 1964 demonstrated, birthright citizens were not guaranteed indefinite status as cultural citizens. For the Zanzibari Swahili, the Luos in Uganda, and Asians in East Africa this delinking between legal citizenship and cultural legitimation within the state raised the question of the performance of citizenship as a condition of national belonging across race, class, and cultural lines.[20]

The uncertainty about legal and cultural citizenship among easily discernible non-African Tanganyikans such as the Asians, as well as the more integrated, hybridized Swahilis with Arab ancestry, would intensify after 1964. Contrary to the policy statement, the transition from minority status to Tanganyikan citizen was more fraught and embattled than was apparent on the surface. This was demonstrated most immediately in two traumatic events that followed shortly after the release of the policy statement on Tanganyikan citizenship.

First, on 12 January 1964, just four months before the scheduled union of Zanzibar and Tanganyika, the Zanzibari African majority overthrew the sultan's constitutional monarchy. The uprising was precipitated by long-standing tensions between Swahilis of Arab ancestry (muhajirina) and those of African and Shirazi (Persian) ancestry, motivated in part by colonial constructions of ethnicity. The Afro-Shirazi Party, headed by Abeid Karume, was Black Nationalist with links to the mainland Tanganyika African National Union and dominated by Swahili of African and Shirazi ancestry. The minority Zanzibar Nationalist Party, led by Ali Muhsin, was the country's oldest party and originated in the Arab Association. Muhsin was rumored to have Pan-Arab sentiments and allegiances to the sultan, with ideas of forming a Muslim union connecting Zanzibar to the Sudan, Somalia, and Egypt. The political landscape was further complicated by the radical Abdulrahman Mohamed Babu's youth wing, the Umma (Masses) Party, with its Cuban and communist influences.[21]

The Afro-Shirazi Party mobilized the revolt, which ultimately forced an exodus of Swahili of Arab ancestry, creating a Swahili diaspora. The resultant confusion over Swahili identity encapsulated the crisis over authenticity, hybridity, and majority citizenship haunting the struggle for national identity, disrupting the smooth narrative of postcolonial citizenship presented by Nyerere.

Simultaneously, tensions were brewing in Tanganyika in response to Nyerere's 7 January policy paper and soon exploded into full-scale rebellion. At the center of the controversy was Nyerere's stated intention of ending the policy of Africanization in government hiring:

Two years ago we introduced a form of racial discrimination into the civil service. For both recruitment and promotion we gave Tanganyika citizens of African descent priority over other Tanganyika citizens. There were good reasons for this action then, which we fully explained. It was necessary to counteract the effects of past discrimination against citizens of African descent so that our civil service could develop a "local look," and there was also an unavoidable uncertainty about which people of non-African descent were really committed to Tanganyika.

The time for this compromise with principles has now past. The reasons which were valid in 1961 are not valid in 1964. Most of all, there is no longer any doubt about who is a citizen of the Republic of Tanganyika.

It is natural that we should distinguish between those who are, and those who are not, citizens of our country. . . . We cannot allow the growth of first and second class citizenship.

The distinction between citizens of African descent and citizens of non-African descent must now be ended.

This means that discrimination in civil service employment, both as regards recruitment, training, and promotion, must be brought to an end immediately. . . . The only distinction which can in future be accepted is that between citizens and non-citizens.[22]

This move created pandemonium in the trade, railway, and government employee unions, which considered it a step backward and against the interests of indigenous citizens. The resulting discontent escalated into an armed takeover staged by the Tanganyikan army. The uprising, quickly repressed, was interpreted as a mutiny, a coup, and a strike that went out of control. Most important, it dramatized the state's vulnerability in the face of emerging subjectivities and contentious sites of citizenship such as the Tanganyikan army.[23]

These two events—the revolt against Nyerere's nondiscrimination decree, and the violent exodus of the artificially constructed minority Arab Africans from Zanzibar compelled by the majority Black Nationalist Party—brought home to Tanganyikan Asians their precarious claim on citizenship. Henceforth, their legitimation as Tanganyikans would depend on their public performance as citizens with political stakes in nationalist politics. This performance would involve refuting public mythologies of Asian passivity and indifference. Conversely, it would also require a personal commitment to Nyerere's vision of a raceless Tanganyika ("the race quarrel is a stupid quarrel"), even as Asians were expected to accept immigrant minority status and trust in the good will of the majority. Such contradictory demands—self-effacement and public displays of allegiance—emerged as the components of political citizenship in Tanganyika.

Writing from a position of nomadic citizenship himself, Frantz Fanon once remarked that, while the Black subject can imagine himself a cosmopolitan, the shock induced by the primordial construction "nigger" will return him immediately to a place of abjectness.[24] The experience of East African Asians in the 1970s resonates with this sudden abjectness. Their narrative of Tanzanian citizenship collapses into a primordial identity in the face of a single word—*banyani*, or commercial usurer. It is the linguistic and rhetorical shift from *banyani* to *Wahindi*, or Tanzanian Asian, that creates a space for activating cultural citizenship within emerging modern identities.

Revisiting this struggle for cultural legitimation exposes the vulnerability and tensions of belonging through which national and postcolonial identities are constituted. Becoming Tanzanian Asian was a gradual process entailing the physical mediation and phantasmic aspects of legal, cultural, and economic citizenship. Asian anxiety was somewhat assuaged by the presence of Sophia Mustapha, the TANU officer nominated as an electoral candidate in Arusha during the final years leading to independence, and Amir Jamal, Nyerere's finance minister. But the scarcity of Asian images in the public discourse of citizenship raised the strategic necessity of political representations of Tanzanian Asian subjectivity, of dramatically demarcating the line between prior histories as *banyani* and their future as Tanzanian Asians.

The move to separate the stereotype of the *banyani* from the complex identity of Tanzania's Asians involved an intricate archive of communities in disaffiliation. Because minority Asians were a heterogeneous community with caste and class divisions that replicated its own logic within the racist preindependence society of British East Africa, the relationship between them and majority Africans had been one of interdependence as well as complex interethnic prejudices, more nuanced than a Black-white colonial discourse of race would allow. Solidarities and biases weighed on both sides. Tanzanian Asians were certainly not innocent of feudal, racist hierarchies nurtured through Hindu ideologies of caste, class, regionalism, and race. Darker Indians, non-Hindus, and southern Indians in general were discriminated against within the Indian community. Such nonprogressive race politics did not help their forays into democratic nonsectarian local politics, which involved redressing their own complicity in perpetuating the racist system that sustained them in East Africa. Added to this was their public stance of disengagement from nationalist politics, and the African majority's suspicions of Asian self-interest, marked by ethnically insular business investments. The stereotypical impact of Asians as a commercially successful mercantile community made them suspect as a vestigial colonial presence in the ensuing struggle for nonracial local representations.

These negative public perceptions were hard to combat, despite the fact that the history of colonial struggle in East Africa had often included politically enlightened, antiracist, secular, and democratic Asians who believed themselves to be African, with varying investments in progressive decolonization. Consequently, the burden that fell on the early production of political representations—exemplified by Mustapha and Jamal, for instance—were many. These representatives offered East Africans for the first time new public images of Asian subjectivity and reflected the changing face of independent Africa. They also reiterated the importance of engagement in the cultural politics of the state, something that immigrant communities had largely steered clear of, barring a few committed activists. These few but groundbreaking Asian public presences, most effectively embodied by Jamal, counteracted the pervasive sense among Asians of being discredited on racial grounds (as had been the colonial practice), which threatened to jeopardize Asian participation in the nationalist phase of postindependence rule.

Dar es Salaam: Transoceanic Links

The city of Dar es Salaam embodies a quiet ferment of syncretic culture. The Indian Ocean link brought African, Arab, Omani, German, British, Asian, Portuguese, Muslim, Christian, and Ismaili influences that combined to create an eclectic postcolonial city with architecturally hybrid resonances. This cultural hybridity contrasted with the city's spatial organization.

Under laws such as the Colonial Labor Utilization Ordinance of 1923, African urban migration had been tightly controlled. Preindependence urbanization policies worked in tandem with colonial labor laws, restricting development in the administrative centers of the colonial state.[25] Hence, colonial urban space and the provision of social services developed in racialized and class-determined ways. The physical geography of the city reflected the social geographies of class and race. White neighborhoods like Oyster Bay were attractive and luxurious residential areas surrounded by gardens, social clubs, golf courses, and recreational facilities. Asian sections like Upanga and the present Samora Avenue were the commercial and business centers, and next in preference for urban social services. In marked contrast to the Uzungini and Uhindini areas of town, the majority

African neighborhoods suffered serious neglect. Africans were forced to live in high-density, often unplanned residential settlements initially located west of the commercial center of Kariakoo on the outskirts of the colonial city and expanding rapidly toward Magomeni and Ilala. From here, Africans commuted to town on foot or bus to work. Their neighborhoods were often without public amenities like street lamps, electricity, tap water, or a sewage system. Such racially demarcated urban social demographics dramatically embodied the severe psychic and material disparities that the postcolonial state would struggle to undo.

The fact that former racist segregation laws had enabled predominantly Asian mercantile and business communities to congregate around the port and commercial center of Dar es Salaam became a source of resentment after independence. Perceived as beneficiaries of a racist system, Asians personified the legacies of colonial spatial organization. These tensions became visceral as local Tanzanians, looking for housing closer to the center, began migrating into neighborhoods like Upanga, upsetting Asians' numerical dominance in the area and bringing with them an increasingly palpable anti-Asian sentiment.

Spatially, Dar es Salaam bore its syncretic colonial legacies and hybrid ethnic geographies in the genealogies of its buildings. Its Asian influences were seen in its Hindu temples; the Darkhan Jama'at-Khana on Mosque Street; Karimjee Hall, which housed the Legislative Council before independence and later became the National Assembly; the Bunge; the Goan Institute; and various schools sponsored by the Patels, Ismailis, Bohoras, and the Aga Khan, later given local Tanzanian names. Some of these locales were pronouncedly Asian in their demographics. Porous sites of social encounter, diasporic in their identifications with former identities and newly politicized socialist citizens, they comprised the broad range of Muslim, Christian, secular, and indigenous communities. At the same time, certain secular and educational forums were selectively open, prescribing the very racist categories that they objected to at a policy-making level. For instance, some Asian schools continued to privilege Asian students over other ethnicities.

These avenues of minority citizenship were simultaneously tenuous and entrenched, racist and open-minded, anxious about and fully absorbed in the formation of the new state. They were the dispersed expressions of civil society that allowed alternative forums outside the officially sanctioned spaces of the state. Their longevity lay in the fact that they posed no threat to the nation's security, nor were they considered potential dangers to the stability of the state. Their apparent passivity in political repre-

sentation both allowed them visibility as a private community and generated resentment among other Tanzanians as well as among politicized
members of the Asian community.

For many politically committed Tanzanian Asians, their public image
as a community disaffiliated from other Tanzanians was a stigma to be
contested in the small details of everyday engagements. Their attempt to
build credibility as cultural citizens was constantly shadowed by an African
nationalism that sharply delineated an anomalous though historically ac-
countable Asian presence. With a long and troubled history of involvement in colonial East Africa, the role of the Tanzanian Asian was a nascent
possibility to be realized in the new nation-state. The emerging credibility
of Asians in Tanzania would have to counter a history of disinformation
and divisiveness nurtured by British colonial administrators like F. D.
Lugard and Lord Hailey in the interest of curbing Asians' growing commercial power in colonial East Africa.[26]

Under the British, Asians were projected in the popular imagination as
opportunistic, ruthless businessmen, ardent capitalists with no political
allegiances to either the Europeans or Africans. Further, their own complicity with the Arabs in the East African slave trade, their interests in establishing a colony in East Africa during the 1920s (instigated by the Aga
Khan, G. K. Gokhale, Sarojini Naidu, and others), and their prejudiced
attitudes toward Africans and other Indian ethnicities derived from caste
and class divisions in India made it difficult for these new political subjects
to emerge as democratic and progressive without considerable politicization on their part as a community in East Africa. On the other hand,
Indian humanitarian interests in native paramountcy in Africa, supported
by B. G. Tilak, B. P. Pal, Gandhi, and C. F. Andrews; their tenacious struggle to achieve Indian equality throughout the Empire; their continuous involvement with East African politics demonstrated by Isher Dass, a prominent Indian leader who accompanied Jomo Kenyatta to London in 1929;
and the flourishing alliances between Asian, African, and African American
nationalists during the 1940s and '50s in London, Paris, and Bandung—all
these factors helped to create new progressive histories of allegiances and
solidarities.

Considerable numbers of publicly involved, antiracist Asian radicals in
Kenya such as M. A. Desai, editor of the *East African Chronicle*, who collabo-
rated with the young Kikuyu Central Association led by Harry Thuku
during the mid-1920s, were pushed out of public consciousness by the rise
of fervent nationalisms. A. M. Jeevanjee, H. S. Virji, L. J. Amin, B. S. Varma,
Mangal Dass, G. B. Tadwalkar, K. N. Jani, and many others in East African

history were soon forgotten. The activism of Indian leaders in East Africa like J. M. Nazareth, A. B. Patel, M. A. Desai, and others who worked to bring Asians and Africans into a collaborative nationalist struggle against racial discrimination during the 1920s was overlooked. Many of these political activists supported and aided in peripheral ways the struggle for African self-determination. For instance, Indians helped in printing the newspaper *Muiguithania*, edited by Jomo Kenyatta, on behalf of the Kikuyu Central Association. The powerful Kenyan trade unionist Makhan Singh, who organized East Africa's trade union movement in 1936 and initiated the Mombasa dock strike in 1939, supported the Kenya African Union.

Despite such committed political allegiances across national interests, Asians' commercial success and prominence as a landed community that owned many of the buildings in major East African towns from Bagamoyo, Tanga, and Dar es Salaam to Nairobi and Mombasa, situated them in tense relation to the battle for territorial sovereignty waged by Africans deprived of rights to land. Later, nationalization policies marked them as an exploiting community. In such tenuous political times, the contentious but productive presence of Asians in East Africa was overshadowed by the stereotype of the feudal, caste-entrenched economic migrant.

This powerful stereotype paved the way for the public disavowal of Asians as cultural citizens in East Africa during the early years of independence, as economic nationalism increasingly demarcated its financial enemies. Home Affairs Minister Leweri Sijaona's 1967 campaign to deport more than three hundred Tanzanian Asians coincided with the more serious anti-Asian policies in Kenya and Uganda. Most of these Tanzanian deportations were later nullified.[27] But in Kenya, Jomo Kenyatta's eviction of Asians in 1968 led to Britain's discriminatory Commonwealth Immigrants Act, which restricted the entry of Kenyan Asians holding British passports. This important legislation allowed the British government to disavow responsibility for certain of its citizens on the basis of skin color. A special clause in the act, however, granted former colonials with white skin the continued right of entry. For the first time, British as well as East African politicians were forced to admit separately that there was a racial basis to their respective policies.[28]

In 1972, Amin's sweeping orders expelling Ugandan Asians created a new nomadic community—which included many formerly affluent merchants, often hastily dispersed and taking no possessions—moving across the Indian Ocean and the Atlantic. The resulting mass migrations from the late 1960s to the early '70s to former homelands such as Pakistan, India, and Bangladesh, or new states of domicile such as Britain, Canada, and

Australia represented a new culture of dispossession within this diaspora already many times uprooted.[29] Since most of these exiled peoples did not return to their countries of origin, this floating postnational community demonstrated that national and ethnic identity are not equivalent entities. It also aggravated a new arena of contention around the subject of modern citizenship—that of postnational identifications. Here, the idea of a community no longer organized around a homeland or a state of entrenched citizenship begins to take shape. Instead, a more inchoate arena of floating identifications—tenuous and unstable, temporary or enduring—coalesces and disperses as these new postcolonial nomadic citizens form transidentities such as the Indian Ocean link or the transatlantic connection, organizing metaphors that produce a historicity across discontinuous trajectories.

The voluntary and coerced nomadisms of Asians from the Indian subcontinent in the late twentieth century shift older arguments of class, race, and economic migrancy onto new ground. Nomadism in this agglomeration of communities encapsulates the multiple locations of class, race, and communal affiliation through which individuals within these communities realized their daily lives. Materially, East Africans occupied shifting class statuses as they moved back and forth between peasant and mercantile backgrounds in former homelands to the position of a landed, racially privileged class under East Africa's colonial and later nonracial policies. Their ambivalence about and resistance to the Black-and-white spectrum of race politics informed their repressed histories of complicity and disaffiliation within the colonial agenda of East Africa.

But many East African Asians have reinvented themselves in their new countries of domicile. In Canada and Britain, Asians aligned themselves with a politics of Blackness in the 1970s and '80s, as a second generation of British-born Asians came into political consciousness. Staking their claims as Black British and Canadian subjects is a radical departure from their prior history as nomadic subjects of inauthentic Black subjectivity. In the United States, their transition from nomadic to locally invested political citizen has faced greater obstacles. The relation between the history of Black migration to the West and the narrowing of the spectrum of African subjectivity through the lens of Afrocentricity has tended to include only particular notions of race and culture in Africa, reducing the history of Asians in Africa to an accident rather than a part of the emerging hybrid fabric of modern migrant identities in contemporary African citizenship. Hence, Asian immigrants from East Africa to the United States have had to contend with both forging new political identities within U.S. minority discourse and creating a space within the range of Black and Asian American subjectivity available in the United States. This has by no means been easy. Further, East African–Asian allegiance to existing categories of identity as either Asian American or African American has been tenuous, since neither fully allows for the complexities of Afro-Asian identity formation.

The diasporic movement of peoples from one context to another sometimes unconsciously frees these communities to explore new realms of self-invention while older fears haunt their search for immigrant solace. In the next few chapters, I will show how this radical displacement of political culture, race relations, and histories of estrangement foregrounds aspects of cultural citizenship in new ways. Instead of operating within the often segregated, privatized spheres of cultural engagement of Asians in Tanzania, these migrant groups find themselves struggling for citizenship in the public realm in Britain, as workers, working-class subjects, and raced immigrants. This cultural shift, from a position of relationality within race discourse in East Africa to one of generic dehistoricized abjectness, creates new currents of opposition and active participation, fueled by a sense of having to take a stand this time in the realm of the political as citizens with stakes in the state.

The connecting of Afro-Asian histories in Africa with the histories of Black and Asian cultural formation in the United States is slowly emerging through various coalitional alliances, but the political pitfalls and tensions en route are many. On the other hand, there are enormous gains to be made through a better understanding of the complex histories that shape both South Asian and African identities in Africa, as well as their late-twentieth-century inroads into U.S. minority culture. These contingent histories will enrich the ways in which future identities and possible citizenships in the twenty-first century will shape their own relationship to past histories of citizenship, whether nomadic or located within a specific nation.

6

Staging the Postcolony

Black British Citizenship and Britain's Transnational Migrations

Ghana became the first African state to acquire independence in 1957. Chairman Mao died in 1976. The nineteen years in between mark a crucial period in the development of Black diasporic visibility in Europe and internationally. It was a time of passionate involvement in global solidarity movements and the formulation of radical itineraries for national sovereignty and self-determination. The cumulative effects of three centuries of slavery, indentured servitude, and colonial subjection galvanized Third World peoples into international socialist and Pan-African coalitions. A transnational cadre of Black radicals developed a political framework within which to articulate concerns about economic and cultural rights, simultaneously charting new modes of citizenship.

Much of this activity occurred in the heart of the crumbling empire. In Anglophone countries such as Tanzania, Britain had always loomed as a port of call. Historically, Britain functioned as a meeting ground for Third World nationals from colonized, newly independent, or transitioning Anglophone states, a relatively hospitable place to convene and exchange notes. From the 1930s to the '50s, London and Paris were transit points for emerging anticolonial figures like W. E. B. Du Bois, Jawaharlal Nehru, Ho Chi Minh, Gandhi, George Padmore, Léopold Senghor, Kwame Nkrumah, and C. L. R. James. Later, decolonizing Third World communities migrated to Britain for economic and educational reasons, bringing with them ideas of political participation and a desire for new kinds of cosmospolitan citizenship. Depending on the conditions of migration (forced or voluntary), the process generated levels of psychic and political dislocation making it difficult to mesh with the political and cultural fabric of British life.

But these traumatic dislocations offered opportunities as well. In newly independent states like Tanzania, Kenya, or Uganda, the urgency to create a cohesive national culture discouraged public expressions of dissent, narrowing the public sphere in the interests of the state. Former colonial host states like Britain, however, bore antagonistic, interdependent, and permeable relations with former colonial subjects, creating new—though no less troubled—avenues for individual autonomy and dissent. The heterogeneous history of Britain's Black populations catalyzed transnational ideas of citizenship and belonging that far exceeded the boundaries of the British state. Nationally bound notions of British citizenship collided with the transnational relationships of Britain to its former colonies, invoking other histories of cultural citizenship in the process. Concepts of citizenship shaping cultural dialogue in states such as Tanzania, combined with new discourses adopted by East African–Asian and Caribbean migrants, provoked heated debate on the nature of the postcolonial state. The idea of Britain itself as such an entity gained currency. That celebrated British insularity and its attendant claim to cultural purity—"Englishness"—slowly gave way to notions of a postcolonial Britishness incorporating its Subcontinental, African, and Caribbean influences, upsetting conventional notions of where the First World ended and the Third World began.

The Black arts movement in Britain developed in the context of this self-conscious struggle for an expanded public culture and broadened concepts of citizenship. According to Kwesi Owusu, editor of *Storms of the Heart*, a survey of Black arts since the 1950s, Black cultural work has been accomplished despite deplorable public funding, weak infrastructures, and what Owusu calls the "disorganic effects of state culture," a pointed critique of Britain's attempts to contain its postwar immigrant populations through hostile policy and ideological scapegoating.[1] The development of Black arts in Britain has occurred in implicit or overt engagement with these machines of governmentality, critiquing, resisting, and protesting the regulatory regimes through which Britain's immigrant communities have had to produce their own subjectivities.

During the early postwar years, Black arts functioned as a mantle for a diverse array of immigrant constituencies. Members of the Caribbean arts movement (CAM), for instance—including Edward Kamau Brathwaite, Doris Brathwaite, Andrew Salkey, John La Rose, Orlando Patterson, Sarah White, and Ngugi wa Thiong'o—orchestrated a lively diasporic cultural renewal.[2] Although primarily an experimental venue for writers and poets from the Anglophone Caribbean, CAM self-consciously tried to include Francophone and Iberian Caribbean compatriots as well. The forums organized by CAM covered topics ranging from the responsibility of West Indian writers to the masses, theories of creolization, the influence of the Harlem Renaissance, the negritude movement, and Cuban negrissimo, to the more militant separatist wing of Black Power that emerged after Stokely Carmichael's visit to Britain in 1967. These energetic and often volatile discussions reflected the unique dilemmas of postcolonial citizenship experienced by communities in migration, simultaneously forging new affiliations with the adopted home, maintaining fragmented connections to other nations or landscapes, and absorbing provocative concepts of global Black solidarity generated by Third World and African American liberation movements.

The British Immigration Act of 1971 dramatically altered the climate in which Black diasporic culture had so far developed. The legislation, designed to stem the flow of Kenyan Asians into Britain, actually halted all primary immigration from former colonies. Only Blacks contracted to do specific work were allowed entry, and then for no longer than twelve months. Under the act, police and immigration officials were granted considerable leeway to harass migrants, incarcerate them without trial, and separate families. Women were subjected to humiliating vaginal examinations to determine whether or not they were virgins. Peter Fryer describes the experience of an eleven-year-old girl who, after enduring such an examination to the accompaniment of British officials' mocking laughter, was told that she would not be granted an entry certificate to join her mother and siblings.[3] Such events, laws, and policies—propelled by Enoch Powell's notoriously racist diatribes—reiterated the dilemma of cultural citizenship for Black communities in pressing ways.

Moreover, by the mid-1970s, two out of every five Black persons living in Britain were born there.[4] These changing demographics radically transformed the very ground on which a previous generation of Black immigrants—such as CAM's members—had formulated concepts of community and nation, and strategies of political activism. The '70s marked a shift away from Blacks as immigrants to the realization that a generation of young Black Britons were now old enough to demand rights in Britain as Brits. This was their home, they were here to stay, and consequently their relationship to their parents' concerns was distanced by different ideas of cultural citizenship. What the new generation of Black British inherited and would have to contend with was a legacy of racism and discrimination in education, housing, employment, cultural misrepresentation, and institutional delegitimation.

Within this context of increasingly belligerent state action and growing xenophobia among Britain's "natives," a wide range of writings, theories, visual art, aural experimentations, and performances emerged from the 1970s onward, informally defining broader areas of Black British inquiry. Invoking discourses related to the histories and cultures of peoples historically produced as "Black" or, at times, loosely as "Third World," in a postindependence, postcolonial, and post–civil rights framework, Black British culture has generated counterpublic spheres of collaborative interaction to forge an arena of Black British concerns. These debates and critical inquiries have consolidated a historically new space of Black cultural studies in Britain.[5]

Black cultural studies addresses the interests, concerns, ideologies, and locations of Black cultural work within a national and global context. Although no specific theory posits a separate discipline called Black cultural studies, the analysis and critique of work around questions of race and ideology, race and culture, race and material practice, race and gender emerged out of—and within the absences and legacies of—existing critical and cultural studies. But where race was merely incidental to the axis around which different trajectories of cultural studies emerged, a Black cultural studies accounts for the crucial role of race in feminist, Marxist, psychoanalytic, and postcolonial theories of culture.

Within the broader arena of cultural studies, contingent developments have contributed to the emergence of race as a pivotal component of a politically informed practice of culture. British cultural studies, in its many inflections through the 1970s and early '80s, tended to overlook—or include only peripherally—the intersections of race, sexuality, and gender within a class- and political economy–based analysis of culture. But a broad expanse of writings, generated through political clubs, art collectives, community centers, labor unions, academic institutions, prompted a more rigorous consideration of race and gender. In the United States, the popularization and diffusion of the term *cultural studies* produced numerous U.S.-based versions, with various genealogies and intellectual formations. Critical practices committed to exploring the cultural production of minorities have developed as part of a broader post–civil rights discourse. As such, the articulation of a Black cultural studies has occurred in tandem with an Asian American cultural studies, a Latino/Chicano cultural studies, and so on, not as independent developments but as deeply imbricated by U.S. political and legal rhetorics. Within these recent critical practices (which I am locating primarily within the academy and other institutions of culture), the impact and pertinence of race in the study of popular culture has been an important aspect.

Black British cultural studies has functioned as a bridge linking a U.S. politics of race and a Commonwealth history of race relations and left politics. It has also been foundational in developing a transnational and globally inflected idea of citizenship within the North. The work of Stuart Hall and other Black intellectuals like A. Sivanandan, Paul Gilroy, Kobena Mercer, Hazel Carby, and Pratibha Parmar; publications such as *Policing the Crisis, The Empire Strikes Back, There Ain't No Black in the Union Jack, Charting the Journey, The Real Me, Black Film/British Cinema, Race and Class;* the writings of C. L. R. James, Erroll Lawrence, Homi Bhabha, Jim Pines, Angela McRobbie, and Dick Hebdige; the productions of film and video collectives like Ceddo, Black Audio, Sankofa, Star, and Retake; informal modes of exchange through the work of playwrights/performers Benjamin Zephaniah, Mustapha Matura, Yvonne Brewster, Hanif Kureishi, photographers David Bailey, Monika Baker, Sunil Gupta, and visual artists Sonya Boyce, Zarina Bhimji, and Sutapa Biswas—all created a cultural milieu that was locally based and theoretically engaged with questions of aesthetics, practice, audience, and ideology.

Stuart Hall's far-reaching contribution to the critical development of British cultural studies is intertwined with the history of the University of Birmingham's Centre for Contemporary Cultural Studies (where Hall served as director in the 1970s, as well as an editor of *New Left Review* from 1957 to 1961) and the trajectory of the New Left in Britain. As a leading Black intellectual in postwar Britain, Hall's extensive writings emerged out of the tensions between the socialist humanism of Raymond Williams, Richard Hoggart, and E. P. Thompson, and the antihumanism of Louis Althusser's structural Marxism. His political and intellectual commitment to Marxism offers a materialist theory of ideology and discourse, grounded in a new reading of Antonio Gramsci, that draws on both psychoanalysis and deconstruction.[6] As a major theorist of the politics of contemporary British culture and society, Hall's intellectual contributions lie in his broad-ranging collective projects and their appropriations by social movements within and outside academia, and his incisive analyses of the dynamics of cultural change have impacted intellectual movements well beyond the borders of Britain, influencing currents in the United States, Taiwan,

Australia, and India. Although numerous political struggles, ideological issues, and forms of collective work shaped and extended Hall's writings beyond the confines of traditional left inquiry, his work reflects the complex ways in which race intersects with gender and class relations in the larger intellectual formation of British Marxism.[7]

Focusing on the ideological functions of mass media, popular culture, consumption, and visual pleasure within various subcultures as well as within dominant structures of power during the 1970s and '80s, Hall opened different avenues of investigation regarding violence, terror, the nature of subject formation, concepts such as Eurocentrism and the West, and the limits of rationalist ideology in Margaret Thatcher's Britain.[8] His work embodies the confluence of different trajectories of political engagement. Merging theories of dependency and structural adjustment with poststructuralist thought, Hall raises central issues around the dilemma of citizenship in relation to contemporary modernity. In *Policing the Crisis*, for example, Hall, in collaboration with Chas Critcher, Tony Jefferson, John Clarke, and Brian Roberts, demystifies mass media narratives that frame immigrant Black populations as aberrant. In this groundbreaking collaboration, the media reifies a homogeneous British state now threatened by its colonial history come home to roost. While the colonial project officially ended with the relinquishing of territories, what has risen in its place are the elaborate economies of mystification and deviance through which the disenfranchised former colonial must be read.[9]

Hall's extraordinarily insightful readings of the pathologies of authority put the British state under the ethnographic microscope, establishing a methodology of political analysis central to Black cultural studies. But to reiterate, the development of Black cultural studies in Britain was not merely an academic exercise. Cultural producers worked side by side with critics and theoreticians, carving out informal institutional spaces from which to challenge the hegemony of Englishness. In this charged atmosphere, the politics of drama were radically transformed by a theater movement that questioned both mainstream and left conventions in the performing arts.

Unhinging the Historiography of British Theater

The theaters of the state and stage have always drawn on each other for signs of the time. During the early nationalisms of modern states, theaters rigorously staged and debated the genres of national culture. Some of the players in these much publicized furors were playwrights who often considered themselves spokespersons for a certain cultural milieu. The disagreements between Vladimir Mayakovsky and the Soviet state, Wole Soyinka and the Nigerian government of Sani Abache, Ngugi wa Thiong'o and Daniel arap Moi's Kenya all staged the collisions between the playwright, genres of cultural citizenship, and ideologies of the state.

During the early postwar years, with increasing migration across states, British theater provided a fertile and provocative venue for staging the travails of immigrant and minority citizenship. Britain itself embodied a commonwealth theater-in-the-round, staging the Empire's demise as well as its reincarnation through its diasporic identities. Because of its history of colonialism, Britain became a productive site for transnational culture. Peoples from Africa, the Caribbean, Asia, and the Middle East struggled for recognition as cultural citizens in the emerging postcolonial British state, in the process destabilizing simple notions of the *post* in postcolonial and other paradigms such as First World/Third World and the West/ non-West. The mobilizing of Black consciousness in public displays of citizenship like the Notting Hill Carnival, workers' strikes, political rallies, cultural performances, presses such as New Beacon, Bourgle L'Ouverture, Presence Africaine, and journals such as *Race Today, Savacou, New Left Review,* and *Race and Class* generated articulate and politicized struggles for gaining access to representation within the dominant culture.

Within this context, Black British theater emerged as a crucial site for performing the postcolony, a strategic arena for representing the psychic and legal struggles of Britain's immigrant and minority constituencies. It provided a forum for decoding and rehistoricizing the tensions experienced by the Third World immigrant, who, straddling two countries, must acquire cultural citizenship by becoming British. At a time when broader commercial markets were unprepared to accommodate minority producers or audiences, Black theater presented the dilemma of being Black and British. Its playwrights shaped the mise-en-scène of their audiences within feminist, left, and working-class culture. And they persevered despite the material realities of Black cultural production, which restricted these artistic forays to the peripheries of urban life through exclusionist policies that persisted up to the 1980s.

When I began my ethnography of Black British theater in the mid-1980s, there was surprisingly little documentation of this vibrant community-based movement.[10] Apart from the brief review of a production, few historicized accounts, critical writings, or even published plays could be found, in striking contrast to the high visibility of Black British cultural critics, filmmakers, and visual artists both locally and internationally.

Yet the debates on citizenship and belonging staged in postcolonial theater during the 1970s and '80s are integral to contemporary British theater history. Britain's status as a postcolony developed in tandem with early dramatic contributions by Mustapha Matura, Linton Kweisi Johnson, Yvonne Brewster, Derek Walcott, Jatinder Varma, Alfred Fagon, Tunde Ikoli, and Benjamin Zephaniah, voicing the unnameable and marking the forgotten in the national imaginary. These works challenge not only mainstream theatrical conventions, but the orthodoxies of British left theater as well. Immigrant producers complicated the preoccupations of left playwrights—class, labor, left politics, the welfare state—with the diasporic history of immigration, assimilation, race, colonialism, and transnational memories of arrival. Forced by inadequate structures of commodification to depend on local communities for patronage and circulation, this community groundedness enabled Black playwrights to elaborate on the transnational connections and open-endedness of immigrant culture, ultimately forging a diasporic identity of Britishness.

Performing in the Interstices: Mustapha Matura and Black British Theater

The border paradigm is an effective means of accounting for the slippage or excess of what is framed as British theater. The border perpetuates visual territories of the past and present, situating postcolonial British theater in a more complex geography of the vanished empire. To grasp the question of borders, we must account for memory that cannot be contained, that overruns the border's limits. Such memory complicates our understanding of the ways in which generations of immigrants have contested and/or assimilated into the dominant culture.

Exemplary of the border-memory dynamic in Black British theater, Mustapha Matura's work rejects any monolithic argument about culture such as the dominant versus the marginal or the colonizer versus the colonized. Matura's work is the first body of dramatic texts to emerge out of Britain and challenge British theater culture on racial and ethnic grounds. Born in Trinidad, he arrived in England in 1960. Positioned by the dominant culture as merely "Black," Matura had to create a space to articulate the complex politics of difference and the wide and disparate histories of blackness among Britain's Black communities. His hybrid genealogy crosses over into his experiments with the theater as his plays explore the in-between and transitory spaces of postcolonial culture and the conflicts of identity and tradition in both Trinidad and Britain.

Beginning in 1971, when his first full-length play *as time goes by* was produced at the Traverse Theatre Club in Edinburgh and the Royal Court in London (winning both the George Devine and the John Whiting awards that year), Matura's work emerged as an intervention on the British fringe. *Black Pieces* (1970), *Bakerloo Line* (1972), *Nice* (1973), *Play Mas* (1974) (which won the London *Evening Standard*'s Most Promising Playwright Award and was transferred to the West End), *Black Slaves White Chains* (1975), *Rum an' Coca Cola* (1976), *Bread* (1976), *Another Tuesday* (1978), *More* (1978), *Independence* (1979), *Welcome Home Jacko* (1979), *A Dying Business* (1980), *One Rule* (1981), and *Meetings* (1982) brought Matura recognition as a major playwright. His visibility in the United States would establish him as a crucial voice in the development and practice of Black theater in the transatlantic context as well.

Matura's work is a collection of multivoiced narratives that explore the precolonial, colonial, and postindependence moments in Trinidadian culture. It raises questions about decolonization and cultural identity by constantly juxtaposing the past and the present, Trinidad and England. Each of Matura's plays can be read as part of a larger voyage of recovering and confronting both private and social history. From *as time goes by*, which traces the ideological and personal implications of migrancy for the first generation of Caribbean immigrants to Britain, to *Play Mas, Meetings*, and *Independence*, which critique colonialism and its aftermath in Trinidad, Matura's work unfolds as an oral map of the subaltern's personal memories in the postcolonial moment.[11]

BORDER CULTURES/BORDER WRITING

Positioned at the borders of both Trinidad and England, Matura's plays construct an alternative dialogue to the dominant discourse of 1970s British theater. Not just class but race and ethnicity (Black nationalism, in particular) problematize the contemporary British experience. His texts continually transgress familiar constructions of Englishness, exploring the limits and possibilities of cultural transition. Simultaneously British and more than British, they occupy the interstices of cultural interchange, as they shift and alter British and, by extension, urban Western cultural norms through a privileging of Afro-Caribbean and Asian cultural codes. Matura coerces into discussion the rhetorics of empire and what constitutes postcolonial British identity by constructing the Black British presence as the dominant force in his texts.

Matura's plays foreground the blind spots of British theater culture and crowd the blank spaces of mainstream drama with the bodies of other territories on the edges of British society (Black skinheads, Black bus conductors,

Black council dustmen), and from other cultures (Afro-Caribbean, Indian, "Trini," Pakistani, Black working class). In this remapping of culture and geography, the borders of empire are revealed as a construct at once fixed and mutable. The margins are centered and "England" relegated to the periphery. The "disorderly" neighborhoods of Britain's borders—Brixton, Southall, Shepherd's Bush, East London, Notting Hill, the Portobello Road, the London Underground—become a globally dispersed center, and England a colony on its fringe. The geography of this dispersed center is imagined through the discursive spaces of its nations. Various characters are "Trini" or "English"; a woman from the Asian or African diaspora, located within the frames of patriarchy, immigration policy, and class politics; from the imaginary homelands of "Africa," "India," and "Trinidad." The former colonies and postcolonial history are reframed as a complex, heterogeneous series of imagined boundaries and maps outside as well as inside Britain's borders, interrupting and altering the very terrain of contemporary British culture.

Matura further complicates this remapping by highlighting the syncretic nature of the cultures invoked. Various hybrid ethnicities of Afro-Asian communities insert themselves into British culture through gestures and linguistic variations to mark their specificities. For instance, patois, Gujarati, and British working-class accents deliberately interrupt and inscribe the language of Englishness in *as time goes by* and *Play Mas.*

The implications of occupying the border shifts in these texts from economic necessity to cultural and political strategy. Initially constructed and positioned as other, as "Black," as "them," by the 1970s the postcolonial immigrant has appropriated the term Black as a potent political signifier. Deepening engagement in British political life alters notions of ethnic specificity and difference. No longer merely "Black," the ethnicities of this "Blackness" soon blur the distinctions between border and core. The composite nature of Britain's "Black" cultures redefines notions of identity and national culture.

SPATIAL BORDERS / TRAVEL STORIES

In these plays about passage, the unpredictable and unwritten emerge from the cultural dislocations of border crossings. Here, travel becomes a theoretically enabling idea. It implies the construction of borders, involves spatial displacement, and positions the body in moments of transition that variously challenge, alter, alienate, and distort the individual and the familiar. Travel implies a refraction of time, both historical and local.

Within the shifting, transitional space of the traveler, borders must be re-drawn constantly.

Travel in Matura's writings is woven into the narrative through tales of arrival and departure told from the transitory spaces occupied by charac-ters who tend to come from former colonies and inhabit very tenuous po-sitions in the new culture. In *as time goes by,* for instance, almost all of these positions are junctions between points of travel in the British transport system, be it bus, train, or garbage disposal. In effect, immigrants become sites of passage while in transit themselves. They have scant material pos-sessions and function merely as checkpoints of arrival and departure, lit-eral manifestations of the term *en route.*

In these intermediary traveling spaces of London's subaltern exis-tence, the telling of the tale becomes the moment of recovery. Fiction and memory, improvised and transformed into a celebratory return through the oral narrative, are Ram's prescription for his subaltern "patients" in *as time goes by.* An eclectic shaman of various gods, Ram's invocation-cum-salutation announces: "Ram, Ram, salam, wale com, shalom, peace, hi, hello, good evening, welcome to the house of truth and reality, come in." Ram occupies a liminal space at the fringes of this city of travelers and dis-placed people. Here in Ram's front room, "lavishly decorated with reli-gious objects and pictures," a subaltern such as Arnold, dressed in the de-humanizing uniform of the London Transport Underground Guards, can humanize his invisibility. "Well brother Ram," Arnold declares, "if a could only no why she left me a would feel good but anyhow ita good talking to you a start to feel good already."[12] Within the fantastical space of Ram's living room, *as time goes by* becomes a series of vignettes about Black British experience.

The oral narrative, populated by travelers and nomads, has a long ge-nealogy in non-Western cultures and becomes crucial to historicizing the dialogues of migrants, refugees, immigrants, and the displaced in Matura's writing.[13] As a form of textuality, the oral narrative occupies the most elusive, precarious position, that of transitional utterance. It can carry the burden of a culture yet is elastic enough for fashioning subjectivity, as Ram suggests in his gesture of welcome: "What you need I provide. What you provide I need. What you desire I recommend. What you recommend I de-sire. My thoughts are at your service. Come in."[14] Any word spoken must alter itself in transition from one speaker to another, from one moment to another. The minimal material condition, that of being able to speak and be spoken to, constructs the oral narrative as an archetype of dispersed cul-tures. It takes up space but cannot be owned or bought. Always in transit, it becomes charged through speech. To utter is to act and engage. To speak locates the speaker in time and history. Voice is agency.

Orality has a special status in the creation and dissemination of culture in colonial and postcolonial societies. Western configurations of non-Western cultures have been redressed by indigenous peoples through orality. The oral emerges as a powerful weapon of subversion, one that is immensely malleable, tensile, with a thousand heads, impossible for the colonizer to appropriate or suppress entirely. Under colonialism, oral narrative becomes a means of cultural survival, of preserving otherwise unrecorded events. It is also the primary mode of exchange for those with little educational opportunity. The power to represent requires access to the means of representation. The immigrant Black communities who comprise a section of the working class are considerably limited by their minimal access to representation. This is particularly true of the wave of postcolonial immigrants from the Caribbean, Africa (especially petit bourgeois East African–Asian entrepreneurs), and India during the 1970s. Hence Matura's privileging of the oral over the written.

As time goes by stages the ways in which orality unwrites Englishness in a predominantly literate culture where access to narrative power is linked to the magic of print. By foregrounding certain kinds of stories, Matura raises the question of whose oral narratives are sanctioned in the official spaces of British culture that lie outside his texts. Through the heteroglossia of oral traditions, Matura performs the rewriting of England with diasporic English, buttressed by Hindi, patois, pidgin, creole Tamil, butchered Arabic, and working-class dialects.

Independence illustrates how Matura allows voices from the fringes of both Black British culture (through the use of Black British actors) and Trinidadian society (through the mise-en-scène) to speak for themselves in a way that positions them as active agents rather than as subjects over-determined by circumstance or passive participants in the colonial machine. The play demystifies both the colonial and postcolonial moments by juxtaposing two characters rooted firmly in different generations— Drakes, part of the colonial legacy, and Allen, the future of independent Trinidad—with different political vectors. Written eight years after as time goes by, Independence unfolds as a series of parables about colonialism and the decompressing economic effects in a newly independent country. The narrated story is the only way to preserve and transfer unofficial history from the colonial to postcolonial phase. Both Drakes and Allen have worked as pool barmen in the Grand Hotel in independent Trinidad. But while Drakes's storytelling is firmly fixed in the colonial past, which he glorifies,

Allen's stories are dreams about the future of independent Trinidad—and his place in its economic and cultural life—based on a critique of imperialism and slavery. In act 11, the former pool bar, now in ruins, becomes the link between the colonial and postcolonial moments for Allen: "I en' romantising dis place, a tell yer wet it was like wit me, an I was here at de end but I hear stories wen I was here about how worse it was."[15]

With restricted access to literacy, storytelling is the primary mode of communication in colonial and postindependent Trinidad for Drakes's generation.[16] Through anecdotes, gossip, riddles, banter, and jokes, Drakes slowly reveals to Allen the unwritten and rapidly receding history of material relations between colonial subalterns and colonizers. The poolside bar becomes the mise-en-scène of Drakes's narrations and a crucial site for Allen's mapping of his own history later on:

> I do' love dis place, but dis is where I saw—we here—we come from, dis place, yes, I needed dis place ter show we where we come from an where we going yes, we need places like dis dat is one a de jokes about it, we need de horror ter show we or else we could never know, my eyes open in dis place, ter wet we was, wet we used ter be an I value it fer dat ter push off, push off from it, yes I need it, I need dis place, an anodder one a de jokes about it is dat de more dis place treat yer like a boy is de more I felt like a man, de more I wanted ter be a man, I felt alive here, I saw sings clear here fer de fist time in my life how de system operated how it killed people, dere used ter be a feller here working wid me call Drakes. I en, know wet happen ter him, but he was one, he was somebody who dis place enslave, because he couldn't see how it worked, but he help me, he is a man. I would never forget him an fer men like him it was too late fer dem, dey was born inro it, but we lucky we had a chance ter look at sings an see dem clear fer de first time, but fer dem who give us dat chance, all de Drakes a dis world.[17]

The oral narrative functions as "informal" knowledge, local knowledge, which in turn is shaped against the dominant form of information, the written word. Its plasticity turns the oral narrative into a powerful vehicle for unmapping space, as people like Drakes give the mapped their own configuration. For instance, in the hands of a former colonized subaltern, the subject of cocktails becomes an exposé of colonial power relations. For Drakes, "it was happiness in dose days" when "everbody had dey own territory," referring to "de old days wen it was a pleasure ter serve drinks, ter see de pleasure on people's faces wen yer place de drink in front a dem an dey start ter run." The colonial period as evoked by Drakes is a moment of excess and plenty, unclouded by a critique of the systematic enslavement of native populations. Drakes's ambivalence as a colonized subject is entangled with his mastery of the art of mixing cocktails and the sense of power this gives him:

> Wat you know bout sparkle, yer do' know dey have Black cocktail, dull cocktail, cocktail you could see through, cocktail yet car' see through. . . . I could make any Linda cocktail. I could make drinks change color right before yer eyes an yer car, remember wet it was before. . . . If a had me ingredients Ed show yer wet cocktail was all about. I'd hit yer wid so much cocktail . . . dat yer would feel like yer was de Prince of Wales. (46)

Cocktails signify Englishness for Drakes, as his description of "Rapid Rage" suggests: "Dat is white rum, wid brown rum, wid Coca Cola separating de sides, like de United Kingdom, an wen dey hit yer belly, is war yer see" (46). Englishness and colonialism become synonymous as he describes the "Planters Punch" to Allen: "You en' know wet a Planters Punch is an you want ter be a farmer. Dat is wet after yer ride all day over yer plantation yer man servant come an put before yer after he stable yer horse, man." Englishness inscribes the system within which Drakes found a function under the old order of colonialism; it becomes the mark of his redundancy within the contemporary context, revealed in the ironic coda to act 1:

HARPER: Brother Drakes, today is the eighteenth of September, Nineteen Seventy-Eight, you agree.
DRAKES: Yes, Brother Harper.
HARPER: Good. Champagne. Bollinger RD 69.
DRAKES: None.
HARPER: Roederer Crystal Brut 73.
DRAKES: None. . . .
HARPER: Veuve Clicquot Gold Label 73. (Lights begin slow fade.)
DRAKES: No. (55)

Drakes accepts Harper's dismissal as someone whose "special skill is not one dat is easy to use in a Developing Progressive Society." Says Drakes: "It mean a might en' get another job, cat's wet, or one a know how ter do. A might end up sweeping Frederick Street, or de market." As a member of a generation that came into middle age during colonialism, Drakes finds himself in a tragic position of being relegated even further to the margins of the new society by the likes of Harper: "An he also drop a hint bout a man of my age, how difficult it is, everyting difficult." Neither "here" in the sense that Allen is, engaged in the contemporary struggle for power, agency, and visibility in independent Trinidad, nor able to use the past in a marketable way, Drakes is symptomatic of the chaos that unfolds on the borders of postcolonial society. His inability to qualify for even a pension—because "it came in after independence" and he "didn't make enough units, I started too late"—foregrounds the unaccountable history of the subaltern who occupies the interstices of society and gets junked like an obsolete appliance during the transition phase (57).

Oral speech becomes the primary mode of anticolonial resistance in Matura's *Independence*, the originary site for ruminations on anti-imperialism and decolonization. The Molotov cocktail is the only type of cocktail that interests Allen. His conversations with Drakes reveal the past to him in all its contradictions, forcing him to devise a plan of action for the future. What Allen puts into practice from the borders of Trinidadian society as a subsistence farmer, eventually to sell in the market, instances the way in which power gets redistributed and redefined within the new social relations of independent Trinidad.

While Allen and Drakes are situated in the contradictory spaces of a decolonizing nation, Matura unambiguously asserts that the only way to escape the old dispensation is a radical erasure of the former structures by the same means that created them, namely violence. Only out of the ashes of violence can a culture begin to construct new subjectivities. Matura projects Frantz Fanon's problematic notion of therapeutic violence into the postcolonial context through Drakes's suicide, which demolishes the Grand Hotel at the same time. Such an unconditional choice of engagement with history contrasts with the character of Harper, who conducts a project of exploitation in postcolonial Trinidad without a ruffle in his existence. For Allen, however, Drakes's gesture is both nihilistic and necessary. Allen comprehends Drakes's choice. He realizes that for Drakes only by annihilating the source of oppression—the Grand Hotel—however symbolic it may be, can the ghosts of colonialism be banished. Returning to the remnants of the hotel a year later, Allen normalizes the moment of violence as inevitable in a narration of his colonial experience to his companion Yvonne:

> It used ter be bad it was everthing a told yer about it wid Black people spending dey whole life running about ter serve white people, till dey dead but look at it now look at it, it dead now it harmless, I wouldn't a bring you wen it was still standing because in dem days just ter come near it, yer had ter change, yer had ter, yer manner had ter be different, ter come in, cat's de kinda effect it had on people an dat went on fer whole generations a people dis place affect. (69)

Independence constructs the oral narrative as a safety valve for the logic of violence that structures life under colonialism and during the transition phase that follows. Through narration and storytelling, the anger and violence of history can be routed into productive channels. Allen insists on this process of recounting and coming to terms with experience throughout the text. Although he understands, even respects, Drakes's terminal act of confrontation, he elects to deal with history's horror through self-reliance and a committed engagement with the land. These become Allen's alternative to the vicious circle of colonial and postcolonial exploitation in which he finds himself.

By suggesting that violence is the most effective means of recovery, Matura reinscribes the Manichaean logic of binarisms onto the postcolonial space at the same moment that he points to other ways of salvaging a decimated culture. This overall structuring device mirrors the binarisms and multiplicities of the narratives. The demarcation between the old dispensation and the new is simultaneously abrupt, as between Drakes and Allen, and obscured, as projected by Harper. Harper breaks the binary relationship constructed between Drakes and Allen by configuring yet another model of the postcolonial condition. As Drakes describes Harper: "People like you just take over wey de English leave off . . . you an people like you spoil it, all, yer jump in de water like fish an carry on de same ting, power, power in yer mind" (67). Harper embodies one end of the spectrum of ambivalence of the colonized toward the colonial machine. He fully intends to carry on where the colonial bureaucracy left off, but in the name of independence. For Harper, Drakes represents "everyting dat is bad wit de past and wet de Republic is trying to eradicate . . . yer car' change and changes is in de air, if yer car' change, yer go get run over, dat is a promise" (67).

Between Harper, Allen, and Drakes, the oral narrative becomes a conjuncture of different locations, the only link between these people as they converge and then are catapulted into separate orbits. For all three, the systems of power are translated primarily in oral terms. This is why Drakes must act in perhaps the only way he knows how when language no longer makes sense of power. Drakes destroys in material terms what language fails to account for, including his own body. As Drakes says in his final speech:

> I have ter stay here I have ter watch dis place . . . ter see dat notting ever move in dis place, ter see it never rise up again. . . . Nobody must touch it, I is de only one, because I build it, wet man build man could pull down, an I en' only I could pull it down, an I do dat every day . . . in a hundred years

time people go come here an say wet was dis place wet did it stand fer wet did it do, who did it benefit, wet BC was dat or wet AD was cat. Yes an interesting period dat was yer see. . . . On a graph or a chart . . . a date, a date on a map. . . . But we go be still here, so go . . . do' come back . . . you have notting ter look back here for . . . I is de watchman. (72)

Through the mode of storytelling, the border becomes an unmapping space, as the territories of various ethnicities cross and reposition within their shifting material relations. In Matura's writing, social and political forces alter the power relations of various cultural and class divisions. We see this in *Independence* in the context of two moments of transformation in Trinidadian history and culture, while in *as time goes by* the shifts occur in the context of the working lives—as opposed to the private experiences— of subaltern communities in London. In all Matura's texts, dominant British culture and the diasporic Black British culture collide, producing the characteristic tensions of British race relations during the 1970s and '80s.

Afro-Asians and the Politics of Blackness

Dispelling essentialist ideas of Blackness as singular and homogeneous is integral to all of Matura's plays. In *Party*, for instance, various Black characters represent different political positions, ranging from indifference (characters A and B) to moderate (character C) to left (V) to the radical militancy of Malcolm X and the Black Power movement (as preached by Z). *Party* demonstrates how power roles alter visibly when whites enter Black territory. Within the space of the party, the white middle and working classes and the Black working class play out the frictions of race politics, exposing the limitations of both white liberalism and Black nationalism within the context of Britain. Sue and P are positioned as committed liberals, supporters of the antiapartheid movement whose solidarity with Blacks is challenged by Z's violent repudiation of their lip-serving political correctness. Z's oversimplified indictment of hegemonic culture suggests the impasse inevitably reached on either side of a binary political configuration:

Well I say their turn has come, because your white God is either a racist or he color blind, or he is just a nice, little excuse for your white liberal conscience. First it was fear of the unknown so you killed, then you killed to convert us to your God of Love, then you killed us because we didn't want to be slaves, now it's God's will, so the poor Black man have to wait until you run out of reasons to kill him. Well my Black god say it is his will that we kill . . . and stop givin' you our blood while you act out your fantasies on us. . . . My Black god say you are a savage and a devil and you should be destroyed, chopped up in little pieces and eaten. . . . So, you take your nice convenient little white God, and ask to help yer, and you tell him you don't think it's right that all these Black people should suffer and see what he says, and come and tell me if you find me.[18]

This diatribe drives Sue to betray her own deep prejudices concealed beneath the facade of her liberal politics, calling Z a "Black beast." By juxtaposing white liberalism against a range of political positions under the rubric "Black," in *Party* Matura attempts to complicate the idea of Blackness, albeit in a somewhat reductive manner.

In *Party,* Miles Davis, Nelson Mandela, Malcolm X, and the Black Power movement are the key points of reference for white culture to negotiate. Islam and Z's "Black God" are the worldviews against which Sue's feeble liberalism contends. The "holy waters of the Thames" is repositioned according to Z's mapping of London as "Holy what it full a shit and dead people, that's what it full a." In this unmapping of space, what gets foregrounded are the other narratives of Black struggle invoked through Z's signifying dashiki. Z says:

Yer ever see that film report on the Black people starving and dying, their ribs sticking out, their veins bursting, their eyes staring and dead, their legs shot off, their limbs dangling, young babies turn grey with hunger, Black people being clubbed and shot, herded like animals? (105)

South Africa, Biafra, and Guinea become the extended centers of Z's life within the borders of Britain, where "Blackness" signifies resistance and revolution alongside the contradictions of daily existence. As Z's narrative suggests, the borders too are multiple and dispersed, incorporating both essentialized and hybridized constructions of Blackness. Z's rhetoric of Black nationalism constructs a totalizing view of both struggle and resistance, while his own position and affiliations are constantly shifting as he vacillates between vulgar Marxist stances, radical Black politics, sexist overtures, and the disempowering utopia of hashish. Likewise, in Matura's other texts, imagined centers and borders collide and alter each other, as the imagined communities of former colonial African and Asian people are framed within their political, class, and cultural locations (93–110).

Borders are tenuous locations in Matura's plays, blurring the distinctions between here and "back home" at one level and demarcating very clear boundaries at others, such as gender politics. Borders become sites of hybridity, the bricolage of clashing codes. In a sense, they occupy the imagined space of being, as they construct within the confines of their neighborhood the projections of home, self, nation, family, and culture, always "quite but not quite" English or Trinidadian in the case of the first-generation immigrant characters in *Party* and *as time goes by*.[19] The syncretism of these borders is simultaneously fractured by contradictions. Postcolonial Black British subjectivities play out the ambivalences of living in England while retaining aspects of their culture, though in a radically altered form. They multiply their politics depending on their class and gender location and in turn construct independent notions of what nation or "home" means.

The texts discussed thus far raise issues of dislocation, identity, nationality, and the problem of belonging, but in gender-specific ways. The characters with power are predominantly heterosexual men; therefore, their projections of self, culture, and home are constructed along lines that are parallel to rather than conjoining with gender. Let me return to *as time goes by* to expand on what becomes symptomatic of Matura's and, by extension, Black British playwrighting of the 1970s.

Immigrant postcolonial culture in *as time goes by* is primarily articulated through the voices of Black men; Black women are relegated to the background as mere appendages. A reading of the projections of England exposes rifts along gender lines. For Ram, the Trinidadian of Asian descent, England is the site of masquerade, where anonymity has earned him the freedom to transform himself from what Trinidadian society expected of him to what he enjoys doing: being a self-appointed counselor and holy man. Masquerade allows Ram entry into white culture, but only as a commodity, the shaman who can sell a quick fix, be it spirituality or drugs, to "de hippies," "dem long hair people who does wear den funny Linda clothes." For Batee, on the other hand, who is a Trinidadian Hindu, England means the four walls of her kitchen, while home, family, and a sense of belonging are firmly rooted in the island culture she has left behind: "I dying ter go back home, it too cold de people don't like me, dey tink we is dirt an' de treat we like dirt . . . how yer could like a place like dat?" Further on Batee says, "A don't have ter go nowhere ter know dab don't like we . . . but one place dey can't touch me is in my kitchen. Dat's de only place I safe because is mine" (82–83). Batee is rendered powerless by being entirely dependent on her husband. By contrast, the Trinidadian women of Afro-Caribbean descent, Thelma and Una, are dependent and subordinate but have more social leverage. Finally, for "auntie Ruby" back in Trinidad, England has all the classic colonial associations. Ruby sends word to Ram that she is still waiting for "de picture a Buckingham Palace . . .

an' one a de Queen." England, India, and Trinidad are constructed differently by different individuals, depending on the fictions or partial facts they want to perpetuate. Culture emerges as the crucial marker of distinct affiliations; the differences within border cultures demarcate the ways in which alliances are or might be made.

The excess of mimicry and the contradictions of such a position in the construction of nation or home become more explicit in the character Skinhead in *as time goes by.* A second-generation Black British teenager, Skinhead exemplifies the generation gap and the problems of British identity. While Skinhead's father, Albert, is a Trinidadian immigrant who remains very much on the periphery of British culture, Skinhead is more working class than Black in the way he initially positions himself. His preference for reggae, refusal to join the British army, and rejection of his father's working-class aspirations place him in a new category of what it means to be British in postcolonial Britain. For Skinhead, home is neither in Trinidad, which he has never seen, nor white Britain, which offers him no clear place in the emerging postempire society of the 1970s. Skinhead's own politics are ambivalent, as he adopts the style codes of the very sections of society that are known to be racist and xenophobic. Such contradictions serve to problematize further the notions of identity and nationhood, for Skinhead clearly falls outside the dominant discourses of cultural and racial homogeneity of the nation-state in Britain.[20]

With such a proliferation of identities and cultures, Matura's depiction of border cultures in effect constructs these spaces through a series of centers, where the Sikh's Gurudwara, the Muslim's mosque, the Jew's synagogue, and the Christian's church may all be located.[21] The border is continually redefined within what informally separates "us," the "authentic British," from "them," the changing faces of Britain, as communities create multiple focal points of interest and exchange. Borders deterritorialize the city and reconfigure space into new relationships in the housing estates, the suburbs, and the Afro-Caribbean and Asian areas of Britain.

Positioned as outsiders from the inside, charting the arrivals and departures of expatriate life, the storytellers in these texts must inevitably come to terms with the limits of their own self-conceptions, as Ram and Batee demonstrate. England is inscribed within these narratives as the border that must be crossed, coming from or going "back home." In *as time goes by,* the title itself implies the inherent state of flux that for Ram becomes a useful phrase to describe the condition of things to his former colonial working-class clients as well as to his flower-power clients. As time goes by, the borders become centered, acquiring roots, as occurs with Albert and his son Skinhead. As time goes by, the expatriates will become immigrants and in turn will alter the culture around them.

While dispersed in their narrative strategies, Matura's plays both transform and are inflected by mainstream British culture of the 1970s. The legacies of colonialism and neocolonialism, and the projects of cultural imperialism, are the knowns that are given materiality in the writing, contextualized within the local and global politics of living on an island, be it colonial or independent, Trinidad or Britain. The visible military presence of U.S. and British forces in postindependence Trinidad in *Play Mas*, the exploitation of Third World countries as fodder for multinational corporations in *Meetings*, and the struggle for power and legal rights by Black British communities in *My Enemy* instance the multiple ways in which this dynamic is enacted. The hybrid spaces in this writing from the borders evoke the diversity of these cultures and their impact on a hitherto uncontested British identity. Matura's texts explore this syncretic culture to propose a heterogeneous concept of Englishness by disclosing those people and locations inside metropolitan Britain and its former colonies who had remained largely hidden from mainstream representation. Their project is to infuse a measure of "Blackness" into the infamously lily-white (and red and blue) Union Jack.

7

Bodies outside the State

Black British Women Playwrights and the Limits of Citizenship

In his account of Black British cultural production and its transatlantic influences, *There Ain't No Black in the Union Jack,* Paul Gilroy outlines the elaborate regimes of production, consumption, and circulation that make Black Britishness a tangible and pervasive presence within the British state.[1] Hovering around Gilroy's intricate archive are the invisible economies of Black British women's cultural work, demonstrating yet another dimension of cultural citizenship within the modern state. Yvonne Brewster, the grand dame of Black British women's theater, recounts in an interview that she was the first Black female drama student in England, trained at the Royal Academy in 1965. In 1982, Brewster became the first Black woman drama officer on the Arts Council.[2] Brewster's anecdote opens the largely unmapped terrain of Black British women's cultural production and its public circulation from the 1960s to the '90s. Black women's playwrighting, as Brewster suggests, has been an evocative site for enacting the dilemmas of citizenship, linking women to the broader struggle for cultural citizenship in Britain.

Not surprisingly, prior to the early '80s, the discourses of identity and belonging in Black British cultural production were predominantly male narratives, foregrounding Black male subjectivity. The playwright Mustapha

Matura, poet/performers Linton Kweisi Johnson and Benjamin Zephaniah, and playwright/director Jatinder Varma were among the early innovators of Black theater. Along with other media practitioners like Lionel Ngakane, Horace Ove, Menelik Shabazz, and Rasheed Araeen, they dramatized the dilemmas of arrival, class antagonism, Pan-African sympathies, Black identity, and the tensions of masculinity, marking the absence of Black women as subjects with agency.

The thriving Black arts movement, propelled by the Greater London Council's funding initiated in 1981, generated new opportunities for Black British women's cultural contributions. Within the movement, Black women playwrights acquired a new visibility, transforming the gendered rhetoric of belonging in new ways. This reconfiguration of concerns caused a fracturing and proliferation of coalitions along the lines of class, gender, ethnicity, and sexuality. Theatre of Black Women, Talawa Theatre Company, Temba, Umoja, Tara Arts Company, Tamasha Theatre Company, Assati, Black Theatre Co-operative, Carib, Black Mime Theatre (later known as the Women's Troop), Unlock the Chains Collective, Munirah, Double Edge, Roots Theatre, the Women's Theatre Workshop, and Theatre Centre were almost all formed during the '80s and '90s.[3] Yvonne Brewster, Winsome Pinnock, Maureen Blackwood, Stella Dadzie, Hazel Carby, Pratibha Parmar, Amrit Wilson, Ravindher Randhawa, Bernardine Evaristo, and other Black feminists increasingly gained public attention. Their work cumulatively destabilized earlier narratives of Black women as absent in the public sphere with histories of Black women as active agents in British struggles for cultural and legal citizenship.[4]

History and Belonging: Immigration and Cultural Production

Beginning with the dismantling of Britain's empire, and concretely located in the arrival of the first sizeable contingent of West Indian people to England on the SS *Windrush* in June 1948, Britain's colonial legacy came to a crisis on its own shores.[5] In the aftermath of decolonization, migrants from Africa, the Caribbean, and South Asia flocked to Britain either as members of the New Commonwealth or simply as British passport holders. Viewed by the adopted country as a threatening mass to be eradicated or repatriated, these semiskilled or unskilled workers catalyzed a shift within dominant "race" discourse, in turn transforming notions of British citizenship.

The saga of this mass emigration is dramatized and celebrated in the work of Black British women playwrights, notably Winsome Pinnock's *A*

Hero's Welcome (1989), Jacqueline Rudet's *Basin* (1985), Zindika's *Leonora's Dance* (1993), and Bonnie Greer's *Munda Negra* (1995).[6] However, because British immigration laws from the 1960s onward determined the type of immigration possible, much Black British drama focuses specifically on the problem of forging new kinds of multicultural citizenship. Subjects of former colonial nations could no longer claim immigration rights to Britain solely on the basis of having the appropriate papers. By the midseventies, immigration from Africa and Asia was virtually stopped through a series of legislative maneuvers designed to both racialize and restrict the growth of Black communities from both regions. From then on, anti-immigrant rhetoric is racinated in very specific ways, pathologizing Black immigrants and expatriation.[7]

For Black women in Britain, immigration policies worked doubly to block access to legal rights and cultural citizenship. While the first wave of immigration from the West Indies during the 1950s brought large numbers of single, economically active women, subsequent migrations led to the control and restriction of Black women attempting to enter the country. Migrancy was experienced by single Black women of African and Asian descent and men in quite different ways. For instance, in 1968 the British government altered the legal rights of entry for Asians by introducing a voucher system. Vouchers were issued only to heads of households, normally men, and to certain categories of dependents. Consequently, Asian women without kinship ties in Britain were barred entry. This restriction affected not only women migrants but also second-generation female immigrants born in Britain, since many widowed, abandoned, or divorced women encountered enormous obstacles proving they were heads of households. Coupled with patriarchal structures within their own cultures, the complexities of survival in the postcolonial British state severely restricted the movements and access to education for most women from immigrant Black communities.[8]

Although a discussion of the distinctions in visibility politics and how they played out in different mediums such as film, visual arts, and theater is beyond the scope of this chapter, it is important to bear in mind that the particular narrative being mapped here is contingent on the interrelatedness of various art practices. Much Black art of this period is informed by the twin projects of decentering the notion of "Black" culture by challenging preconceptions of who is "British," and coming to terms with the constantly shifting implications of what it means to be "English." Rejecting fictions of cultural homogeneity, Black cultural workers evoke a transforming urban syncretism that is altered and in turn shaped by its various immigrant and indigenous constituencies. The work of film and video collectives such as Retake, Star, Ceddo, Sankofa, Black Audio, and the Women's Collective is particularly noteworthy, pushing the boundaries of representation beyond a mere repositioning of Black identity within the British imaginary. Generating work for many artists in different mediums simultaneously, these collectives complicated received ideas of the postcolonial citizen along the axes of gender, sexuality, generation, and immigrant histories.

The particular economies of race and representation that coalesce to make working across mediums a necessity in the early years of Black cultural struggle in Britain are underscored here. During the 1980s, theater actresses such as Corinne Skinner Carter of *Passion of Remembrance*, Rita Wolf of *My Beautiful Laundrette*, *Burning an Illusion*, and *Khush*, and Meera Syal of *Sammy and Rosie Get Laid* and *My Sister-Wife* worked in film as well, while playwrights such as Tunde Ikoli, Hanif Kureishi, and, more recently, Winsome Pinnock and Meera Syal wrote and directed for film and television while continuing to work in theater. Visual artist Sonya Boyce designed the sets for the film *Dreaming Rivers*, directed by Martina Attile of the Sankofa Film and Video Collective, while filmmakers John Akomforah, Isaac Julien, Robert Crusz, Maureen Blackwood, Attile, Gurindher Chadda, and Pratibha Parmar find themselves charting new critical territories as both theoreticians and practitioners. These interlinking arenas produce a critical mass of work focused on the relationship of Black cultural production to cultural citizenship.

Intersectionality and Individual Rights: Rukhsana Ahmad's
Song for a Sanctuary *and Meera Syal's* My Sister-Wife

In her essay "Woman's Era," Hazel Carby discusses the texts of Black women, from former slave Harriet Jacobs to Anna Julia Cooper, as testaments to the racist practices of the suffrage and temperance movements, indictments of the ways in which white women allied themselves not with Black women but with a racist patriarchal order against all Black people. According to Carby, "only by confronting this history of difference can we hope to understand the boundaries that separate white feminists from all women of colour."[9] Feminist, postcolonial, and queer scholarship over the past two decades has complicated the Black-and-white boundaries that Carby invokes, by opening up the links and crossroads between race, gender, nationality, and sexuality.

Arguing for such an intersection from the context of critical legal theory,

Kimberle Crenshaw observes that the tendency to treat race and gender as mutually exclusive categories of experience and analysis is perpetuated by a single-axis framework dominant in U.S. antidiscrimination law and reflected in feminist theory and antiracist politics.[10] According to Crenshaw, such a one-dimensional analysis flattens the multidimensionality of Black women's experiences and results in their erasure. Using African American women as a reference point, Crenshaw demonstrates how dominant conceptions of discrimination structure notions of subordination as disadvantage occurring along a single categorical axis. This limits inquiry to the experiences of otherwise privileged members of a group. In race discrimination cases, this group tends to be composed of sex- or class-privileged Blacks; in sex discrimination cases, the focus is on race- and class-privileged women. For Crenshaw, only by considering the problems of intersectionality can one begin to embrace the experiences and concerns of Black women in the United States. While Crenshaw's work is specific to the United States in its cultural moorings, her arguments for intersectionality and dismantling the single-axis framework are crucial to an understanding of the political junctures within which British Blacks function. Taken together, the works of Crenshaw and Carby point a way toward a reworking of the single-axis framework and problematizing existing paradigms.

A number of Black British women have articulated in their art what Crenshaw and Carby are reconfiguring in legal and literary theory. Consider Rukhsana Ahmad's moving portrayal of a London women's refuge, *Song for a Sanctuary* (1993).[11] Here, the conditions of immigrant women's lives in Britain slowly unfold through the regulative structures of religion, patriarchy, honor, duty, and community that limit the kinds of citizenship to which they have access. Cocooned within the rigidly patriarchal and dogmatic boundaries of embattled religious ideologies and culturally resilient customs, Ahmad's protagonist, Rajindher, struggles to understand her dependence on an abusive husband and her invisibility as a subject within the state. Rajindher's complex history—fifteen horrific years of domestic violence, trapped by the psychic economies of secrecy and pride that relegate such material conditions to the private realm—poses the difficult question of subjecthood in diaspora. Caught between her culture's punitive traditions and the state's secular intrusions, for Rajindher citizenship in Britain is continually shaped as a negation of her psychic self, from her arrival to her brutal death. Her Punjabi husband, Pradeep, represented as a grotesque caricature, is committed to feudal and agrarian notions of ownership and retribution. After Pradeep stabs Rajindher to death in the refuge with his *kirpaan* (a curved dagger sacred to the Sikhs), he exonerates himself by invoking customary patriarchal rights: "This is not murder, it is a death sentence, her punishment for taking away what was mine. . . . She can't leave me, she's my wife."

Ahmad relentlessly pursues the interstitial realms of women's lives such as the refuge, where the limits of legal, psychic, and economic citizenship impinge on the rights of immigrant women within the state. Rajindher is caught between British concepts of individual rights and her culturally specific realm of experience, where notions of duty and honor supersede (if not entirely displace) Western concepts of individual rights, making it difficult for her to come to terms with her condition, despite fifteen years in Britain. But as Crenshaw's paradigm of intersectionality reminds us, Rajindher's rights as an immigrant are determined by the gendered and heterosexual matrix of British law: she is defined as a dependent by virtue of being married. Seeking refuge from her husband carries the risk of losing status as a legal immigrant. Moreover, should she clear this hurdle and become eligible for state support and housing, she must reconsider her own subjectivity, shaped by the very same ideological regimes of customary practice that produced her husband. Enmeshed in the secular discourses of Western individualism under British common law and those of residual customary practices such as Sikh notions of duty, honor, virtue, and retribution, Rajindher finds herself trapped by culture with tragic consequences. Rajindher's poignant story dramatizes the interstitial ways in which multiple regimes of the self, the secular, and the customary impinge in violent and interlocking ways on the formation of immigrant women's subjectivity.

Ahmad's depiction of a British Sikh family's disintegration points up a crucial aspect of cultural and legal citizenship within the modern state: the tension between common law and customary practice. Rarely the subject of discussion in states such as Britain and the United States—except as a human rights issue, for instance, the volatile debates surrounding clitoridectomy and infibulation—customary practice often works as a regulative economy governing women's bodies regardless of cultural specificity. Customary practice does not translate easily into the legal discourse of Western nations and therefore renders invisible the complex mechanisms through which women from Hindu, Buddhist, Confucian, and Muslim cultures must forge psychic and legal access to individual rights.[12]

Song for a Sanctuary, however, oversimplifies the tensions between the secular and the customary by locating the customary as primordially "native" or "Third World" against the modernity of the British state. This leads to the erasure of the complex layers of the law and the body that shape citizens in democratic states such as India, invoked in *Song for a Sanctuary* as a feudal, nonsecular locale in Punjab. The play offers secularity within Western individualism as the only way out. Consequently, both Rajindher and Pradeep are reduced to the worst colonial stereotypes of Asians as peoples with no civilized (read: secular) notions of rights, entrenched in barbaric practices of customary "tradition." The concluding anachronistic display of Pradeep's sense of righteousness reiterates this stereotypical bind between tradition and modernity. Pradeep's murderous act falls outside the sphere of Western notions of rights (theoretically, at least), as he invokes a feudal though debatably culturally coherent notion of Sikh male ownership in which a wife is a nonperson within the economy of customary law. This closing moment indicts Pradeep as a parochial throwback, a depthless caricature of emasculated immigrant masculinity, reinforcing racist stereotypes even as the narrative attempts to lodge an internal critique of women's oppression within specific communities.

The ambivalent self-hate articulated by Rukhsana Ahmad through the monstrous character of Pradeep reproduces some of the more disconcerting stereotypes about "backward" Asians within British society as much as the text renegotiates a deep anger against men like Pradeep, who have contributed to the demonization of South Asian men through their own feudal and undemocratic perceptions about gender. Ahmad's own ambivalence about Asian masculinity erupts through this scorching critique of the violence embedded in the isolation of immigrant women and their sense of self. *Song for a Sanctuary* works as a reminder of painful orthodoxies that are contorted through the immigrant experience and explode in hideous ways.

Similarly, Meera Syal's dark screenplay *My Sister-Wife* (1993) contends with the irreconcilable forces of individuality and communality as they clash within the domestic spaces of a Pakistani Muslim household in South London. In a series of reversals reminiscent of Genet's *The Maids*, Syal deftly portrays the competing logics of customary practice—in this case, Islamic law—and civil law, the law of the British state. With great wit, Syal sketches the tortuous and circumlocutory ways through which immigrants in Britain negotiate between the customary traditions of former homelands and the less evident, more contemporary orthodoxies of the secular culture within which they must live as British subjects.

The plot is framed by two poles of immigrant British Muslim women's subjectivity. Farah is the modern urban professional woman, born in Pakistan, raised in Britain by cultured, upper-class Pakistani businesspeople. Maryam is a traditional Pakistani bourgeois woman in an arranged marriage to Asif Shah, a wealthy binational businessman who travels between Britain and Pakistan. With this ménage à trois, Syal sets the stage for a psychic struggle between individual rights and customary practice.

What follows is a compelling exploration of the epistemological crevices of competing psychic and sexual economies in which the common denominators are the oppression and interdependence of Black women. Syal's work shreds the illusion that education and modernization can buy middle-class women enough consciousness to opt out of the patriarchal circuits of exchange and subjection. Instead, Syal skillfully lays out the intangible but more compelling psychic economies of cultural insularity, immigrant self-perpetuation, and isolation through which Asif's and Maryam's cultural ambivalence takes root and finally overwhelms Farah's British sense of self and individuality. Syal paints a contemporary picture of interlocking interests of desire and patriarchy, both Muslim and Western (read: secular) through which this particular British Muslim household must determine its fate. And Maryam and Farah eventually do, by killing the source of their discontent, Asif.

Farah and Maryam are enmeshed in a traditional Pakistani Muslim situation, made possible by Asif's right to have more than one wife (interpreted as bigamous and therefore illegal in Britain). Farah, driven to the edge of insanity by Asif's increasing psychological abuse, displaces her agony onto Maryam. Perceiving Maryam as the tormentor, Farah attempts to kill her by adding poison to the pitcher of drinking water kept in Maryam's room. But by a bizarre twist of events, Asif becomes the victim, leaving the women dependent on each other for help and care. This deeply troubling scenario ends inconclusively with Farah's inadvertent murder of Asif and the bleak companionship in which Farah and Maryam find themselves, offering no suggestions as to how their predicament might be resolved within local communities.

As in Ahmad's portrayal of the dilemmas of intersectionality, Syal's text raises further questions about the limits of juridical logic. In Syal's script, the dramatic series of events that unravels in Britain is precipitated by customary practices embedded in Muslim private law. In Pakistan, men can legally marry more than one woman, and divorce is accomplished by the simple ritual of repeating the word *Talaq* three times. Consequently, following the narrative of bigamy dramatized in *My Sister-Wife* to its sordid end, we are left with the disturbing dilemmas posed by cultural relativism, whereby to condone the right to customary practice outside the purview of the secular state is to participate in perpetuating women's oppression. On the other hand, to disregard the regimes of patriarchal control that shape the psyches of immigrant Muslim women in Britain would be to de-historicize the kinds of laws and oppressions through which women's bodies and subjectivities are produced under the secular state.

Like Ahmad, Syal poses difficult questions about immigrants and cultural assimilation within British secularism, presenting modern Muslim identities—as embodied by Farah and her parents—in tension with the feudal Muslim identities of conservative immigrants like Asif and his first wife, Maryam. According to Syal, modern individualism within contemporary Muslim cultures allows for a wide range of lifestyles, as Farah's forward-looking parents and her own subjectivity suggest. Opposed to this are the anachronistic regimes of control presented under the guise of tradition and represented by Asif's mother. Maryam stands at the cross-roads of these conflicting identities, a victim who is determined to survive the circumstances. But, Syal suggests, there is no question that these oppressive regimes of feudal Muslim practice must be abandoned. There is no middle ground for Syal, as neither Maryam nor Farah emerges successfully from the trauma. Like Ahmad, Syal recognizes the regimes of tradition that work to the detriment of women, and both argue for a move away from tradition toward more emancipatory forms of identification through a decolonization of the self. Neither Ahmad nor Syal suggests what that self might be. But the negativity of their critique implies that they see modern secular individualism as the way out. For both playwrights, becoming British means coming to terms with specific histories of oppression while struggling to find new, emancipatory strategies for creating viable British Asian identities.

Positionality and the Critique of Bourgeois Feminism:
Jacqueline Rudet's Basin *and Winsome Pinnock's* A Rock in Water

The notion of positionality struggles between the totalizing narratives of the subject and the eternal sliding of the signifier. According to post-structuralists, the fragmented subjectivity of postmodernity results in the occupying of multiple identities, rendering subjectivity a shifting space of signification and "reality" a simulacra. The deconstructionist perspective, on the other hand, insists on the need for arbitrary closure to instantiate meaning. As Stuart Hall argues, "All the social movements which have tried to transform society and have required the constitution of new subjectivities, have had to accept the necessarily fictional, but also the fictional necessity, of the arbitrary closure which is not the end, but which makes both politics and identity possible."[13] Thus, signification assumes meaning within a specific historical context.

But this process is not gender neutral. Black women, for example, have historically been subsumed under the rubric of race by way of the construction of "the Black community," thereby eliding structures of patriarchal control and oppression validated as custom. For emergent forms of citizenship—in this case, Black British women's—the dangers of a totalizing subjecthood are subordinated to the urgent need to master the rudimentary aspects of acquiring citizenship, such as legal representation and public mobility. Positionality, in this case, implies locating oneself as a subject already overdetermined by various contingent narratives, and self-consciously foregrounding those narratives that demarcate the identities one has chosen to occupy, such as Black lesbian, Black Marxist, Asian feminist, and so on. Positionality is essential to subject formation, since it is only through the realization of a certain series of identifications that one comes into voice. For working-class Black British women who do not write or speak English, this process is a literal one: learning that one has legal rights, learning to use those rights, and learning how to get heard, after which visibility politics become possible.[14]

Locating themselves within what Meenakshi Ponnuswami calls "the Newer Left constituencies of Thatcher's era," Pinnock and Rudet respectively address what Ponnuswami identifies as the failure of British feminist historiography and New Left theater to account for the emancipatory alternative economies of Britain's Black populations. Ponnuswami points out that the white feminist historiography of Caryl Churchill, Pam Gems, the Women's Theatre Group, Monstrous Regiment, Deborah Levy, and Shirley Gee, among others, critiques bourgeois feminism without providing alternative avenues for feminism's more emancipatory intersections. As Ponnuswami rightly observes, the New Left's cursory acknowledgment of feminist practice and its neglect of race have left Black women outside of even progressive discourse.[15]

Elaborating on this exclusion, Rudet and Pinnock elucidate how issues of race and gender are once again subsumed by working-class politics, how the roles of Black women in the politicizing of Black workers are ignored and silenced. By privileging the logic of intersectionality in their distanciation from British left culture, both playwrights critique the foregrounding of class as the prism through which to view the workings of material and social relations. Instead, they unpack the very tangible ways through which gender and sexuality play out in these processes, ultimately erased within the predictable class agendas of left politics. Finally, for

Black British women articulating the politics of positionality, the question of gender was inextricably linked with Anglo-European feminist movements, which invariably excluded Black women and avoided the issues of race and immigration.[16] Pinnock's Black communist feminist Claudia Jones in *A Rock in Water* and Rudet's Black lesbian feminist Susan in *Basin* embody a critique of white British bourgeois feminism, proposing alternative economies of identification and invoking transnational relationships with Black diasporas of the New World.

As representative instances of some of the issues raised by Black women's playwrighting in the 1980s, Rudet's and Pinnock's works merit close attention. They were among the first Black British women's plays available in print (thanks to the efforts of Yvonne Brewster),[17] and they are situated within the context of the diasporic Black experience of the twentieth century. While Rudet's play is structured around the lives of Black lesbian women of Afro-Caribbean descent in postcolonial Britain, *A Rock in Water* highlights Black women's struggles for legal and cultural citizenship within modern secular democracies in a transnational framework.

Rudet's *Basin* (1985) is a linear piece of theater, realistic in form. It was directed by Paulette Randall, a founding member of the Theatre of Black Women, begun in 1982.[18] *Basin* raises epistemological questions about alternative economies of meaning in the postcolonial European city, exploring a distinctly Afro-Caribbean British women's culture through culturally specific paradigms such as the basin and "zammie." The basin, a round, shallow metal container, is presented by Rudet as a common item possessed by Black women across the diaspora. It is invoked here as an archetype that connects them across history and geography. *Zammie* is a patois word used by Rudet to capture the profound bond between Black women that falls outside Western notions of friendship and its boundaries. According to Rudet, "'zammie' is not 'lesbian' in patois. The word refers more to the universality of friendship between Black women; no matter what nationality, no matter what class, all Black women have very important things in common. They're the last in line; there's no one below them to oppress." "Every Black woman is the 'zammie' of every other Black woman," Rudet continues. "It's almost an obligatory thing."[19] While these generalizations about Black women are reductive, Rudet's portrayal of the zammie relationship reflects the more nuanced specificities of everyday life in the city for Black women. Her invocation linking zammie love to the basin references Audre Lorde's prologue to her own ruminations on the subject, titled *Zami*: "When I sit and play in the waters of my bath I love to feel the deep inside parts of me, sliding and folded and tender and deep."[20] *Basin* is a Northern memory of Caribbean women's identity in conversation with its transatlantic counterpart, the biomythography narrativized by the North American writer Lorde: "Madivine. Friending. Zami. How Carriacou women love each other is legend in Grenada" (14).

Positionality in *Basin* is located along the axes of sexuality, class, and cultural specificity. By invoking the basin, Rudet argues for an imaginary history and mythology that link all diasporic Black women. While the premise of commonality is based on an essentialist construction of race, the rupture occurs across gender and sexuality. The idea of zammie is proposed as an alternative economy of desire, outside the heterosexual matrix of Western bourgeois feminism but operating within the experience of Britishness. Similarly, the basin symbolizes a central philosophical tension with English forms of cultural citizenship, by drawing into Western notions of love an expressive system of fragmented epistemological undercurrents from the Caribbean.

In *Basin*, the kinship networks of Black women disarticulate British notions of heterosexual nuclear families, thereby critiquing the founding myths of the British state. All three women in the play are Black British. Susan, a lesbian actress, convinces Mona, whose generous personality leaves her materially abused by men and women alike, to cross the boundary of her own heterosexual assumptions into that of zammie love. This transformation in Mona alienates Michelle, a single mother whose own unbridled and economically desperate heterosexuality is positioned as disempowering and dependent. What emerges is a contradictory space of simultaneously fixed and shifting representations, where Blackness is fixed but sexuality's constructions are dismantled, negotiated, or displaced. *Basin* opens out a dynamic field of identification that contentiously plays out the ideological and epistemological contradictions of postcolonial positionality. It reasserts the claim that if it is difficult for Black men to survive within the deeply hostile British society, Black women are multiply bound within the structures of tradition, the colonizer's culture, British law, the disenfranchised space of the "Third World subject," and the political economy of labor.

As opposed to the privatized sphere of Rudet's *Basin*, Winsome Pinnock's *A Rock in Water* (1989) is situated within the global histories of Black British women and their politicization through international feminisms, radical left politics, the struggles of Black peoples in the Caribbean, the United States, and Africa articulated by Black consciousness, Black Power, and other independence movements, and the work of Black intellectuals like June Jordan, Angela Davis, Maya Angelou, C. L. R. James,

Alice Walker, Toni Morrison, Mahatma Gandhi, W. E. B. Du Bois, Edward K. Brathwaite, Steve Biko, and others. Privileging the transnational cultural formation of Black British identity through the character of Claudia Jones, the play links three different histories of Black struggle in Trinidad, the United States, and Britain during the first half of the twentieth century.

A Rock in Water premiered at London's Royal Court Theatre Upstairs on 12 January 1989. Its protagonist, Claudia Jones, is based on the real-life African American political activist credited with launching the Notting Hill Carnival in Britain, and instrumental in running one of the first Black presses in Britain, the West Indian Gazette.[21] The play demonstrates the range and extent to which Black women were actively engaged in political action in both the United States and Britain during the 1940s and '50s by inserting women from different backgrounds and contexts into a political treatise about the power and surveillance of the democratic state. Rejecting simplistic notions of political identification, it juxtaposes the interests of the state and that of human action along the grids of race, gender, and class. The mingling of capitalist, socialist, and communist ideologies demonstrates the interplay of all these influences in the formation of women's subjectivities. By dramatizing the intersections, the play marks out the ways in which certain social formations generate a discursive authority that sustains the power of particular constituencies—for instance, bourgeois capitalist men.

Structured as a series of Brechtian vignettes, the play episodically unravels Claudia Jones's persecution as a Black communist and radical feminist during the 1950s by the U.S. government, and her deportation across the Atlantic. It moves spatially from the streets of Brooklyn in 1927 to Trinidad, Harlem, Ellis Island, Alderson Prison in West Virginia, and eventually London. Charting Jones's voluntary and involuntary migrations and eventual exile, Pinnock displaces conventional representations of Black women as passive agents outside history. She also challenges the idea that Black women were absent from public politics prior to the 1960s. The works of Ahmad, Rudet, and Syal suggest that the sites of immigrant women's cultural interventions were largely privatized and concealed from the public sphere by virtue of their status as third-class citizens with second-class citizenship. But Pinnock disputes this characterization by dramatizing Jones's encounters with women throughout the city: in factories, in prison, on the streets.

A Rock in Water enacts the contradictions of both intersectionality and positionality, as the political and geographic contexts of Jones's life keep shifting over the years. Through Jones, Pinnock comments on the transnational connections among citizenship, left politics, and the state's policing of Blacks on either side of the Atlantic. Focusing on the material conditions of domestic and undocumented labor, factory work, and state-legitimized coercion, Pinnock unleashes a scathing critique of bourgeois left society. The repressed labor histories of invisible constituencies are revealed in the characters of the Black prison officer, female garment factory workers, their foreman, working-class activists, and Mary, a Southern U.S. Black woman whose employment opportunities in 1927 New York are limited to work as a domestic. These characters operate metonymically, juxtaposing the complex intersectionality through which relations of disempowerment and privilege, legitimacy and disavowal within the state are produced. To the extent that Black women could gain a hearing and have access to publicity or recourse to independence and economic power to determine their own fates, they played an important role in the process of identity formation for Black British citizenship. The common experience of disempowerment along with a similar history of colonial servitude created alliances across class, culture, and language among people of various nationalities reinventing themselves as Black British subjects.[22]

It is no accident that the printed text is the focus of this discussion. The demise of the Greater London Council in 1986, a deepening recession, rabid conservatism, and steep cuts in arts funding have taken their toll on creative ventures on both sides of the Atlantic. However, minority cultural constituencies have proved remarkably resilient. Certainly, the critical mass of Black women's performance work available in print has increased in literally small but symbolically monumental bounds. This has occurred largely because of the commitment and imaginative resources of women like Yvonne Brewster, Kathy Perkins, Roberta Uno, Catherine Ugwu, and Kadija George, not to mention the growing new audiences hungry for artistic work reflecting their experience in the struggle for cultural citizenship.

The scripts I have cited bear the baggage of Margaret Thatcher's Britain, its ungenerosity and xenophobia, while simultaneously articulating global affiliations that exceed the narrow spectrum of British citizenship. All four playwrights I have discussed, Rukhsana Ahmad, Meera Syal, Winsome Pinnock, and Jacqueline Rudet, locate their plays across national boundaries: Punjab and Britain in *Song for a Sanctuary;* Pakistan and Britain in *My Sister-Wife;* the United States-Trinidad-Britain triangle in *A Rock in Water;* Dominica and Britain in *Basin.* In doing so, they foreground the increasing interdependence of cultural transactions across ideologies of belonging. Transnational identifications inform the dialogues in these texts, dismantling older notions of Englishness, nationness, and left politics. Considered together, these texts present the contradictory and pleasurable sites of transnational affiliations, struggling to maintain coherence within the rapidly shifting political and psychic terrains of everyday existence.

8

The Scream of Sycorax

Spirit of Exchange and the Cannibalistic State

As the cultural work of Black British women demonstrates, women are everywhere present but relegated to the background in nationalist and postcolonial struggles for citizenship. The official record of modern state formation is virtually wiped clean of women as active political participants. Moreover, until recently the surreptitious ideologies of nation building uncovered by revisionist historians rarely included gender as a constitutive category.

Sycorax, an often neglected figure in Shakespeare's final play, *The Tempest*, offers a provocative critique of the erasure of women as political participants in the modern state. Sycorax draws our attention to the history of colonial conquest and national liberation that has consigned women to the shadows of modern state formation. Recent feminist reflections on Sycorax are responses to earlier colonial and postcolonial adaptations of *The Tempest*, which reiterate her paradigmatic omission as a transnational condition, focusing as they do solely on Ariel, Caliban, and Prospero. As Roberto Fernández Retamar points out in his essay "Caliban" (1971), the metaphorical power of Caliban/Cannibal—evidenced by Thomas More's *Utopia* (1516), Montaigne's *On Cannibals* (1580), and Shakespeare's rendering—has generated an elaborate reworking of North-South readings of the emerging state in relation to raced and classed colonial and postindependence narratives of state power.[1]

In the twentieth century, Uruguayan writer José Enrique Rodo's *Ariel* (1900), French Jean Guehenno's *Caliban Speaks* (1926), O. Mannoni's *Prospero and Caliban: The Psychology of Colonization* (1950), Martiniquan Frantz Fanon's *Black Skin, White Masks* (1952), Barbadian George Lamming's *The Pleasures of Exile* (1960), Kenyan Ngugi wa Thiong'o's "Africa and Cultural Decolonization" (1971), John Pepper Clark's *The Example of Shakespeare* (1970), David Wallace's *Do You Love Me Master?* (1977), and Martiniquan Aimé Césaire's *A Tempest* (1965) are some of the more notable discussions on the theme of Caliban. The systematic omission of Sycorax in these texts opens a series of meditations on the gendered nature of the struggle for postcolonial statehood across national contexts. As the unspoken source of Caliban's servitude, Sycorax is read through the condition of Prospero's own history of possessing and being possessed. She is the first term of the appropriation of property, the last term of the alchemy of desire.

Sycorax impinges on the terrain of largely male protagonists of nation-state formation as a disruptive presence, more heard than seen. Unlike Miranda, Prospero's daughter, whom Coco Fusco reminds us is the other significant female character in *The Tempest*, Sycorax embodies gendered indigenousness.[2] She is invoked as the primordial occupant of Argier, the precolonial pristine territory outside Europe's cartographic imagination. In its evocative historic import, her emergence as aural Black subjectivity outside Europe's ocularity is already posed as an interlocking system of signs: she is heard, not seen, therefore outside the visuality of Europe's language of logocentric reason. Yet it is the coerced visual silence of her incarcerated "irrational" body on which Prospero's own tenuous reason hinges. Her cacophonous barbarism provides the foil to Prospero's wordy civility. Her sonic silence is deafening, as her threatening "bestiality," ability to reproduce, magical powers, and rights to the land by virtue of her originary nativeness all mark the limits of European as well as male anxiety and must therefore be hidden from history permanently. But, as Sycorax suggests, you can incarcerate the body of the historically disempowered subject, but its aurality cannot be erased.

As a citizen of the emerging New World modernity, Sycorax, the raced, colonized, gendered subject, returns to the scene of her repression. This time her tale is reversed, as she travels to the former Empire-turned-Island-Nation, Britain—and by extension, the West—and interrupts notions of universalist humanism by staging her own modern sorcery: the claim to democratic citizenship. The scream of Sycorax exposes the ideological ambivalence embedded in the democratizing discourses of the West and challenges the limits of Prospero's science of privileged white citizenship in Britain.

The aurality of Sycorax is a powerful diasporic link between African, European, Caribbean, and New World subject formations. Her voice evokes the obscured historic terrains through which subaltern struggles must materialize. She is the resounding force behind the nascent state as she elaborates the selective narration of possessor and possessed, cannibal and cannibalized. Sycorax disarticulates Empire, Englishness, and Masculinity while simultaneously shaping the discourse of modernity, desire, and indigenous rights in the diabolical encounter of Europe with its fantasies of elsewhere.

As a key to unraveling the psychic boundaries of power, gender, and nationalist sentiment, Sycorax is simultaneously native woman and modern subject of the new nation. Her audible screams unleash the unspoken economies of the alchemy of exchange. She forces on the pragmatism of emerging capitalist world systems a nervousness of subaltern agency and resilience. Her presence is one of growing unease for both colonial occupier and indigenous male subject.

If Prospero encapsulates the narratives of Enlightenment and the emergent modern states of sixteenth-century Europe (in this case, Milan and Naples), Sycorax represents the terrifying logic of Prospero's own experience of loss and possession. Sycorax marks Prospero's own disenfranchisement when overthrown by his brother in his state of Milan. She also serves as a reminder of Prospero's unlawful seizure of her territory, yet to be narrativized as state. Shakespeare's Sycorax embodies the diabolical magic of esoteric geographies associated with the pagan god Setabos of the Patagonians, considered to be the "devil himself."[3] Prospero, on the other hand, is white magic, the magic of the legitimated space of Western cartography, the alchemy of Western history.

Sycorax marks the outer limits of Europe's knowledge of itself, geographically and in terms of governance. She makes audible the epistemic and psychic rupture in the written, engraved, etched, and codified world of Enlightenment cartography and its accompanying narratives of European civility and statehood. Collision with Sycorax, whom Ariel announces to be from Argier (or Algiers), erodes Prospero's authority over the known and reveals his own terror of other epistemological realms wrenched open through this encounter.[4] Reduced to the untranslatable witch of the most "unmitigable rage" in Prospero's reading, Sycorax explodes the space of Western knowledge with her grasp of a different epistemological magic.

Her incarceration by Prospero and mysterious, unquestioned death contaminate Prospero's discourse of civilization and conquest through the uncontainable and radical subjectivity of indigenous rage rendered magical. Sycorax manifests the powerful sorcery of self-determination and sovereignty that echoes through the seamless and tumultuous landscape of Enlightenment history.

When she first appears in the play, Sycorax is described as the monstrous materialization of the now usurped Island-Nation, whose imaginative geography spatially compresses the New World, imbricating Algiers and the Bermudas, the site of Blackness. A sign of the unspeakable violence of history, Sycorax is proferred as the tortured gift of the stolen Island-Nation. In turn, her indigenous presence provides Prospero the parameters of fear and prohibition through which to produce his rule. Sycorax's value shifts from sovereign queen to stolen slave, making Prospero's expenditure as unlawful owner/king of the Island-Nation possible. She is the repressed horror at the center of Prospero's terror-filled state, the indigenous agent whose rightful access to the island property is held in petrification through Prospero's magic of state control.

The encounter of Sycorax with Europe in *The Tempest* enacts the alchemy of the cannibalistic state. According to film theorists Robert Stam and Ella Shohat, the Brazilian poet/dramatist Oswald de Andrade's "Anthropophagic Manifesto," launched during the Brazilian modernist period of the 1920s, popularized anthropophagy, or cannibalism, as a theory of exchange.[5] Moving the notion of cannibalism away from the anthropological and anecdotal accounts of colonial travelers, anthropophagy offers an analysis of consumption and desire in the colonial encounter. De Andrade's project was the creation of a national culture through "the consumption and critical elaboration of both national and foreign influences. Imported cultural influences were to be devoured, digested, and reworked in terms of local conditions." In the words of Joaquim Pedro de Andrade, Brazilian director of the film *Macunaíma* (1969), an adaptation of the 1928 modernist novel by Mario de Andrade, "Cannibalism is an exemplary mode of consumerism. . . . Every consumer is reducible . . . to cannibalism. . . . Those who can, 'eat' others through their consumption of products, or even more directly in sexual relationships. . . . The new heroes . . . try to devour those who devour us."[6]

Oswald de Andrade's anthropophagy complicates economic theories of use value and exchange, adding an insurgent, corporeal dimension. His nuanced reading of capital as consumption addresses the violent and reductive realms of conquest and subjugation, confounding simplistic accounts of good colonized/bad colonizer. In anthropophagy's overlapping terrains of desire and repression, Sycorax—like Prospero—is an exiled magician, sharing in an anthropophagous exchange of diabolical magic to possess the other. Each invents the other as evil and the self as righteous. Yet Sycorax's alchemy is reduced to malevolent power. She is described as Cannibal, while Prospero's magic is Art harnessed to Enlightenment science.[7]

In his extensive genealogy of the term *cannibal*, Peter Hulme archives the social histories surrounding the narrativization of cannibalism as the devouring of human flesh, unpacking the ideological role of anthropophagy.[8] By reading scenes of the spiritual, libidinal, legal, and material consumption of indigenous bodies like Sycorax, Hulme exposes the political, social, and narratological process of state formation. Hulme's analysis disrupts the colonizer versus colonized dialectic, revealing a seething cauldron of ambivalent and contested identities and territories. Described through the language of anthropophagy (for instance, the Mandevillian motif "men / Whose heads stood in their breasts?")[9] popularized in numerous travelogues such as the Bermuda Pamphlets of 1610, Raleigh's account of Guiana, and those by John Smith, Christopher Columbus, Magellan, and Samuel Purchase, among others, the New World—Sycorax's Island-Nation—is imbued with what Frantz Fanon calls "maleficent power."

The legality of possession emerges as one arena of struggle in the colonial collision between men in Hulme's archive "Prospero and Caliban." Hulme does not, however, discuss whether or how an ideological cannibalism might actually enable a nonteleological reading. Here, Oswald de Andrade's theory is helpful in thinking through the notion of ideological cannibalism as postcolonial critical practice. De Andrade's anthropophagous irreverence allows Sycorax to tear apart the structuring frame of history between men and rewrite it on radically different terms.

Sycorax challenges her assumed animality, which is linked to her pregnant, maternal body. She exceeds the anthropological and historical anecdotes of cannibalism available by revealing their discursive limits. Sycorax's shriek both manifests the "maleficent power" of the bestialized native and exposes that power. As Fanon observes, in the violent exchange of territorial ownership in the colonial market, the settler bestializes natives; he describes them in zoological terms of foul gestation and breeding swarms.[10] Sycorax as native woman figures in this economy as the "blue-ey'd hag" whose pregnant body produces the free though maleficent labor of "A freckled whelp hag-born—not honour'd with / A human shape" whom Prospero will "keep in service."[11] She emerges cannibalized by the systems of capital through which her enslaved pregnant black body is consumed as free labor. She is the expendable commodity of an unmarked island in the outer peripheries of Europe's imagination.

Sycorax is both cannibal and cannibalized. She physicalizes (or materializes) a critique of the anthropophagic economy of capital through which the production and representation of the sovereign state—one European, the other of the New World (though geographically located in the "uninhabited" old world of North Africa, presumably Algeria in Shakespeare's text)—are forged. Through the deployment of cannibalistic logic, of devouring and being devoured, a colonial, preindustrial, and yet very contemporary theory of use/exchange value can be read in the play. Sycorax, indigenous native of the Island-Nation, is invested with all that the settler is not—Fanon's "maleficent power," radical subalterity.

In this economy, Prospero must project onto Sycorax all that he fears in himself and his modernity. He reads Sycorax as cannibal to enable his own cannibalizing logic of devouring indigenous rights in the Island-Nation. By scarring, torturing, incarcerating, demonizing, mythologizing, and projecting onto the native bodies of Sycorax and Caliban the barbarism of European modernity, Prospero inscribes European law onto his stolen territory. His system of governmentality is replete with the punitive regimes of torture, incarceration, and surveillance on colonial terms.

What gets lost in Prospero's mechanisms of governmentality are the complexities of citizenship of the ruled, the subjugated, and the colonized. The incarcerated body of Sycorax—the "malignant thing! . . . who with age and envy / Was grown into a hoop," the absent presence of woman embodying the nation as the voice of Sycorax, "of sorceries terrible / To enter human hearing"—is erased in the visual rhetoric of statehood.[12] It is this paradoxically familiar act of consumption that draws me to inquire into the way Shakespeare's Sycorax figures (or does not) in the projects of the proletarian revolutions of decolonization.

Writing Sycorax: Disarticulating Empire and the Spatializing of History

Shakespeare broke new ground in the art of harnessing history and literature to the imperatives of conquest and transnational modernization. As Edouard Glissant argues in *Caribbean Discourse*, the ideologies of state formation "concealed *under the surface*" of history writing propel the Bard's great tragedies. Shakespeare's interrogation of the metaphysical questions of legitimacy and succession to the English and Dutch thrones—foregrounded in his history plays, particularly the treatise on perfect kingship in *Henry V*—culminates in his avowal of the superiority of the West, even as the dukedom of Milan collapses through internal feuds in *The Tempest*. In other words, Europe's violent mapping of its elsewhere, projected as the horror and bestiality of the New World, is aided and abetted by a teleological notion of development and progress manifested in *The Tempest*. Caliban is nature from below, with degrees of elevation capped by Prospero as the Western ideal.[13] Glissant gestures toward Shakespeare's gendering of the nature of statehood. This gendering shapes the founding myths of the perfect king, as the antithetical treatises of *Richard III* and *Henry V* demonstrate.

But for Glissant Shakespeare's history plays map the *impossibility* of the ideal state (74–75). *Caribbean Discourse* splits open the "epistemological deficiency" that Glissant traces in his radical reconceptualizing of modernity's self-narrative. In a relentless critique of the economies of exchange that generated modernity's circulation and consumption of black bodies as slave labor, Glissant raises the question of how to write from this epistemological bind. By staging the dramatic geographies of alienation and dispossession behind the slave trade, he poses for us the spatializing violence of the transatlantic migrations from Africa to Europe to the Caribbean to Virginia. In such a monstrous journey, Shakespeare's own tempest gets devoured or, rather, drowned in what Glissant calls the transversality of the Caribbean. By this Glissant means "the implosion of Caribbean history" (66). Glissant's transversality becomes one way to imagine writing in this epistemological bind. The spatially mobile metaphor of transversality locates the transatlantic slave trade as a site of traumatic shock, imploding the notion of a linear and hierarchical History. In his "quarrel with history," Glissant dispels the ridiculous claim that a people "have no history." "History (with a capital H) ends where the histories of those peoples once reputed to be without history come together." The shaping transversality of postcolonialism relieves writing of the seamless illusion of a single History that would run its unique course. Instead, Glissant narrates the "subterranean convergence" of multiple, interlocking histories, unfurling this dispossessed historical space through montaged moments of traumatic shock (64, 66).

The relationship of shock in writing to a dispossessed historical space is most profoundly embodied in Sycorax. Her screams shatter the violent regimes of desire in reading and writing the colonized body, depicted in Kamau Brathwaite's *Barabajan Poems* (1994). Here, Brathwaite performs Glissant's implosion of history through a transversal writing journey. The name of Sycorax in the section "Sycorax // O'Grady" becomes Brathwaite's vehicle of dispossession and transversality as she occupies the crucible of transatlantic naming:

Limuru
Kinta Kunte
Sycorax // O'Grady
Missile // O
NationLanguage
and the fight for
NommO
Name/Nam/Manding
O[14]

Brathwaite raises the ghosts of Sycorax's naming by situating her within the transversality of crossing histories: East Africa, West Africa, the Caribbean, the transatlantic slave trade, emergent narratives defying linearity. In Brathwaite's exegesis on naming, he splits open the forms of ideological cannibalism contained in the naming of Sycorax, native woman whose indigenous name is erased: "Well you all know the Biblical & Shakespearean references to name . . . throughout history . . . you have people concerned with name" (236).

Rerouting this process of writing history at the transverse junctures of an accrued past of slave memory ("Kinta Kunte") and the present within modernity's optic, Brathwaite invokes naming as a means of imploding teleological notions of self. This liminal experience of naming that transforms the New World subject is located, for Brathwaite, in East Africa. Limuru, Kenya, becomes the scene of the poet's reinscription. Brathwaite evokes Sycorax as the medium of his renaming:

> And in the case of my own self—that xperience I had in Kenya—I wd like to share with you a little more about the meaning of my Kikuyu name *Kamau* / given to me at her home, outside in the grounds, on the ground, one afternoon in Limuru by Ngugi wa Thiong'o's grandmother . . . kneeling on the ground with the wind on my face & the great sky of Eden all around me in front of these old women who like ripped open my shirt & like spat upon my chest . . . & began chanting deep deep down inside their chests & deeper down into their very bellies searching for my *nam* so they cd find my name. (236)

The Sycoraxian image Brathwaite materializes through Ngugi wa Thiong'o's grandmother offers a sonorous, incantative reworking of the process of naming. Naming is the phenomenological site of *un*becoming for Brathwaite, through which his name "Kamau" can be arrived at, is unraveled. It situates the poet's own body at the transversal limits of experience and memory, present and past. The ceremony of naming alters the poet's body through Sycorax materialized as sound. For Brathwaite, Sycorax is "perhaps the most important person / element in the drama. The Invisible (she doesn't even APPEAR in Shakespeare), the SUBMERGED MOTHER . . . the Igbo Damballa women I witness (eye of the navel) in D'Ogou, the carpenter's shop in M&Q/ Barbados" (317).

In *Barabajan Poems*, Sycorax is simultaneously bearer of culture/indigenous woman and the metaphoric space of split form, disjunctured selves. The invocation of Sycorax as the space of ritual is synonymously juxtaposed with the spatialized writing of a history hidden from view, embarked on in the dialectical spaces of the *Barabajan* narrative. Sycorax is simultaneously the place of modernity's spiraling present and its repressed past. For Brathwaite, she is both embodied and heard in the chasms between words. Sycorax evokes the archetypal scene of modernity in the same space that her voice dismembers language to forge new dreams of modernity's re-inventions, like "Kamau," the name spun forth.

Writing from a different historical space, that of the poet-citizen envi-sioning a historicity that extends beyond the confines of an Island-Nation, whether Tobago or the Caribbean itself, Canadian Marlene Nourbese Philip wrenches open the kernel of writing itself, located transnationally between islands and continents. She scoops out the tender possibilities of language through the recuperable rites of naming in states of dispersal, in passage across water. Naming in Nourbese Philip's work bears the shock of a histori-cally dispossessed space, the space of Sycorax. Nourbese Philip's *she tries her tongue, her silence softly breaks* (1989) searches the remote peripheries of writing for a way of narrating the inarticulate disjunctures of such a postcolonial wandering. In this archive of dispossession, a whirling vortex of stolen lands, decimated bodies, and anguished mother tongues forged out of many lin-guistic worlds, Nourbese Philip keeps sight of Sycorax hovering in the back-ground. Like Brathwaite, Nourbese Philip archaeologizes naming:

this chattel language	*o as in what am I offered for this*
babu english	*'lot' of slaves*
slave idiom	*OW as in they faced the 'shroud' of*
nigger vernacular	*their future.*
coolie pidgin	*OI as in they paid for their slaves*
wog pronunciation	*with coin.*

(I say old chap how goes it, what ho?)

this lingua franca
arrrrrrrrgot of a blasted soul[15]

Excavating the detritus of history through the layered ruins of language, Nourbese Philip stages a dialogic dance of sonic and ocular reverberations. The anthropophagic logic of modernity that consumed slave bodies also devoured the master's language, spewing forth chattel language, babu english, slave idiom, and coolie pidgin. This cannibalistic space of modernity is the burdened backdrop against which Nourbese Philip's historical excavation unfolds. It is the echo of intertwined history, cutting across colonizer and colonized, then and now. It is the space of writing the present.

Read in the light of ideological cannibalism laid out earlier, Nourbese Philip's decentering of Englishness along with masculinity performs Glissant's transversality. The allegorical wounding continues through Nourbese Philip's rewriting of dispossession, as it is spatialized in transversal relationships within the churning of history:

> oath   moan   mutter   chant
>   time grieves the dimension of other
> babble   curse   chortle   sing
>   turns on its axis of silence
> praise-song   poem   ululation   utterance
>   one song would bridge the finite in silence
> syllable   vocable   vowel   consonant
>   one word erect the infinite in memory (64)

For Nourbese Philip, writing sound is the preferred space for Sycorax's alchemy. Writing itself becomes a sonic reinscription that permeates the allegorical wounding of history, a balm that transfigures even as it returns as an echo of the violent past. As Nourbese Philip enunciates so deliberately, this writing is aural—it reverberates, richocheting off the encrusted walls of the past while impinging on the audibility of the present with a ferocious vocality. Nourbese Philip creates waves of this vocality through the power of enunciation; the axis of silence is rich with the tremors of alternate histories and subaltern movements. The crevices of sound need to be revisited with care, she suggests. Our ocularcentrism has blinded us to other forms of inscribing history, the sonic among them. Nourbese Philip's writing transcribes some of these unheard moments of modernity's intransigence.

Remembering Sycorax: Decolonization and the Erasure of Women

CALIBAN: Uhuru
PROSPERO: What did you say?

CALIBAN: I said, Uhuru!

PROSPERO: Back to your native language again. I've already told you, I don't like it. You could be polite, at least; a simple "hello" wouldn't kill you.[16]

Aimé Césaire's Caliban shouts *uhuru* thrice in *A Tempest* (1969). As a Francophone play about decolonization, it is striking that Caliban's articulation of struggle is the Kiswahili word for freedom. *Uhuru* was the slogan of revolutionary Pan-Africanism, audible throughout East Africa in the turbulent 1950s, with the Mau Mau and the Maji Maji rebellions, and the decolonizing 1960s. A founding concept for two of Julius Nyerere's watershed formulations, *Uhuru Na Umoja* and *Uhuru Na Ujamaa*, the word *uhuru* links the process of indigenization that Cesaire raises in his critique of the master's language, *Discourse on Colonialism*, to the struggle for African independence.[17]

Written after *Discourse*, *A Tempest* explores the masculinist lines along which the independent, anticolonial state is fashioned. The play is structured as an embattled dialectic between Caliban and Prospero; between Ariel, a mulatto slave, and Caliban, a Black slave; between Ariel and Prospero. In Césaire's eloquent travels through the psychic economies of colonialism, woman is absent except as shadow framing the peripheral state. The struggle against colonialism is a struggle of white man against enslaved Black and mulatto men, while the native land emerges as the sensualized embodiment of woman, alive but dreamlike.[18]

Césaire's treatise on decolonization uses as its founding logic Prospero's primordial act of theft. Sycorax's incarceration precedes Caliban's coming to political consciousness and a sense of self through which his claims to indigenous right can emerge. Sycorax figures here only as a prior moment, a precursor to the drama of modernity. She is the native sorceress whose magic cursing terrorizes and haunts the colonizer. Caliban has forgotten how to perform this anticolonial sorcery and must retrieve it by repeating the lessons of his mother (Sycorax) through the colonial encounter between master and slave. This is the curse of the cannibalistic Law of Exchange. Caliban must learn to produce his own alchemy, the language of self, indigenous rights, and property, "To get back my island and regain my freedom" (69).

Césaire avoids grappling with Sycorax in his mise-en-scène of modern nation formation, even though he alludes to her continuing existence through Caliban's conviction: "I know that Sycorax is alive" (15). In *A Tempest*, Sycorax is both a primordial presence and an afterthought that frames the struggle for liberation among men. As the precursor to revolution in Césaire's play, Sycorax marks the limits of representation. She is both hidden from history and invisible though ever present. As a counterpoint to the unfolding of the revolutionary state, invoked by the call for *uhuru*, or freedom, Sycorax's absence can be read as a loud but unheard rejoinder to the masculinist agendas of national liberation and its notion of freedom. Her curses haunt the independent state in its reworkings of national interests.

But learning how to curse, as Retamar points out in his essay on Caliban, is not enough in devising strategies for change. Both Ariel and Prospero are ultimately slaves of the same system and have to realize that social transformation lies beyond hurling curses—in the place of honor among Caliban's rebellious and glorious ranks.[19] The primordial curse—the yet-to-be-contended-with struggle for visibility by women within the modern state—is dismissed as an ancient relic. In their narratives of socialist emancipatory alliances forged between Caliban and Ariel, Césaire and Retamar refuse to hear the meaning in the deafening screams of Sycorax.

Performing Sycorax: Disrupting Masculinity
in the Cannibalistic Postcolonial State

In "Caliban's Daughter: *The Tempest* and the Teapot," Michelle Cliff raises the powerful specter of Sycorax "the aboriginal mother," "the precolonial female." Sycorax, the savage mother of Caliban, witch, "wildwoman," the imagined mother of Bertha Rochester/Antoinette Cosway. Sycorax, the woman "whose fury implodes, the woman who is defined from the outside, who according to that foreign definition cannot be whole, whose dark blood is the source of her betrayal and a constant danger." For Cliff, it is only with "the magic of this precolonial woman that Caliban counters the spells of the colonizer" in Césaire's *Tempest*:[20]

CALIBAN: . . . I know that Sycorax is alive. Sycorax.
Mother.
Serpent, rain, lightning.
And I see thee everywhere! . . .
Often, in my dreams, she speaks to me and warns me.[21]

Cliff's essay makes it possible to consider a feminist theory of the state.[22] She underscores the magic of Sycorax, one that exceeds death and incarceration, as Caliban confirms in Cesaire's *Tempest*. Sycorax's alchemy is too terrible to be remembered except as a shadow of the archetypal scenes of national and colonial encounters. Her alchemy is always narrativized as a struggle between men, between nations: Prospero and Caliban, Caliban and Ariel, Europe and Africa, Algeria and France, Britain and India. Sycorax corporealizes the always allegorized masculinity that takes for granted the presence of women as backdrop in the performance of statehood.

Nuanced by Cliff's critique, this reading of Sycorax raises interesting questions about the translatability of state power. As woman, Sycorax is invisible as the arbiter of statehood for Prospero. Yet it is his fearful perception of her presence that motivates his acts of incarceration and state control. Sycorax's intranslatability marks the dilemma of bodies without official history through which the state is produced. She is the material enactment of the terrified state. From the founding moment of the fledgling nation, the rhetoric of modern statehood assumes certain unequivocal rights, such as universal franchise, which again obfuscate the specific ways through which the gendered state materializes: always as the body of woman (as in Eugène Delacroix's image of Liberté leading the Nation), but with the Hobbesian head of the king, the feminized body politic but irrevocably masculine head of state.[23]

Within the imperialist logic of colonialism and patriarchy, natives are cannibals to be civilized. The extremity of this barbarism is the body of the indigenous woman, on the one hand virgin landscape, on the other the absolute site of abjectness through which notions of nationness emerge, both invisible, "banish'd," and hypervisible "blue-ey'd hag." The bloated and emaciated body of Sycorax—first to be sacrificed on the altar of nationness, last in line for sovereign selfhood—encapsulates the dilemma of indigenous struggles in modern nation-states.

9

Transnational Migrations

Aesthetic Hybridities—Performed Syncretisms

In response to neocolonial relations of knowledge, emerging postcolonial states in the imperial histories of the twentieth century generated new conceptions of the citizen, language, and ways of being in the world. Issues of *métissage* and *creolité* in the Francophone Caribbean; concepts of anthropophagy and the carnivalesque in Brazilian discourses about modernization during the 1920s and '30s; phenomenologies of negritude and negrissimo and the impact of writings by Aimé Césaire, Frantz Fanon, Leon Damas, Birago Diop, and Léopold Sédar Senghor; and notions of indigenous national consciousness promoted by Kwame Nkrumah, Jomo Kenyatta, and Sékou Touré, among others, contaminated other nascent ideologies of nationness with long-term repercussions in the struggles for heterogeneous citizenship within the fictionalized, sovereign, monolithic postcolonial state.

Since the 1930s, various conceptual frameworks for galvanizing ideas of plurality and multicultural citizenship against monocultural national identities within the state have been pursued, by positing notions of a "third" space politically, geographically, and historically. The idea of a third space in aesthetics, political affiliations and the international political economy haunts the seamless narrative of oppressed and oppresser, colonized and colonizer, First and Third World, dominant and subaltern.[1]

From the debates on third cinema and Third World aesthetics that inspired the third cinema conference in Edinburgh in 1986, to the idea of third theater explored by Eugenio Barba, Augusto Boal's theater of the oppressed, Indian street theater forms such as *Jatra*, Paolo Freire's pedagogy of the oppressed, Rustom Bharucha's experiments in third space for postcolonial theater, Vijay Tendulkar's protest theater, Jerzy Grotowski's notion of a poor theater, Guillermo Gómez Peña's border *brujo*, the Border Arts Workshop's border activism, Ngugi wa Thiong'o's notion of "orature," and Penina Mhando's conception of theater for development, cultural practitioners have struggled to destabilize economic reductionism in the interests of new cultural hybridities.[2]

In many postcolonial states, alternative art movements have privileged a retro-nationalist move toward indigenization in the search for native roots in disrupted precolonial cultural forms. Merging vernacular languages, folk arts, European avant-garde forms, and secular concerns, these postcolonial playwrights, directors, visual artists, and performers offer a variety of interpretations of contemporary aesthetics across national borders. For instance, Badal Sircar's incorporation of *Jatra* in Calcutta and Girish Karnad's blending of Sanskrit folk mythologies into English Indian theater in Bangalore share various hybridizing influences with Jatinder Varma's experimental work with the Tara Arts Group in London. All three directors employ Indian mythology, use English as well as Indian languages as vehicles of performance, and explore Indian dramatic forms as vehicles for presenting contemporary life in London, Calcutta, or Bangalore.[3]

Other concepts of hybridity such as Oswald de Andrade's anthropophagy, Homi Bhabha's mimicry, Kobena Mercer's creolizing practices, Stuart Hall's new ethnicities, Paul Gilroy's syncretism, Manthia Diawara's Afro-kitsch, Edouard Glissant's transversality, Marlene Nourbese Philip's babu english, Roberto Retamar's Caliban, Antonio Benitez-Rojo's supersyncretism, Assia Djebar's nomad memory, Arjun Appadurai's global ethnoscapes, Lisa Lowe's heterogeneity, José Martí, Nicolás Guillén, and Françoise Lionnet's uses of métissage, Néstor García Canclini's cultural reconversion, Celeste Olalquiaga's Tupinicopolitan aesthetic, Robert Stam's carnivalesque, and Michelle Cliff's ruination, to name a few, have specifically addressed issues of contemporary hybridities in relation to state sovereignty and transnational movements of peoples.[4]

Many of these conceptual hybridities move beyond the idea of the nation to reveal the interdependent ways in which transnational circulations of commodities operate. As a result of the increasingly mediated globalizing economy, these ideas of hybridity destabilize authoritarian forms of control, while interrogating the parameters and limits of the democratic state. Instead of working within the narrow boundaries of the state, these theories of hybridity pose a challenge to the limits of the sovereign state. By proposing alternative economies of aesthetic and political viability through ideas of a third space, these theorists of hybridity offer ways out of narrowly defined ideas of artistic possibility. Rather, they pose broader syncretic identities such as international feminist (Assia Djebar, Michelle Cliff, Marlene Nourbese Philip), Third World, Asian American (Lisa Lowe), postcolonial, and socialist as a means of creating alternative international communities through which to create social, aesthetic, and political communities.

Hybridity, Diaspora, and U.S.–South Asian Culture

While this idea of hybridity offers temporary or utopian avenues for personal and communal self-invention, the practices of cultural hybridity pose troubling questions for citizenship in national contexts. In Britain as well as the United States, cultural hybridity—invoked by words like *mestizaje, dingo, mongrelism, creolization, syncretism*—has forced open the fault lines of migrant identity within the state.[5]

Since the mid-1980s, with Hanif Kureishi's *My Beautiful Laundrette* and *Sammy and Rosie Get Laid*, the consumption of British Asian cultural commodities has exploded in the United States, opening up for public scrutiny the expressive cultures of this previously obscure diaspora. While Kureishi's contributions to theater revealed the spectrum of anxieties about hybridity in British Asian culture, his films and recent television success with *The Buddha of Suburbia* (1990) have found an eager market of U.S. consumers as well.

Kureishi heralded an increasingly visible crop of young cultural workers who have cleared a space for diasporic Asian culture in North America. At the junction of a cumulative history that includes Bandung, nonalignment, postcolonialism, American civil rights discourse, and the dispersed histories of nationalisms and diasporas, this conglomeration of communities embodies a postmodern compression of history. Their resulting hybridizations challenge easy conceptions of national longing within specific new immigrant cultures as these artists accrue a visual historicity and slowly gain public legitimacy as citizens of North America. Because of their histories of dispersal and arrival, and their experience of in-betweenness, the consumption, circulation, and production of their work invariably involve moving between national contexts. This critical mass of North American–South Asian cultural work unashamedly probes the broader implications of the possibilities and limits of cultural citizenship, incorporating East Africa, the Caribbean, Britain, India, Canada, and the United States as part of its imaginative geography.

Viewed through a transnational lens, the condition of hybridity compels a critical reevaluation of the binarisms around race and the West/non-West. While the rhetoric of binarisms shapes the international economy of labor, as evident in the increasingly divergent North-South discourse, the lived reality of contemporary hybridity concretizes and inflects ideas of oppression and domination. Oppressed peoples are not in positions of subordination every waking moment. Rather, they exist in relation to different economies of pleasure and consumption. Subaltern agency creates informal avenues of disavowal and affiliation, which in turn create pleasure within hybrid conditions. The performance of hybridity allows for malleable forms of negotiation with structures of domination through a style politics and elusive economies of consumption. Performed hybridity rejects the developmental model of modernity in which everyone is always "catching up" with the West. Instead of reproducing "peoples without history" or peoples always out of sync, performed hybridity levels the playing field, with simultaneous or contingent modernities, where Brazil, India, and Trinidad are as much a part of the dialogue as Europe or the United States. Performed hybridity questions authenticity even as it claims credibility for New World subjects.

Diasporic South Asian cultural practices in North America raise questions about how the production of new political identities destabilizes ethnocentric ideas about gender, sexuality, and nation through the formation of counterpublics. As a multiply located community of peoples from Fiji, Singapore, Guyana, Trinidad, East Africa, and Britain in North America, they present a gargantuan map of communities in dispersal. Their cultural commodities foreground the anxieties of displacement, of being labeled in excess of one's lived identity as a raced new immigrant or second-generation Asian American, an experience that haunts many such multiply migrated communities. The cultures catalyzed by these different influxes express the need to be cosmopolitan, as they reinvent personhood through the detritus of mobility. At the core of these cultural commodities generated within the South Asian diasporic communities of North America is a preoccupation with the notion that agency needs to be mobilized before any gesture of belonging can be performed. This self-consciousness stems from the awareness of second-generation North American constituencies that such agency is often left nascent and unarticulated, or expressed through a public disavowal, as in the case of their parents' political reticence in former countries of domicile such as Uganda, Kenya, Tanzania.

Commodities such as bhangra music, for instance, have popularized the African, Caribbean, Latin American, Punjabi, and British connections of the South Asian diaspora with North America, concretizing some of these historical and political links to these regional histories. Bhangra introduced a range of British Asian musical innovations to North America, experimenting with disco, hip-hop, house, funk, and Punjabi folk music during the 1980s. The fluidity of bhangra music's capacity to flow and circulate through communities gradually generated emerging counterpublics of youth drawn together under the aegis of bhangra as a diasporic phenomenon of pleasurability. In New York during the 1990s, clubs like Soca Paradise, Sounds of Brazil, Club Demarara, Den of Thieves, and other locales catalyzed this growing subcultural identification with a distinctly diasporic form. Local New York DJs like D. J. Rekha, D. J. Gita, and D. J. Mike emerged as regulars, while the explosion of musical genres from bhangra to chutney, jungle, and other forms has made the New York bhangra music culture popular among consumers, since few bhangra musicians are U.S. based.[6]

A growing renaissance of writers, performers, visual artists, and media practitioners such as Allan deSouza, Sanjay Lovexi, Ian Rashid, Shani Mootoo, Bina Sharif, Amitav Ghosh, Chandra Mohanty, Deepa Mehta, Meera Nanji, Mira Nair, Shishir Kurup, Pratibha Parmar, Meena Alexander, M. G. Vassanji, Shaheen Merali, and Gurindher Chadda, to name a few, have engaged with the performance of these hybrid identities in relation to Caribbean and African experiences, while critiquing narratives of nation embedded within those identities. The Canadian M. G. Vassanji's *Uhuru Street* (1991) explores how hybrid identities are shaped in excess of national boundaries, while the Asian American novelist and poet Meena Alexander's *Manhattan Music* (1997) unravels the intricacies of nomadic citizenship in states of physical and psychic dislocation.[7] Canadian Shani Mootoo's videos, short stories, and visual work probe lesbian and feminist experiences of migrancy and cultural contamination, while Ian Rashid's poetic interrogation of sexuality and political community in Britain, Canada, and India similarly foregrounds the intersections of hybridity, sexuality, and nomadic citizenship. Both Mootoo and Rashid highlight the dissonances of syncretic cultures as they travel across nation-state formations.

For many of these performers, writers, filmmakers, and visual artists, political visibility is a performative act. As these cultural practitioners demonstrate, political visibility makes it possible to stake claims for cultural legitimacy because it operates from a sense of belonging within the state. Visibility politics deploy strategic identities in the interest of cultural citizenship. The forging of communities, alliances, and discrete identities such as queer Asian American is one such tenuous arrangement through which the pedagogical performance of cultural citizenship is realized. But the narrative of coming out, an enactment of political visibility, is neither transparent nor the only avenue through which complex identities express themselves as citizens. On the contrary, such a performance of visibility hinges on very North American notions of self and its relation to the social.

For diasporic South Asian cultural producers in North America, the dilemma of cultural legitimacy is staged in relation to dominant and minority notions of self in the United States and Canada. For those with histories of travel and residence in numerous countries before their arrival in the United States, the process of cultural citizenship is elusive and troubling, though necessary. It produces a host of concerns around the politics of representation that are essentially different from concerns of legal citizenship.[8]

Political visibility is neither immediately available nor easily maintained for new social identities. For many diasporic South Asians like Allan deSouza, now a resident of the United States, political visibility involves struggling between the legal and the unofficial, between multiple categories of identity such as Asian American, Goan, East African, queer, Black British, and the arenas of ambiguity and disaffiliation generated around sexuality, nationality, and belonging.[9] This is further complicated if one is part of a relatively obscure diaspora, such as as the East African–Asian diaspora. DeSouza's work foregrounds the nomadic affiliations embedded in diasporic communities that have migrated three or four times across different national boundaries—in desouza's case, Kenya, Britain, Portugal, and the United States. Cultural citizenship for a Black British/Asian American visual artist from East Africa might mean identifying simultaneously with the affiliations Asian American, Black, South Asian, East African Asian, Afro-Asian, queer, thereby complicating any easy allegiance to a single political identity.

As many of the above-mentioned practitioners demonstrate, the dilemma of forging political visibility has allowed for new possibilities. This informal network of cultural workers has probed the open arenas of coalitions and strategies that have animated and continue to inform new conceptions of politically engaged work through expressions of hybridity. In the theater, these alliances have generated new voices transatlantically. The cross-medium work of actors, playwrights, and screenwriters like Sarita Chaudhuri, Zia Mohyeddin, Rita Wolf, Farrukh Dhondy, Hanif Kureishi, Meera Syal, Biha Sharif, Alaknanda Samarth, Pratibha Parmar, Roshan Seth, Jatinder Varma, Saeed Jaffrey, and Amol Palekhar during the 1990s generated new avenues for experimentation in the United Kingdom as well as within the United States. The availability of Channel Four programs like Kureishi's *Buddha of Suburbia*, the word-of-mouth popularity of these actors, films, plays, music, and other commodities, and the rapid circulation of these products across national borders have opened up a transnationally connected arena of cultural practice. There now exists a broader sense of the communal and the collaborative extending beyond the borders of the United States, Canada, or Britain. Diasporic South Asian work is slowly forging transnational networks of consumption incorporating the United States, Canada, and Britain as a dispersed but linked cultural market.

Transatlantic Performance Culture in the 1990s

In what ways does the experience of multiple migrations shape the narration of stories? This question frames the work of Shishir Kurup, a Los Angeles–based performer whose meditations on cultural citizenship form a continuous dialogue about the disaffections and imaginings of new immigrants in the United States. An innovative participant in the flourishing Asian American performance art scene in Los Angeles during the 1980s and '90s, Kurup draws on images and languages reminiscent of East Africa, India, Britain, and the United States. Using Malayalam, English, Hindi, Swahili, Gujarati, and "American," Kurup's work raises the broader question of how imaginary homelands reinvent the idea of home and what it might mean to reside there.

Both *Assimilations* (1991) and *Exile* (1992) perform the displacements of diasporic belonging. To be a citizen of the United States and a nomadic storyteller embodying many genealogies of arrival; to speak of here, echoing memories and fragments of many migrations; to be produced as an African-Asian-American emerging out of a complex history of being from Africa, which exceeds the available narratives within Asian American history—these are some of Kurup's thematic preoccupations.

In *Assimilations*, a one-man show produced by Kurup and directed by Page Leong at the performing space Highways in Los Angeles in 1991, the Public Theater in New York in 1992, and London's Institute of Contemporary Arts in 1995, Kurup unravels little vignettes of cultural collision titled "Mythic Fears," "My Father's Name Is . . ," "Africa," "Mombasa," "Mzee," and "Siam," among others. Structuring his scenes as fault lines in the tectonic planes of citizenship, Kurup sketches vibrant pictures of the Everyperson nomad, caught in postmodernity, where time future and time past collide in time present, in the City of Angels, trying to capture former life histories and memories. Through an intricate series of gestural movements, he performs the condition of being a participant in transit cultures sloughed off in multiple disruptions before arrival in the United States.

Dispelling any myth of originary culture, Kurup explores the tensions between transplanted and reinvented traditions by narrating a series of incidents from the life of a wandering immigrant. Kurup's autobiographical narrator, Shishir, acquires a mythic, archetypal dimension as he unfolds the complexities of his coming into political consciousness as a "raced" American. Caught between being produced as a new political subject (both Black and Asian, depending on the context) and being a child of the postcolonial world, Shishir pulls the audience into his volatile consciousness, made political before he even recognizes the shape of these politics, growing up in small-town America.

Assimilations commands attention from its opening scene. A poignant, sacred prayer, sung in an unfamiliar South Indian language (Malayalam), fills the empty space as the performer rushes onstage holding a can of powder:

> (*Out of the dark we hear a sweet Malayalam song*)
> *Pambegal Ku Malam Induh*
> *Paravuhgul Kagashum Induh*
> *Manusha Puthren Um Talah Chaikan*
> *Manil Idum Illa, Manil Idum Illa (Repeat)*
>
> *Mame* I'm going out to play
> Put some powder on *mone*
> But I'm just going out to play
> Be a good boy now and put some powder on
> But I hate powder
> Be my golden son now.[10]

This opening sequence is striking in its historic implications. Here, the narrative of race is literally etched in skin tones, reminding one of Frantz

Fanon, Aimé Césaire, Nina Simone, W. E. B. Du Bois, Langston Hughes: light skin, dark skin, how one powders oneself to "whiteness," literally and metaphorically, politically and psychologically. Kurup's emergence out of the dramatic shadows of the stage reveals the epidermal logic behind floating affiliations with the Indian Subcontinent and Africa—now *kathakali*-like, now minstrelsy-like, with the bitter twist of history to humor it. The secret of assumed historical origins gets translated in everyday life into repressed conversations about race and blackness for a polylingual U.S.–South Asian diaspora.

Kurup's multilingual script embodies the debris of migrancy in its irreverent mishmash:

> Jambo, Habari, Muzuri. Shiro, puri, jalebi, tala dood pakkh. Huyu iko watu wa America. Si, senor mimi ido watu wa America. Me shire toh nehi. . . .
> *(Music ends. Lights crossfade)*

Mobility inflects language as words are altered, made hybrid. Heteroglossia shapes the viewpoints of Kurup's myriad scenarios. Kiswahili, Punjabi, Arabic, Gujurati, Hindi, Spanish, and English create the creole culture of this diasporic experience, the East African–Asian American. Here, the limits of U.S. discourses of citizenship and belonging are thrown into question—where the specificities of ethnicities and their histories collide with contemporary forms of citizenship. In *Assimilations*, this is posed as the dilemma of belonging to the nation. Through Kurup's performance, the language of U.S. race rhetoric refracted through particularly U.S. Black-white binarisms of race gets dispersed into a non-U.S. idea of "Blackness," an ideological and political construct that produces different ethnicities and peoples as "Black" in different contexts, at different historic moments, in the United States. To be reduced to a category of race that can neither fit nor accommodate the lived relations of actual hybrid ethnicities, this seems to be part of the condition of the narrator of *Assimilations*.

Kurup's one-man show brilliantly stages the complexities of coming into "the fact of Blackness," as Frantz Fanon put it.[11] Being called "Little Richard" and "my favourite little nigger" at school, as Kurup remarks in one vignette, demonstrates how categories of ethnicity are always less than and more than the constituted political subject: in this case, an African-Asian-American. As Kurup's highly stylized, narratively fractured renderings of urban American racism unfold, new borders, new psychic maps get drawn: Mombasa, Nairobi, Kerala, Milwaukee, Los Angeles, Burger King, class politics, immigration all become the markers, the navigation points for his political journey of cultural citizenship.

Assimilations tangibly performs the elisions within Asian American discourse about who can legitimately occupy the category Asian American (as more conventional histories of Asians in the United States elide the changing demographics of Asia/America) and the more informal ways in which other histories, other memories of the changing kaleidoscope of peoples of Asian descent in the United States continuously erode, forge, and bring into new horizons the conversation about identity, immigration, belonging, and citizenship. As Lisa Lowe suggests, the 1990s can afford cultural specificities within Asian American dialogue now that, for strategic political purposes, the alliances of various Asian American ethnicities have come to be recognized as a valid constituency.[12] But *Assimilations* demands a more complicated rendering of how the different histories of Black peoples around the world link, intersect, are artificially separated by sociologically erroneous categories of race, and shape the cosmopolitan cultures of New York, Los Angeles, Kingston, London, Dar es Salaam, Port-au-Prince, Nairobi, and Rio de Janeiro. It raises questions about how diasporas are formed at the invisible crossroads of migration, indentured servitude, slavery, sugar plantations, cotton plantations, internments and incarcerations, and colonial and postcolonial histories in the United States.

Assimilations dispels the notion of unilinear narratives of race by questioning identity categories before arrival in the United States. Kurup questions how the politics of Blackness and the rhetoric of Asian American identity may be negotiated for peoples of South Asian descent who hail from Africa, Britain, the Caribbean, or Latin America and have a different relationship to the history of Blackness from that of African Americans. He performs the blurring boundaries of everyday race relations in the United States, where it is not a question of either/or but, rather, one of sometimes this and sometimes that and sometimes in between this and that.

In the section on the practices of naming for multiply migrated peoples titled "My Father's Name Is . . ," Kurup shows how names are distorted, mutated, and take on new shapes and sounds as peoples arrive to new shores and take on new identities, such as Miami, New York, Los Angeles. Kurup performs the transformation of his parents' names from India to Africa to the United States, from Karipottu Thaivalipill Ravindran Kurup to Ravindran Karipottu to Ray Karapot. His mother's name mutates from Leela Bhavani Nair to Bhavani Ravindran to Bonnie Ravindran. This brilliant critique of how culture is both lost and syncretically renewed is staged with great wit and pathos. We laugh at our own mutations, our own transformed "americanizing" cultures, in their cacophonous mutations in the barrios, in the streets, in the dhabas, in the Little Tokyos and Little Hong Kongs, something sloughed off, something formed anew, from block to block, despite the myths of homogenization, the promise of monopolized spaces of pleasure. Kurup performs the tensions of name changing for racinated Americans. What does it mean to change one's name for "America," meaning dominant America, to be not white, not quite, as one's name is racinated?

> Shishir Ravindran Kurup became Shishir Kurup or *(pulling out yearbook)* Shish, C.C., SeSe, Shishir, Shishink, Shirsha, Hosh Hosh, Sheer Energy, Shiser Krup, C.C. Corruption, Little Richard, Tutti Frutti, My favourite little nigger, and last but not least . . . Shitsmear Karap. *(Black out)*

Kurup makes the point that while immigrants—whether Indian, Pakistani, Bangladeshi, or Sri Lankan—in diasporic affiliations may change their names by whitening them, dominant culture resists this whitening by racializing them within the available discourse of race in the United States.

Assimilations is a stringent postcolonial critique of American hegemony in the international waters of global migration as Kurup performs his particular "mythic fears" of "coming to America":

> Mythic fear number one: Americans loved to go streaking.
> Mythic fear number two: Americans spoke in an English so slanged, we would have a very difficult time understanding them. They loved double negatives . . . "I didn't do nothin."
> Mythic fear number three: Like the British they didn't wash their ass, just wiped it with toilet paper. This frightened us. This frightened my mother, this frightened my father and this terrified me.

This scatological critique of the West's reproduction of itself in the non-West and the return of its repressions through the arrival of immigrants takes on the language of waste and excess, desire and terror. As Kurup stages the debris of American hegemony in its global backdrops of invisible spaces such as Africa, India, Latin America through the proliferation of icons such as Bruce Lee, Clint Eastwood, Carlos Santana, Elvis Presley, Charles Bronson, loaded with ideological venom, he brings back into our perceptual imaginary the "mythic fears" of being "in America," of having arrived but being nowhere in particular, politically or otherwise. To have traveled from immigrant to citizen, he inverts the mythic fear of arrival to one of perpetual nostalgia, a retrospective meditation on loss, invention, and the creating of new stories from the peripheries of contemporary urban American life, such as Malayalee Los Angelenos forging alliances with other nomadic, more than thrice migrated and not so legal Los Angelenos. From Vietnam, the West Bank, Iran, China, Africa, Tijuana, Haiti, Thailand, the map extends into the disappearing horizons of Kurup's pan-national conceptions of demystifying the secret fears of "coming to America."

10

Postnational Reverberations

Migration has become a way of life for many in the latter part of the twentieth century. The large-scale displacement of peoples from the rural to the urban or across nations has heightened the precariousness of arbitrary boundaries while fueling contemporary identifications with ossified national identities. The 1970s in particular witnessed a global reconfiguration of national citizenship. As new nations contended with older ones, new geopolitical arrangements—neocolonialism, globalization, structural adjustment—shifted relations of power in less unilateral directions, creating multiple nodes of transnational interrelatedness. In the process, peoples around the world have aspired to conceptions of world citizenship while also asserting their particular social identities. With increased democratization of citizen rights across many states since the end of the Cold War, and the tendency toward permitting more individualistic expressions of self in formerly collectivist or socialist societies, the notion of citizenship practically begs consideration.[1]

For a critical examination of contemporary citizenship, the decade of the 1970s resounds with particular historic significance. It was the moment of rupture in former relations of power and knowledge for postcolonial states as well as for Western states radically renegotiating conceptions of democratic citizenship. Minority rights movements in Canada, the United

States, and Britain were inspired by the revolutionary struggles for political and economic rights in Tanzania, India, and other Third World countries. The relation between national and social development–experimented with in Cuba, Nicaragua, Tanzania, Mozambique, Ghana—was thrust onto the world stage. Some postcolonial ideologies of the '70s attempted to develop alternative, sustainable modernities outside the networks of consumption driving the emergent global economy.

The impact of the 1970s as a moment of political experimentation that offered tenuous articulations of these alternative modernities is a little-theorized aspect of our cultural history. As a period, it generated new kinds of pan-identities that were broader than the borders of the nation and linked more intimately with notions of alternative circuits of political networks, whether socialist, nonaligned, anti-imperial, Third Worldist, or regionally transnational. The 1970s laid the groundwork for the current mechanisms of globalization through which many Third World states continue to operate.

As these chapters demonstrate, the past thirty years mark a visible shift away from empire to an interdependent, geopolitically demarcated system of local, national, and transnational citizenships. These cultural flows attest to the fact that they are not determined entirely by the relations of center and periphery, where "the West" is always the point of arrival but, rather, by different micronetworks of circulation through which legal, political, and cultural citizenships are negotiated. The relationship between First World economies and formerly Second World socialist and communist publics is complicated by considering kung fu cinema, soul music, and Black British dramatic works. The point is not to privilege these cultural activities as categorical examples that represent a singular national experience. On the contrary, they are tenuous forms—transient, publicly consumed, of the moment, and dispersed. For that reason, they interrupt the coherence of the state and the privileging of national boundaries in the reading of a particular historical moment. They work as symptomatic instances of how the relation of state to minor citizen transpires through transnational networks.[2]

Modern migrations, urban and translocal, have played out the full extent of the borderlands between the legal, cultural, and political, while revealing a largely inarticulable informal dimension to citizenship as a lived practice. These movements of people across geopolitical borders have blurred the discrete categories of the "civil element," "political element," and "social element" laid out by Thurgood Marshall as a schema for twentieth-century citizenship. In Marshall's genealogy, social rights emerge as a result of the tumultuous democratization processes of this century.[3] While Marshall's structural separation of the political, social, and civil aspects of contemporary citizenship is far from the blurry lived reality of citizen-subjects as entities acted on and embodied within the state, the contingent ways in which each of these categories continue to operate as discursive frameworks cannot be dismissed.

The impact of modern migrations on the idea of citizenship as a juridical category has been a reworking of concepts such as legal, political, and cultural citizenship to find their points of intersection. Dislocated communities, refugees of dissolved nations, immigrants many times displaced, locals relocated to others parts of the state—all underscore the act of modern citizenship as an activity rather than just an imagined community. This is not to claim that the state no longer matters or that transnational structures of being have appropriated the role of the state. As Toby Miller suggests, there is little agreement over what nations are, what national identity is, or how to rationalize national movements.[4] Consequently, transnational forms of citizenship are sometimes available to us in ways that the state is not. As I hope has become clear through the cultural readings presented here, the state is no longer the sole arbiter of citizenship. The recent histories of citizenship in many postcolonial states reiterate the tension between the myths of nation building and the need for a strong state, on the one hand, and the heterogeneity of the state's citizenry on the other. In practice, the interstitial ways in which enactments of citizenship exceed the legal boundaries of the state and often involve multiple states in a single act, formally or informally, complicate earlier understandings of the correlation between subject and citizen.

For many people who have never left the state but are travelers within the national imaginary, as well as most urban migrants, the enactment of citizenship has assumed an import it never had before. These urban nomads experience citizenship either as a voluntary or mandatory act. As subjects of the state often invisible because they are frequently unpropertied, these categories of urban citizen demand a careful interrogation of the sorts of subjects that stand in for the state when citizens are named. Urban migrants are often the first affected by the strategic production of good citizens, since migrants are often produced as weak or inauthentic subjects, wanting in their public displays of citizenship. By exploring the mechanisms whereby people are admitted into the nation as citizens, in contingent and marginal ways, the layered relationships between the citizen and state are brought to the fore.

Citizenship resituates questions of national belonging as political cultures mediate traditions. Tanzania, where ideas of socialist citizenship came up against Africanization policies even as the postcolonial state forged alternative ideological points of contact with China, the Soviet Union, Cuba, Eastern Europe, and Pan-Africanists, is an example. Influenced by the Leninist and Maoist models of centralist forms of governance, the redistribution of property and ownership in Tanzania created a complex transition from decolonizing state to socialist modernity through attempts to delink strategically within the global economy. The question of political citizenship in Tanzania before 1985 meant a careful negotiation between socialist and nationalist sympathies often in tension with each other. In such a milieu, political—that is, socialist—citizenship might differ from the legal and cultural aspects of Tanzanian citizenship, as these forums of citizenship contradict, cohere, and superimpose established ideas of how to perform the self within the state. For Tanzanian Asians, the concerns of minority belonging during the 1970s focused primarily on legal citizenship and the enforced climate of political citizenship. Issues of cultural and social citizenship were submerged under the pressures of political belonging. Cultural practices were regarded as largely private efforts to forge religious and social counterpublics rather than politicized efforts to mobilize consciousness, a perspective that underestimated the power of cultural representations to engage with notions of who the citizen is, and what kinds of citizenship could be imagined.

As my discussions in the latter part of this book shift to British concerns, it allows us to view how a left politics opposed to the centralist culture of socialist states opened up alternative forms of political action for minority citizens. The migration of East African Asians to Britain and North America politicized subsequent generations of this nomadic community. Issues of cultural rather than just legal citizenship became the subject of broad public debates in Britain and the United States, as second-generation Asian British and U.S.–South Asian subjects struggled to forge historically new public realms of affiliation across race and class divides. The recent exhibition *Transforming the Crown: African, Asian, and Caribbean Artists in Britain, 1966–1996*, held in New York City from October 1997 to March 1998, presented some of these new directions in film, visual culture, and media practices. The first full-fledged transatlantic exhibition of its kind, *Transforming the Crown* demarcates various realms of cultural contestation through which ideas of British citizenship have been expanded by second- and third-generation British and U.S. cultural producers. The work of many of these practitioners probes the unspoken limits of representational possibilities. The critical presence of former East African

Asians like the Kenyan-born Bhajan Hunjan, Tanzanian Shaheen Merali, Ugandan-born Said Adrus, Kenyan Allan deSouza, Kenyan-born Pratibha Parmar, Kenyan Juginder Lamba, Zanzibari Lubaina Himid, and Ugandan Zarina Bhimji suggests the increasing permeability of legal and cultural expressions of citizenship. These visual artists have selectively foregrounded their sense of locale, selfhood, and civic commitment in their work in ways that one could argue are allowing for new conceptions of transnational identities to emerge.[5]

Postnational Forays

People need to think beyond the nation, Arjun Appadurai argues. The kinds of nationalisms available, from the decolonizing postcolonial state of the late 1940s and '50s to the postindustrial nation of the millennium, have been altered irrevocably, even as trenchant ethnic nationalisms and totalitarian discourses of identity surge in antidemocratic ecstasy. The concept of the nation has been scrutinized and irreverently disavowed at many levels through international flows of capital, goods, arms, and desire, while the sovereignty of the state has taken on new forms of expression. These new forms, in conjunction with the transnational flow of culture, result in what Appadurai terms the "emergent social forms" that compel us to think postnationally.[6]

As I've argued in this book, within the rubric of global migrant citizenship in the twentieth century, a sense of belonging for many has been forged under duress. For nomadic communities, the concept of a postnational condition of existence was already a way of life by the time of decolonization in the 1960s and '70s. Even as the nation was emerging as a desirable object, many of its postcolonial citizenry migrated with fractured conceptions of what the homeland was or what the new place of residence would be. Consequently, these emergent social forms are less likely to be grounded in the official discourses of print and more probably to be found in the popular and communal genres of music, cinema, urban culture, and theater.

The notion of the postnational departs from national, contained forms of belonging in a self-conscious and contingent way. It allows some of the fault lines between transnational exchanges within the state and the globalizing processes that determine how bodies get read in transit between states to emerge. This is not to deny the continuing presence of the national or to delegitimize the majority experience of citizenship within the state but, instead, to scrutinize those affiliations through a reexamination of what has always fallen outside the purview of the national—the transnational impact of different aspects of citizenship on citizens of a particular state. Postnational identifications open up those arenas that do not belong to the state by way of the notion of nation and point to those forces that replace the state in some instances, under the rising influence of a globalizing logic that is based less and less on popular conceptions of the nation.

Foregrounding the postnational underscores the active effort people have to undertake in order to belong to a state.[7] It separates the struggle for citizenship from mythic assumptions of a national community and reconfigures it as a political process of participatory enactment that is increasingly broader than its territorial borders, and that is linked to other states through networks of migration. The concept of the postnational demystifies citizenship as a social good and demands a reconsideration of the categories, assumptions, and practices of citizenship as a social agent in a transnationally interdependent world. Citizenship here is a performed and continuous process of becoming as much as it is a fictive and imagined state of being. It is simultaneously bound up by the mythography of the nation and mediated by the social biographies of its heterogeneous populace. Its conditions of possibility are enacted through laws as well as through cultural practices, fracturing coherent categories of citizenship. At once nationally determined and often expressed in the form of global entities such as international organizations, nongovernmental organizations, multinational corporations, and the internationally dispersed workplace, citizenship as an embodied practice in urban contexts operates at the junction of the local and the postnational.

Notes

CHAPTER 1: THE PERFORMANCE OF CITIZENSHIP

1 See Thurgood H. Marshall, "Citizenship and Social Class," in *Class, Citizenship, and Social Development* (New York: Harper and Row, 1965), 78 ff; George Armstrong Kelly, "Who Needs a Theory of Citizenship?" in *Theorizing Citizenship*, ed. Ronald Beiner (Albany: State University of New York Press, 1995), 89; Toby Miller, "Civic Culture and the Postmodern Subject," in *The Well-Tempered Self: Citizenship, Culture, and the Postmodern Subject* (Baltimore: Johns Hopkins University Press, 1993); Will Kymlicka, "Multination States and Polyethnic States," in *Multicultural Citizenship: A Liberal Theory of Minority Rights* (Oxford: Clarendon Press, 1995).

2 Arjun Appadurai, "Global Ethnoscapes: Notes and Queries for a Transnational Anthropology," in *Modernity at Large: Cultural Dimensions of Globalization* (Minneapolis: University of Minnesota Press, 1996), 31, 33, 49.

3 Lauren Berlant, *The Queen of America Goes to Washington City: Essays on Sex and Citizenship* (Durham, N.C.: Duke University Press, 1997), 10, 56.

4 Michael Ignatieff, "The Myth of Citizenship," in *Theorizing Citizenship*, 62.

5 Lisa Lowe, "Immigration, Citizenship, Racialization," in *Immigrant Acts: On Asian American Cultural Politics* (Durham, N.C.: Duke University Press, 1996), 19, 21, 22.

6 William A. Shack, introduction to *Strangers in African Societies*, ed. William A. Shack and Elliott P. Skinner (Berkeley and Los Angeles: University of California Press, 1979), 6–13. See also Fantu Cheru, *The Silent Revolution in Africa: Debt, Development, and Democracy* (London: Zed Books, 1989), 4–7.

7 Sanjay Suri, "Expelled Asians Returning on Anniversary," *India Abroad*, August 29, 1997.

CHAPTER 2: CITIZEN NYERERE

1 H. H. Gerth and C. Wright Mills, eds., *From Max Weber* (London: Oxford University Press, 1946), 245.

2 See Shawky Saad Zeidan, "Charismatic Leadership and Political Participation: The Case of Nasser's Egypt," *Journal of South Asian and Middle Eastern Studies* 11, no. 2 (Winter 1978): 63–64; Bruce Lincoln, *Authority* (Chicago: University of Chicago Press, 1994), 2; Gerth and Mills, *From Max Weber,* 245–47.

3 F. A. Hayek, "The Great Utopia," in *The Road to Serfdom* (Chicago: University of Chicago Press, 1994), 31.

4 A. W. Singham and Shirley Hune, *Non-Alignment in an Age of Alignments* (Westport, Conn.: Laurence Hill, 1986). See also R. R. Ramchandani, ed., *India and Africa* (Atlantic Highlands, N.J.: Humanities Press, 1980).

5 See Siba N'Zatioula Grovogui, "Native Rights to Dispose of Themselves" and "Partial Recognition to the Barbarous," in *Sovereigns, Quasi Sovereigns, and Africans* (Minneapolis: University of Minnesota Press, 1996), 71, 80. See also T. O. Elias, "The Evolution of Law and Government in Modern Africa," in *African Law: Adaptation and Development,* ed. Hilda Kuper and Leo Kuper (Berkeley and Los Angeles: University of California Press, 1965).

6 Kristin Mann and Richard Roberts, eds., *Law in Colonial Africa* (Portsmouth, N.H.: Heinemann, 1991). See also Robert H. Jackson, "A New Sovereign Regime," in *Quasi-States: Sovereignty, International Relations, and the Third World* (Cambridge: Cambridge University Press, 1990).

7 Julius K. Nyerere, *Freedom and Development* (Dar es Salaam: Oxford University Press, 1973), 206–7.

8 See Mahmood Mamdani, "The Native Authority and the Free Peasantry," in *Citizen and Subject* (Princeton: Princeton University Press, 1996), 130–41.

9 Ibid., 139.

10 See S. W. Frederick, "The Life of Joseph Kimalando," *Tanzanian Notes and Records,* no. 70 (July 1969): 28. The Asian lawyer was perhaps Zafferali, for whom Kimalando worked before joining another Asian advocate, Trivedi, in Moshi, Tanzania.

11 Ibid., 23. Kimalando's colleague Rawson Watts was contemptuously ejected from the New Africa Hotel in Dar es Salaam, an incident that provoked African civil servants to find a way of securing and maintaining their rights against racist policies of segregation.

12 Ibid., 25.

13 See Mamdani, "Indirect Rule," in *Citizen and Subject,* 62. The British version of indirect rule was consolidated by Lord Lugard, the architect of indirect rule. However, the practice of institutional segregation predates Lugard's version and was not restricted to British colonies. The French and the Boers had their versions of this, called "association" (French colonies) and "apartheid" (in the Boer colonies in Africa).

14 Stuart Hall, "Minimal Selves," in *The Real Me: ICA Document 6* (London: Institute of Contemporary Arts, 1988), 44. See also Homi K. Bhabha, "Commitment to Theory," in *Questions of Third Cinema,* ed. Jim Pines and Paul Willemen (London: BFI, 1989), 121.

15 See photo inserts in Julius K. Nyerere, *Freedom and Socialism / Uhuru Na Ujamaa* (Dar es Salaam: Oxford University Press, 1968), 256–57. These observations stem from my student days in primary and secondary school in Dar es Salaam and Arusha from the early to mid-1970s.

16 Julius K. Nyerere, "The African and Democracy," in *Freedom and Unity / Uhuru Na Umoja* (Dar es Salaam: Oxford University Press, 1966), 104.

17 Ibid., 103.

18 Ibid., 103, 104.

19 Nyerere, "*Ujamaa*: The Basis of African Socialism," in *Freedom and Unity*, 170–71.

20 Lionel Cliffe, "The Political System," in *One Party Democracy*, ed. Lionel Cliffe (Nairobi: Makerere Institute of Social Research / East African Publishing House, 1967).

21 As a student at the Forodhani Primary School during the late 1960s and early '70s, I can attest to the palpability of change. History books were rewritten, the language of schooling was shifted from English to Swahili, road signs and school names were changed. The city was being literally rewritten with great rapidity.

22 Daudi Mwakawago, "Dar-es-Salaam: Two Urban Campaigns," in *One Party Democracy*.

23 Ibid., 256–57.

24 Ibid., 219.

25 Joe Lugalla, *Crisis, Urbanization, and Urban Poverty in Tanzania: A Study of Urban Poverty and Survival Politics* (Lanham, Md.: University Press of America, 1995), 13–18.

CHAPTER 3: UJAMAA AND SOUL

1 J. K. Obatala, "U.S. 'Soul' Music in Africa," *The African Communist*, no. 43, (1970).

2 Walter Goldschmidt, ed., *The United States and Africa* (New York: Praeger, 1963), 27. See also Colin Legum, "Regionalism versus Globalism," in *African Crisis Areas and U.S. Foreign Policy*, ed. Gerald J. Bender et al. (Berkeley and Los Angeles: University of California Press, 1985), 279–80.

3 See Ed Guerrero, *Framing Blackness: The African American Image in Film* (Philadelphia: Temple University Press, 1993), 91–103; Manthia Diawara, ed., *Black American Cinema* (London: Routledge, 1993); and Mark Reid, *Redefining Black Film* (Berkeley and Los Angeles: University of California Press, 1993).

4 See Paul Gilroy, *There Ain't No Black in the Union Jack* (London: Century Hutchinson, 1987); Manthia Diawara, "Afro-Kitsch," in *Black Popular Culture*, ed. Gina Dent (Seattle: Bay Press, 1992); Ngugi wa Thiong'o, *Moving the Centre: The Struggle for Cultural Freedoms* (London: James Currey, 1993); Julius K. Nyerere, *Crusade for Liberation* (Dar es Salaam: Oxford University Press, 1978).

5 Julius K. Nyerere, *Freedom and Unity/Uhuru Na Umoja* (Dar es Salaam: Oxford University Press, 1966), 85.

6 Julius K. Nyerere, *Freedom and Socialism/Uhuru Na Ujamaa* (Dar es Salaam: Oxford University Press, 1968), 231.

7 Ibid., 179–410.

8 See Nyerere, *Crusade for Liberation*, for further elaboration of Afro-American and African alliances.

9 Miriam Makeba, *Makeba: My Story* (New York: Penguin Books, 1987), 163.

CHAPTER 4: KUNG FU CINEMA AND FRUGALITY

1 Shishir Kurup, "In Between Spaces," in *Let's Get It On: The Politics of Black Performance*, ed. Cathrine Ugwu et al. (Bay Press: Seattle, 1995), 34.

2 Ali A. Mazrui, "Cultural Forces in African Politics," in *Africa and the West*, ed. Isaac James Mowoe and Richard Bjornson (Westport, Conn.: Greenwood Press, 1986). See also Ali A. Mazrui's *Cultural Forces in World Politics* (Nairobi: Heinemann, 1990) and *The African Condition* (Cambridge: Cambridge University Press, 1980).

3 While there were many spheres of youth practice, my observations are inflected

primarily by my experiences as a Tanzanian youth schooled under *ujamaa* in Dar es Salaam and Arusha. The rhetoric of a classless and raceless society worked to conceal as well as to foreground the kinds of racisms and classisms that developed under the transforming structures of Tanzanian civil society.

4 Julius K. Nyerere, "*Ujamaa:* The Basis of African Socialism," in *Freedom and Unity/ Uhuru Na Umoja* (Dar es Salaam: Oxford University Press, 1966), 170.

5 Julius K. Nyerere, "The Arusha Declaration," in *Freedom and Socialism/Uhuru Na Ujamaa* (Dar es Salaam: Oxford University Press, 1968), 247.

6 Donatus Komba, "Contribution to Rural Development: Ujamaa and Villagisation," in *Mwalimu: The Influence of Nyerere*, ed. Colin Legum and Geoffrey Mmari (Trenton, N.J.: Africa World Press, 1995), 36.

7 See Joe Lugalla's excellent study of *ujamaa's* effects on urbanization, "The Post-Colonial State and the Urbanization Process, 1961–1993," in *Crisis, Urbanization, and Urban Poverty in Tanzania: A Study of Urban Poverty and Survival Politics* (Lanham, Md.: University Press of America, 1995), 37–39. Lugalla emphasizes the neglect of urban restructuring through the ambivalent state policies toward urbanization during this time. Consequently, rather than benefiting the marginalized urban majority, urban planning in Dar es Salaam simply perpetuated the colonial legacy of town planning. See also Knud Erik Svendsen, "Development Strategy and Crisis Management," in *Mwalimu*, ed. Legum and Mmari, 109.

8 John Iliffe, "Urban Poverty in Tropical Africa," in *The African Poor: A History* (Cambridge: Cambridge University Press, 1987). See also Lugalla, *Crisis, Urbanization, and Urban Poverty in Tanzania.*

9 A. G. Ishumi and T. L. Maliyamkono, "Education for Self-Reliance," in *Mwalimu*, ed. Legum and Mmari, 52, 53, 54.

10 Nyerere, "Frugality: 26 April 1965," in *Freedom and Socialism*, 332.

11 Geoffrey Mmari, "The Legacy of Nyerere," in *Mwalimu*, ed. Legum and Mmari, 178. Mmari suggests that Nyerere's style in dress was considered a copy of Chairman Mao's. My observations are based on personal experience as a kung fu fan and spectator at many a wrestling match performed at Kivukoni Beach. Kung fu also inflected styles of dancing in Dar es Salaam, where simulated kung fu arm and leg movements were incorporated into the bumps, free style, and disco.

12 I am indebted to Gordon Tait's recent unpublished work on subcultural theory for laying out the groundwork on this issue.

13 See *The Empire Strikes Back: Race and Racisms in 70's Britain* (London: Hutchinson Education, 1982); Stuart Hall and Tony Jefferson, eds., *Resistance through Rituals* (London: Hutchinson, 1976).

14 Ishumi and Maliyamkono, "Education for Self-Reliance," 51–53.

15 Nyerere, *Freedom and Unity*, 162, 258, 316, 332.

16 Ibid., 159, 162, 323, 332.

17 See Ishumi and Maliyamkono, "Education for Self-Reliance," 47–49. They point out the serious educational poverty afflicting Tanganyika on the eve of independence; Nyerere, *Freedom and Socialism*, 262, 337, 385.

18 Dan Nabudere, "The Politics of East African Federation, 1958–1965," in *Imperialism in East Africa* (London: Zed Books, 1982), 111.

19 Nyerere, *Freedom and Socialism*, 256–57.

20 V. I. Lenin, *The Tasks of the Youth League* (Peking: Foreign Language Press, 1975), 3.

21 Ibid., 19.
22 Ibid., 18–20.
23 Ishumi and Maliyamkono, "Education for Self-Reliance," 52.
24 Schools such as Forodhani Primary School and Azania Secondary School in Dar es Salaam, as well as the Arusha Secondary School, implemented some of these practices.
25 The Arusha Secondary School was an interesting site in terms of the transnational flow of Soviet and African American teachers.
26 Andrew Hindes, "Hong Kong Invasion at US Box Office (Feb 23–25)," Variety, 26 February 1996.
27 Mahmood Mamdani, Imperialism and Fascism in Uganda (Trenton, N.J.: Africa World Press, 1984); and Isaac Shivji, Class Struggles in Tanzania (New York: Monthly Review Press, 1976).
28 Bruce Thomas, Bruce Lee, Fighting Spirit (Berkeley, Calif.: North Atlantic Books, 1994).
29 Hsiung-Ping Chiao, "Bruce Lee: His Influence on the Evolution of the Kung Fu Genre," Journal of Popular Film and Television 9, no. 1 (Spring 1981): 37–38.
30 Nyerere, "Frugality," in Freedom and Unity, 332–33.
31 The term state-saturated societies is borrowed from Samir Amin, who uses it to describe states in which ideologies permeate every aspect of everyday life, and whose institutional pervasiveness determines the lives of their citizens. Former communist and socialist societies are obvious examples. See Samir Amin, "The System in Crisis: A Critique of Sovietism, 1960–1990," in Re-Reading the Postwar Period (New York: Monthly Review Press, 1994).
32 Michel Foucault, Technologies of Self (Amherst: University of Massachusetts Press, 1988), 19.
33 Ibid., 20.
34 Ibid., 20–21.
35 Ibid., 35.
36 Ibid., 37.
37 Chiao, "Bruce Lee," 33.
38 I use the term new historic subjects to imply both the new political subjects and the historically new conditions that create new subjectivities, as Ernesto Laclau and Chantal Mouffe have elaborated on in Hegemony and Socialist Strategy (London: Verso, 1985).
39 See Ed Guerrero, Framing Blackness (Philadelphia: Temple University Press, 1993); Manthia Diawara, ed., Black American Cinema (New York: Routledge, 1993); and Mark Reid, Redefining Black Film (Berkeley and Los Angeles: University of California Press, 1993).
40 Ishumi and Maliyamkono, "Education for Self-Reliance," 53.

CHAPTER 5: NOMADIC CITIZENSHIP
1 Mahmood Mamdani, Imperialism and Fascism in Uganda (Trenton, N.J.: Africa World Press, 1984), 65–66.
2 Peter Fryer, "The Settlers," in Staying Power: The History of Black People in Britain (London: Pluto Press, 1984), 383.
3 See Mamdani, Imperialism and Fascism in Uganda; Jessica Kuper, "'Goan' and 'Asian' in Uganda: An Analysis of Racial Identity and Cultural Categories," and Ali A. Mazrui, "Casualties of Underdeveloped Class Structure: The Expulsion of Luo Workers and

Asian Bourgeoisie from Uganda," in *Strangers in African Societies*, ed. William A. Shack and Elliott P. Skinner (Berkeley and Los Angeles: University of California Press, 1979); Pratibha Parmar, "Gender, Race, and Class: Asian Women in Resistance," in *The Empire Strikes Back: Race and Racisms in 70's Britain* (London: Hutchinson Education, 1982), 241.

4 Abdul Sheriff, *Slaves, Spices, and Ivory in Zanzibar: Integrations of an East African Commercial Empire into the World Economy, 1770–1873* (London: James Currey, 1987), 40. According to Sheriff, the presence of East African slaves in Porbandar, Gujarat, the Kutch port of Mandvi, Bombay, and Diu in the early 1800s suggests that the exchange in labor was not onesided.

5 R. R. Ramchandani, ed., *India and Africa* (Atlantic Highlands, N.J.: Humanities Press, 1980); see introduction. See also John Middleton, *The World of the Swahili: An African Mercantile Civilization* (New Haven, Conn.: Yale University Press, 1992).

6 In her extensive work on Indian migrants in the British empire, Marina Carter discusses the coercive and violent means through which this "voluntary" labor was created. See Marina Carter, *Voices from Indenture: Experiences of Indian Migrants in the British Empire* (London: Leicester University Press, 1996), 45, 49, 85. See also Marina Carter, *Servants, Sirdhars, and Settlers: Indians in Mauritius, 1834–1874* (Delhi: Oxford University Press, 1995).

7 Robert Gregory, *India and East Africa: A History of Race Relations within the British Empire, 1890–1939* (London: Oxford University Press, 1971). See also Mazrui, "Casualties of an Underdeveloped Class Structure"; Carter, *Voices from Indenture.*

8 Sheriff, *Slaves, Spices, and Ivory in Zanzibar*. See also James Kirkman, *Fort Jesus: A Portuguese Fortress on the East African Coast* (Oxford: Clarendon Press, 1974), 128–49, 159–62; Middleton, *The World of the Swahili*, 97, 19, 67, 75, 185.

9 Mazrui, "Casualties of an Underdeveloped Class Structure."

10 Kuper, "'Goan' and 'Asian' in Uganda," 245.

11 Ali A. Mazrui, "Changing the Guards from Hindus to Muslims," in *Cultural Forces in World Politics* (London: James Currey, 1990), 210–11. See also Vijay Gupta, "Non-Alignment to Collective Self-Reliance," in *India and Africa*, ed. R. R. Ramchandani, 47.

12 Tanganyika became independent in 1961 and merged with Zanzibar to form Tanzania in 1964. To avoid confusion, throughout this section on the early post-independence period, I will refer to the country as Tanganyika.

13 Jean-François Bayart, *The State in Africa: The Politics of the Belly* (London: Longman, 1993), 5.

14 Census records of 1957; see Lionel Cliffe, "The Political System," in *One Party Democracy*, ed. Lionel Cliffe (Nairobi: Makerere Institute of Social Research / East African Publishing House, 1967), 5.

15 Julius K. Nyerere, "Oral Hearing at Trusteeship Council, 7 March 1955" and "Oral Hearing of Trusteeship Council, 18 June 1957," in *Freedom and Unity/Uhuru Na Umoja* (Dar es Salaam: Oxford University Press, 1966), 38, 47.

16 Nyerere, "Oral Hearing of Trusteeship Council, 1957"; see also "The Race Problem in East Africa," in *Freedom and Unity*, 28.

17 Nyerere, "The Race Problem in East Africa," in *Freedom and Unity*, 29.

18 Nyerere, "The Race Problem Demands Economic Action," in *Freedom and Unity*, 73, 74.

19 Nyerere, "Tanganyika Citizenship," in *Freedom and Unity*, 259.

20 See Alamin M. Mazrui and Ibrahim Noor Shariff, *The Swahili: Idiom and Identity of an*

African People (Trenton, N.J.: African World Press, 1994), 132–35. Mazrui and Shariff map out the Afro-Arab culture that produced Swahili culture on the East African coast. They foreground the colonialist categories that created anti-Arab sentiment along an Arab-African axis within the coastal regions, leading to the artificial demarcation of African and Arab peoples among the hybrid Swahili of Zanzibar. Mazrui and Shariff suggest that non-Swahili, non-Zanzibari Africans capitalized on the colonial polarization between Swahili with Arab ancestry and Swahili with African and Shirazi (Persian) ancestry for their own gain. They point out that the 1964 revolution in Zanzibar was induced by non-Zanzibaris like John Okello.

21 William Edgett Smith, *Nyerere of Tanzania* (London: Trinity Press, 1973), 92.
22 Nyerere, "Tanganyika Citizenship," in *Freedom and Unity*, 259.
23 Smith, *Nyerere of Tanzania*, 108–21.
24 Frantz Fanon, *Black Skin, White Masks* (London: Pluto Press, 1986), 109.
25 Joe Lugalla, "Colonialism and the History of Urbanization in Tanzania," in *Crisis, Urbanization, and Urban Poverty in Tanzania: A Study of Urban Poverty and Survival Politics* (Lanham, Md.: University Press of America, 1995), 11.
26 Ramchandani, ed., *India and Africa*, 15.
27 Smith, *Nyerere of Tanzania*, 198.
28 Fryer, "Surrender to Racism," in *Staying Power*, 383.
29 Smith, *Nyerere of Tanzania*, 198. See also Fryer, *Staying Power*, 384–87.

CHAPTER 6: STAGING THE POSTCOLONY

1 Kwesi Owusu, ed., *Storms of the Heart: An Anthology of Black Arts and Culture* (London: Camden Press, 1988).
2 See Anne Walmsley, *The Caribbean Artists Movement, 1966–1972* (London: New Beacon Books, 1992), for a thorough history of the CAM years.
3 Peter Fryer, *Staying Power* (London: Pluto Press, 1984), 385.
4 Ibid., 389.
5 See Kobena Mercer, *Welcome to the Jungle: New Positions in Black Cultural Studies* (London: Routledge, 1994).
6 Lawrence Grossberg, "The Formation(s) of Cultural Studies," *Strategies*, no. 2 (1989): 114–49. For a selection of Stuart Hall's work, see *The Empire Strikes Back* (London: Hutchinson, 1982); *Policing the Crisis* (London: Macmillan, 1978); *Resistance through Rituals*, ed. Stuart Hall and Tony Jefferson (London: Hutchinson, 1976); *Culture, Media, Language*, ed. Stuart Hall et al. (London: Hutchinson, 1980); "Cultural Studies: Two Paradigms," *Media, Culture, and Society* no. 2 (1980): 55–72; "Notes on Deconstructing the Popular," in *People's History and Socialist Theory*, ed. R. Samuel (Boston: Routledge and Kegan Paul, 1981); "The Rediscovery of 'Ideology': Return of the Repressed in Media Studies," in *Culture, Society, and the Media*, ed. M. Gurevich et al. (New York: Methuen, 1982), 56–90; "Signification, Representation, Ideology: Althusser and the Post-Structuralist Debates," *Critical Studies in Mass Communication* 2, no. 2 (1985): 91–114; "The Toad in the Garden: Thatcherism among the Theorists," in *Marxism and the Interpretation of Culture*, ed. Cary Nelson and Lawrence Grossberg (Urbana: University of Illinois Press, 1988).
7 See David Morley and Kuan-Hsing Chen, eds., *Stuart Hall: Critical Dialogues in Cultural Studies* (London: Routledge, 1996), 3.

8 See Hall et al., *Policing the Crisis.*

9 Hall et al., "Towards the 'Exceptional State,'" in *Policing the Crisis*, 323.

10 See *Black Plays* and *Black Plays Two*, ed. Yvonne Brewster (London: Methuen, 1987–1989).

11 This discussion is based on the following editions of Matura's work: *as time goes by and Black Pieces* (London: Calder and Boyars, 1972); *Play Mas, Independence and Meetings* (London: Methuen, 1982).

12 Matura, *as time goes by*, 9, 12.

13 See Manthia Diawara, "Popular Culture and Oral Traditions in African Film," *Film Quarterly* 41 (Spring 1988): 6–7. Diawara discusses the oral tradition in the context of African cinema. This cultural tradition emerged in syncretic forms within Afro-Caribbean and Black British spaces.

14 Matura, *as time goes by*, 59.

15 Matura, *Independence*, 70.

16 For primarily oral cultures, the spoken was still an important link in the exchange of information during colonial occupation, especially with literature being available only to privileged natives. Recognizing this, the women of the Sistren Theater Collective in Jamaica have done extensive work in exploring their oral history by speaking for themselves through informal and oral modes of communication. See Sistren, with Honor Ford Smith, *Lionheart Gal* (London: Sister Vision, 1987). The collective is composed of women primarily from working-class communities. Similarly, I view Matura's technique of dialogue from the borders as having both a contemporary and an archival importance.

17 Matura, *Play Mas, Independence and Meetings*, 70–71. All subsequent passages will be cited by page number in the text.

18 Matura, *as time goes by and Black Pieces*, 105. All subsequent passages will be cited by page number in the text.

19 Homi K. Bhabha, "Of Mimicry and Men: The Ambivalence of Colonial Discourse," *October*, no. 28 (Spring 1984): 126. Bhabha argues that the discourse of mimicry is construed around an ambivalence and that in order to be effective, "mimicry must continually produce its slippage, its excess, its difference." Bhabha states that colonial mimicry is "the desire for a reformed, recognizable Other, as a subject of a difference that is almost the same, but not quite."

20 See Paul Gilroy, *There Ain't No Black in the Union Jack* (London: Century Hutchinson, 1987), for British race politics in the 1970s and '80s.

21 See Salman Rushdie, "Handsworth Songs," in *Imaginary Homelands* (New York: Penguin, 1991), 117.

CHAPTER 7: BODIES OUTSIDE THE STATE

1 Paul Gilroy, *There Ain't No Black in the Union Jack* (London: Century Hutchinson, 1987).

2 Stella Oni, "An Interview with Yvonne Brewster, O.B.E.," in *Six Plays by Black and Asian Women Writers*, ed. Cheryl Robson (London: Aurora Metro Press, 1993), 18.

3 Kadija George, Introduction to *Six Plays by Black and Asian Women Writers*.

4 Beverley Bryan, Stella Dadzie, and Suzanne Scafe, *The Heart of the Race: Black Women's Lives in Britain* (London: Virago Press, 1985).

5 Peter Fryer, *Staying Power: The History of Black People in Britain* (London: Pluto Press,

1984), 372–86. See also Errol Lawrence, "Just Plain Commonsense: The 'Roots' of Racism," in *The Empire Strikes Back: Race and Racism in 70's Britain* (London: Hutchinson, 1982), 68–71.

6 Winsome Pinnock, *A Hero's Welcome*, in *Six Plays by Black and Asian Women Writers*, 44. On a nameless West Indian island in 1947, Stanley, Minda, and Sis fantasize about England and finally succumb to 'The Motherland Needs You' posters pasted all over the island. See also John Solomos et al., "The Organic Crisis of British Capitalism and Race," in *The Empire Strikes Back*, 14–16, 30.

7 Lawrence, "Just Plain Commonsense," 70; Fryer, "The Settlers," in *Staying Power*.

8 Pratibha Parmar, "Gender, Race, and Class: Asian Women in Resistance," in *The Empire Strikes Back*, 241, 245–47. See also Amrit Wilson, *Finding a Voice: Asian Women in Britain* (London: Virago Press, 1984); Shabnam Grewal et al., *Charting the Journey: Writings by Black and Third World Women* (London: Sheba Feminist Publishers, 1988).

9 Hazel Carby, "Woman's Era," in *Reconstructing Womanhood* (London: Oxford University Press, 1987), 6.

10 Kimberle Crenshaw, "Demarginalizing the Intersection of Race and Sex: A Black Feminist Critique of Antidiscrimination Doctrine, Feminist Theory, and Antiracist Politics," *University of Chicago Legal Forum* (1989): 139–67.

11 Rukhsana Ahmad, *Song for a Sanctuary*, in *Six Plays by Black and Asian Women Writers*, 181.

12 For further elaboration on the distinction between civil law and customary practice, see Mahmood Mamdani, *Citizen and Subject* (Princeton, N.J.: Princeton University Press, 1996), 109–10, 112–19. A bipolar system of justice developed under British indirect rule. Customary law was meted out to natives by chiefs and British commissioners, while modern justice was handed down to nonnatives by white magistrates. This dualism in legal theory emerged out of two distinct but related forms of power, the centralized modern state and the locally governed native authority. Civil law marked the secularity of the modern state, while customary law and practice was the elaboration of local customs, mores, and tribal authority. Customary law emerges during and after colonialism as the complex and indeterminate collision with the secular and the modern, as narrativized by British common law. Examples of customary practice include Muslim law in colonial African states like Nigeria, African law in Lesotho, customary law in Tanzania, and customary courts for all "tribesmen" in Botswana.

13 Stuart Hall, "Minimal Selves," in *The Real Me: ICA Document 6* (London: Institute of Contemporary Arts, 1988), 45.

14 *Breaking the Silence: Writing by Asian Women* (London: Centerprise Publishing Project, 1984) documents the early consciousness-raising efforts by Black women to acquire cultural and legal rights. See also Bryan et al., *The Heart of the Race*.

15 Meenakshi Ponnuswami, "Feminist History in Contemporary British Theater," *Women and Performance*, no. 14–15 (1995): 287–305.

16 Pratibha Parmar, "Black Feminism: The Politics of Articulation," in *Identity: Community, Culture, Difference*, ed. Jonathan Rutherford (London: Lawrence and Wishart, 1990), 103–5.

17 Jacqueline Rudet, *Basin* in *Black Plays* (London: Methuen, 1987), and Winsome Pinnock, *A Rock in Water*, in *Black Plays Two* (London: Methuen, 1989). Both collections are edited by Yvonne Brewster.

N o t e s

18 Elaine Aston, *An Introduction to Feminism and Theatre* (London: Routledge, 1995), 88.
19 In Brewster, ed., *Black Plays*, 114.
20 Audre Lorde, *Zami: A New Spelling of My Name* (Freedom, Calif.: Crossing Press / Freedom, 1982), 7.
21 Brewster, ed., *Black Plays Two*, 46–47.
22 Hazel Carby, "White Woman Listen! Black Feminism and the Boundaries of Sisterhood," in *The Empire Strikes Back*.

CHAPTER 8: THE SCREAM OF SYCORAX
1 Roberto Fernández Retamar, *Caliban and Other Essays*, trans. Edward Baker (Minneapolis: University of Minnesota Press, 1989).
2 Coco Fusco, *English Is Broken Here: Notes on Cultural Fusion in the Americas* (New York: New Press, 1995), 6–7.
3 *The Tempest*, 1.2.321, 375.
4 Ibid., 1.2.261–65.
5 See Ella Shohat and Robert Stam, *Unthinking Eurocentrism: Multiculturalism and the Media* (New York: Routledge, 1994), 307–10.
6 Joaquim Pedro de Andrade, "Cannibalism and Self-Cannibalism," quoted in *Brazilian Cinema*, ed. Randal Johnson and Robert Stam (New York: Columbia University Press, 1995), 82.
7 Peter Hulme, "Prospero and Caliban," in *Colonial Encounters: Europe and the Native Caribbean, 1492–1797* (London: Routledge, 1992), 114–15.
8 Ibid., 87.
9 *The Tempest*, 3.3.46–47.
10 Frantz Fanon, *The Wretched of the Earth* (New York: Grove Press, 1968), 42, 55.
11 *The Tempest*, 1.2.275–86.
12 Ibid., 1.2.259–64.
13 Edouard Glissant, *Caribbean Discourse* (Charlottesville: University Press of Virginia), 74–75.
14 Kamau Brathwaite, *Barabajan Poems* (Kingston and New York: Savacou North, 1994), 235.
15 Marlene Nourbese Philip, *she tries her tongue, her silence softly breaks* (London: The Women's Press, 1993), 47. Originally published in 1989.
16 Aimé Césaire, *A Tempest*, trans. Richard Miller (New York: Ubu Repertory Theater Publications, 1986), 13. Originally published in 1969.
17 Césaire, *Discourse on Colonialism* (New York: Monthly Review Press, 1972).
18 *A Tempest*, 15.
19 Retamar, *Caliban*, 45.
20 Michelle Cliff, "Caliban's Daughter: *The Tempest* and the Teapot," *Frontiers* 12, no. 2 (1991): 40–42. Cliff draws on Jean Rhys's reading of Bertha Rochester/Antoinette Cosway from *Wide Sargasso Sea*, in her reworking of the significance of Sycorax.
21 Césaire, *A Tempest*, 15.
22 Such a theory of the state is being narrativized by Michelle Cliff, Gayatri Spivak, Mervat Hatem, Assia Djebar, Norma Alarcón, Gloria Anzaldúa, Leslie Marmon Silko, and Fatima Mernissi, among others.
23 My thanks to Radhika Subramaniam for pointing this out to me.

CHAPTER 9: TRANSNATIONAL MIGRATIONS

1 See Françoise Lionnet, *Autobiographical Voices: Race, Gender, Self-Portraiture* (Ithaca, N.Y.: Cornell University Press, 1989), 9–10, 15–17, 176; Edouard Glissant, "An Exploded Discourse," in *Caribbean Discourse* (Charlottesville: University Press of Virginia, 1992), 24, 25, 109; Ella Shohat and Robert Stam, *Unthinking Eurocentrism: Multiculturalism and the Media* (New York: Routledge, 1994), 309; Aimé Césaire, *Discourse on Colonialism* (New York: Monthly Review Press, 1972); Frantz Fanon, "Racism and Culture," in *Toward the African Revolution* (New York: Grove Press, 1967); Colin Legum, "Culture and Politics," in *Pan-Africanism* (New York: Praeger, 1965), 95; Kwame Nkrumah, *Consciencism: Philosophy and Ideology for Decolonization* (New York: Monthly Review Press, 1964); Jomo Kenyatta, "The New Religion in East Africa," in *Facing Mount Kenya* (New York: Vintage Books, 1965); Sékou Touré, "International and Pan African Objectives," in *Sékou Touré* (London: Panay Books, 1978), 139–40. See also Edward Soja, *Thirdspace: Journeys to Los Angeles and Other Real-and-Imagined Places* (Oxford: Basil Blackwell, 1996); David Harvey, *The Condition of Postmodernity* (Oxford: Basil Blackwell, 1990); Henri Lefebvre, *The Production of Space* (Oxford: Basil Blackwell, 1991), for extensive discussions of postmodernity and space.

2. See Jim Pines and Paul Willemen, *Questions of Third Cinema* (London: British Film Institute, 1989); Ian Watson, *Towards a Third Theatre: Eugenio Barba and the Odin Teatret* (New York: Routledge, 1995); Augusto Boal, *Theatre of the Oppressed* (London: Pluto Press, 1979); Paolo Freire, *Pedagogy of the Oppressed* (New York: Continuum, 1993); Rustom Bharucha, *Theatre and the World: Performance and the Politics of Culture* (New York: Routledge, 1993); Vijay Tendulkar, *Ghasiram Kotwal* (Calcutta: Seagull Books, 1984); Jerzy Grotowski, *Towards a Poor Theater* (New York: Simon and Schuster, 1968); Guillermo Gómez-Peña, *Warrior for Gringostroika* (Minneapolis: Graywolf Press, 1993); Ngugi wa Thiong'o, *Decolonising the Mind: The Politics of Language in African Literature* (Portsmouth, N.H.: Heinemann Educational Books, 1986); Penina Mhando, "Theater for Development," unpublished paper.

3. *Jatra* is a form of street theater popularized by director/playwrights such as Badal Sircar, Utpal Dutt, and various street-theater proponents in Calcutta. The form became a popular experimental vehicle in Madras, South India, during the early 1980s. See Badal Sircar, *Three Plays: Procession / Bhoma / Stale News* (Calcutta: Seagull Books, 1983); Kirtinath Kutkoti's introduction to Girish Karnad, *Hayavadana*, in *New Drama in India* (Calcutta: Oxford University Press, 1975). I am referring here to the production of *The Little Clay Cart*, directed by Jatinder Varma, Tara Arts Group, London, late 1980s. Jatinder Varma, personal interview, London, summer 1989.

4 See Shohat and Stam, *Unthinking Eurocentrism*, 309; Homi Bhabha, *The Location of Culture* (New York: Routledge, 1994), 87; Kobena Mercer, *Welcome to the Jungle: New Positions in Black Cultural Studies* (New York: Routledge, 1996), 63; Stuart Hall, "New Ethnicities," in *Stuart Hall: Critical Dialogues in Cultural Studies*, ed. David Morley and Kuan-Hsing Chen (London: Routledge, 1996), 441; Paul Gilroy, *There Ain't No Black in the Union Jack* (London: Hutchinson, 1987), 217; Glissant, *Caribbean Discourse*, 66; Marlene Nourbese Philip, *she tries her tongue, her silence softly breaks* (London: Women's Press, 1993), 47; Roberto Fernández Retamar, *Caliban and Other Essays*, trans. Edward Baker (Minneapolis: University of Minnesota Press, 1989); Benitez-Rojo, *The Repeating Island* (Durham, N.C.: Duke University Press, 1992), 12;

Assia Djebar, *Fantasia: An Algerian Cavalcade* (Portsmouth, N.H.: Heinemann, 1993), 226; Arjun Appadurai, *Modernity at Large: Cultural Dimensions of Globalization* (Minneapolis: University of Minnesota Press, 1996), 48; Lisa Lowe, *Immigrant Acts: On Asian American Cultural Politics* (Durham, N.C.: Duke University Press, 1996), 60; Lionnet, *Autobiographical Voices*, 9–10, 15; Néstor García Canclini, "Cultural Reconversion," in *On Edge: The Crisis of Contemporary Latin American Culture*, ed. George Yúdice et al. (Minneapolis: University of Minnesota Press, 1992); Celeste Olalquiaga, *Megalopolis* (Minneapolis: University of Minnesota Press, 1992), 83; Michelle Cliff, *No Telephone to Heaven* (New York: Vintage, 1989), 1.

5 Chandra Mohanty, Norma Alarcón, Judith Butler, Hortense Spillers, Gayatri Spivak, Peggy Phelan, Gloria Anzaldúa, Marlene Nourbese Philip, Ketu Katrak, Ania Loomba, Rey Chow, Ella Shohat, Coco Fusco, Hazel Carby, Pratibha Parmar, Michelle Cliff, Assia Djebar, and Angela Davis, among others, have elaborated extensively on these issues.

6 For a more extended reading of bhangra music, see Gayatri Gopinath's essay, "Bombay, U.K., Yuba City: Bhangra Music and the Engendering of Diaspora," *Diaspora* 4, no. 3 (1993). See also George Lipsitz, *Dangerous Crossroads: Popular Music, Postmodernism, and the Poetics of Place* (New York: Verso, 1994), 126–27.

7 M. G. Vassanji, *Uhuru Street* (Portsmouth, N.H.: Heinemann Educational Books, 1991); Meena Alexander, *Manhattan Music* (San Francisco: Mercury House, 1997).

8 See *Amerasia Journal* 20, no. 1 (1994), issue titled *Dimensions of Desire*; Russell Leong, ed., *Asian American Sexualities* (New York: Routledge, 1996); *Our Feet Walk the Sky*, ed. Women of South Asian Descent Collective (San Francisco: Aunt Lute, 1993); Andrew Parker et al., eds., *Nationalisms and Sexualities* (New York: Routledge, 1992). These anthologies address some of the ambivalences around the politics of representation, and the relation of self to cultural citizenship in terms of incomplete, partial, or strategic identities.

9 See Chandra Mohanty, "Defining Genealogies: Feminist Reflections on Being South Asian in North America," in *Our Feet Walk the Sky*.

10 Shishir Kurup, *Assimilations*, as performed at Highways and the Public Theater. All further citations are from this version.

11 Frantz Fanon, *Black Skin, White Masks* (London: Pluto Press, 1986).

12 Lowe, *Immigrant Acts*, 83.

CHAPTER 10: POSTNATIONAL REVERBERATIONS

1 Will Kymlicka, *Multicultural Citizenship: A Liberal Theory of Minority Rights* (Oxford: Clarendon Press, 1995), 191.

2 Ulf Hannerz, *Transnational Connections: Culture People Places* (London: Routledge, 1996), 128.

3 Thurgood H. Marshall, "Citizenship and Social Class," in *Class, Citizenship, and Social Development* (New York: Harper and Row, 1965), 78 ff.

4 Toby Miller, *The Well-Tempered Self: Citizenship, Culture, and the Postmodern Subject* (Baltimore: Johns Hopkins University Press, 1993), 107.

5 Mora J. Beauchamp-Byrd, "London Bridge: Late Twentieth Century British Art and the Routes of 'National Culture,'" in *Transforming the Crown: African, Asian, and Caribbean Artists in Britain, 1966–1996*, by Mora J. Beauchamp-Byrd and M. Franklin Sirmans

(New York: Franklin H. Williams Caribbean Cultural Center/African Diaspora Institute, 1997).

6 Arjun Appadurai, *Modernity at Large: Cultural Dimensions of Globalization* (Minneapolis: University of Minnesota Press, 1996), 158.

7 My thanks to Randy Martin for drawing my attention to this idea.

Index

Created by Eileen Quam

Nationalism: in East African countries, 90; and transnationalism, 39, 157–58
Nation-states: and forced migration, 6; as male territory, 128
Nyerere, Julius, 12, 14; on African historicity, 77; on African rights, 77–78; background, 31; biography, 21; as charismatic leader, 23, 24, 26, 29; on citizenship, 79; on class hierarchy, 32; and crowds, 32–36; on democratic participation, 32–33; and East African–Asian identity, 36; on education, 56; as founding father, 25–29; on government hiring, 80–81; on individualism, 27–28, 30; power of, 27–28; public persona, 24–25; published speeches, 77; soul music ban by, 37–38; visit to China, 58, 63; visual modernity of, 29–32; on youth, 55–57. See also Ujamaa

Obote, Milton, 70
Oral tradition, 100, 166n13, 166n16
Owusu, Kwesi, 90

Pan-Africanism, 42–43, 50, 89
Pateman, Carole, 14
Performance: ontology of, 13; as political, 145–46; as self-conscious, 14–15; transatlantic, 147–52. See also Movement theory
Philip, M. Nourbese: she tries her tongue, her silence softly breaks, 135–36
Pinnock, Winsome, 120; Rock in Water, 122–24
Politics: ambivalent, 10; identity, 71; participatory, 4, 15–16; as visible, 145–47. See also Democracy
Ponnuswami, Meenakshi, 120
Popular culture. See Soul culture
Public sphere, 34

Racism: in Tanzania, 36, 77–78, 161–62n3
Randall, Paulette, 121
Rashid, Ian, 145
Reid, Mark, 39, 67
Resistance, 23; anticolonial, 29

Retamar, Roberto Fernández, 127, 138
Return of the Dragon, The (film), 54, 62
Rousseau, Jean-Jacques, 14
Rudet, Jacqueline, 120; Basin, 121–22, 124

Sammy and Rosie Get Laid (film), 143
Schumpeter, Joseph, 14
Self-reliance. See Ujamaa
Shakespeare, William: Henry V, 132; Richard III, 133; Tempest, 127, 128, 133. See also Sycorax
Shiuji, Issa, 14
Sijaona, Leweri, 86
Sircar, Badal, 142
Slavery, 71, 164n4
Socialism: Tanzanian, 3, 24, 25, 33, 72
Soul culture, 38–40; influence on Asian youth, 45–46; as transnational, 39, 41, 42, 47–48
Soul music, 37–38, 43
South Asians: and British colonial rule, 72–73; diasporic culture, 144–47
Storms of the Heart, 90
Superfly TNT (film), 43, 47
Swahili, 2, 56, 164–65n20
Syal, Meera: My Sister-Wife, 117–19, 124
Sycorax (fictional figure), 127–39; and cannibalism, 130–34, 139; on Europe's self-knowledge, 129; historical space in, 133; as indigenous, 128, 130; lack of study of, 128; naming of, 134–35; scream of, 128–29

Tanganyika/Tanzania: Asian cultural life in, 35, 45, 72, 156; Asian eviction from, 1–2, 19; colonial policies, 29; Dar es Salaam as syncretic, 83–84; Dar es Salaam expansion, 38; independence, 35–36, 40, 76, 162n17, 164n12; land rights, 78; name change, 40, 164n12; nationalism in, 90; socialism in, 3, 24, 25, 40–41; as state-saturated society, 64; uburu na umoja, 46; urban planning in Dar es Salaam, 162n7; youth culture, 45–46, 49–58. See also Nyerere, Julius
Tanganyika African National Union

MAY JOSEPH is assistant professor of performance studies at the Tisch School of the Arts, New York University. She is coeditor (with Jennifer Natalya Fink) of *Performing Hybridity* (Minnesota, 1999). She has been a guest editor of *Women and Performance* and is on the editorial boards of *Cultural Studies* and the *Journal of Sports and Social Issues*.